Imagining Animals

Art, psychotherapy and primitive states of mind

Caroline Case

Routledge
Taylor & Francis Group

LONDON AND NEW YORK

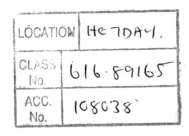
First published 2005
by Routledge
27 Church Road, Hove, East Sussex, BN3 2FA

Simultaneously published in the USA and Canada
by Routledge
270 Madison Avenue, New York, NY 10016

Routledge is an imprint of the Taylor & Francis Group

© 2005 Caroline Case

Typeset in Times by RefineCatch Ltd, Bungay, Suffolk
Printed and bound in Great Britain by TJ International Ltd,
Padstow, Cornwall
Paperback cover design by Sandra Heath

This publication has been produced with paper manufactured to
strict environmental standards and with pulp derived from
sustainable forests.

British Library Cataloguing in Publication Data
A catalogue record for this book is available from the British Library

Library of Congress Cataloging in Publication Data
Case, Caroline, 1948-
   Imagining animals : art, pyschotherapy and primitive states of mind /
Caroline Case.–1st ed.
      p. cm.
   Includes bibliographical references and index.
   ISBN 1–58391–957–0 (hbk) – ISBN 1–58391–958–9 (pbk)
1. Art therapy for children. 2. Imagery (Psychology) in children.
3. Animals–Psychological aspects. 4. Animals–Therapeutic use. 5. Autistic
children–Rehabilitation. I. Title.
   RJ505.A7C37 2005
   616.89'1656'083–dc22
                        2005003622
ISBN 1–58391–957–0 (hbk)
ISBN 1–58391–958–9 (pbk)

For David, with love

The Haddock Song

I once had a haddock called Pete, called Pete
I once had a haddock called Pete
I once had a haddock called Pete, called Pete
I once had a haddock called Pete

I loved my haddock called Pete, called Pete
I loved my haddock called Pete
I loved my haddock called Pete, called Pete
I loved my haddock called Pete

I got hungry at home one day, one day
I got hungry at home one day
I got hungry at home one day, one day
I got hungry at home one day

I boiled my haddock called Pete, called Pete
I boiled my haddock called Pete
I boiled my haddock called Pete, called Pete
I boiled my haddock called Pete

I served up my haddock called Pete, called Pete
I served up my haddock called Pete
And then I sat down to eat

I missed my haddock called Pete, called Pete
I missed my haddock called Pete
I missed my haddock called Pete, called Pete
I missed my haddock called Pete

I fished up a haddock and called it Pete
I fished up a haddock and called it Pete
I fished up a haddock and called it Pete
I fished up a haddock and called it Pete

I loved my haddock called Pete, called Pete
I loved my haddock called Pete
I loved my haddock called Pete, called Pete
I loved my haddock called Pete

Swing song at the play-park: Kate and Isobel

Contents

List of Illustrations

Acknowledgements

Many people have helped and supported me through the writing of *Imagining Animals*. There is a huge debt to children and families who have helped me to understand something of what they needed, and who have kindly given permission for material to be discussed. Friends and colleagues have facilitated the development of ideas, as well as allowing me to think my differences. This support has fostered my own thinking. My special thanks to Barbara Greenman, for her relationship with clay, and Hugh Spendlove, potter, for his creative clay workshops. In child psychotherapy, George Crawford, Joan Herrmann, Chris Holland, Anne Hood, Ann Snedden, Sheila Spensley, and Jean Robinson deserve special mention for the opportunities to discuss clinical work in different settings. Crossing boundaries, in a like way, are friends and colleagues who have dual qualifications in art therapy with a separate analytic training, special thanks to Tessa Dalley, Joy Schaverien and to Kathy Killick particularly, who read the manuscript for me at a crucial stage. I am grateful for support from different work settings, in particular from Paul Barrows, David Dunbar, David Hadley, Hugh Jones, Iris O'Brien, Suzanne Sproston, Gail Walker and everyone at the Knowle Clinic. Lastly, this would not have been possible without the support and love of my family, Josh and Miranda, and especially, David and Isobel who have heard much too often the phrase 'when the book is finished'.

I would like to thank the following authors and publishers for their permission to reprint from published works:

The Spirit Level by Seamus Heaney, with permission of Faber and Faber Ltd.
The Amazing Maurice and his Educated Rodents by Terry Pratchett and Lyn Pratchett (2001, p. 45), published by Doubleday. Used with permission of The Random House Group Ltd.
The Once and Future King by T. H. White (1939, p. 45), with permission of David Higham Associates.
A version of 'Animation and the location of beauty' by Caroline Case from

Journal of Child Psychotherapy 28(3):327–43 (Chapter 3 this volume) © 2002 used with permission of Routledge.

A version of 'Authenticity and survival: Working with children in chaos' by Caroline Case from *Inscape* (8)1:17–28 (Chapter 8 this volume) © 2003 used with permission of Routledge.

Every effort has been made to trace copyright holders and to obtain permission to quote from, Walter de la Mare *The Listeners*, and from A. A. Milne *Winnie-the-Pooh*. Any omissions brought to our attention will be remedied in future editions.

Part I

Working with children who are hard to reach

Introduction: working with children who are hard to reach

This book brings together some apparently divergent themes that emerged in my early career as an art teacher, then work as an art therapist for over thirty years and as a child psychotherapist for ten years. The clinical work took place in the statutory services of education, social services and child and family health, but also in charitable foundations and private practice. These have not been described in detail, in order to aid confidentiality for the children and parents who kindly gave permission for their material to be included in the book.

The children described in the book encompass some different aspects of being hard to reach in clinical work, in that they have lived through situations where hope has been lost. Two of the children, Colin and Lucy, came from backgrounds of neglect with known physical abuse (Colin) and suspected sexual abuse (Colin and Lucy); both had parents living in hard drug cultures. Two of the children, Henry and Sally, had had early environments where there had been prolonged maternal depression, following traumatic bereavements. Henry was referred following delinquent behaviour, and Sally with a puzzling combination of symptoms. Several of the children had had adverse circumstances around their births; Simon had been a premature baby, born with fears for his own and his mother's life, Wendy and Ian had been born with fear and expectation that they might be handicapped. The children in Chapter four presented differently, and are included in the book to illustrate some other aspects of closeness and separation, on the theme of duality-unity. They had sleep difficulties, and were characterised by being extremely sensitive; Rebecca, Ian, Alice and Lizzy. The work with Sally, which forms the core of Part three gives a narrative of her therapy, a child with a mother with prolonged depression due to adverse circumstances in her own childhood and bereavement trauma. Sally was referred with symptoms including: learning difficulties, autistic traits, muteness, incontinence and speech difficulties.

THEORETICAL APPROACH

The theoretical approach which informs the work with the children and their families is psychodynamic, synthesising certain aspects of art therapy and child psychotherapy. The focus is on interaction through play and the making of images in therapy. Central to this is the knowledge through my own art work, sculpture and painting, that art both expresses and finds forms for feelings but is most importantly a way of thinking and reflecting on life experiences nonverbally. Images, both metaphorical and concrete, are the building blocks of emotional learning, expressions of felt life. This develops in parallel to verbal, abstract modes of naming and thinking.

Stern (1985) writes that, poetry aside, language usually focuses on one sensory mode, thus fracturing the amodal global experience of the child. With the advent of language the infant gains entrance to a wider cultural membership, but at the risk of losing the force and wholeness of original experience. Stern explores the slippage between personal world knowledge and official or socialised world knowledge as encoded in language, because the slippage between these two is one of the main ways in which reality and fantasy can begin to diverge.

> Infants' initial interpersonal knowledge is mainly unshareable, amodal, instance-specific, and attuned to nonverbal behaviours in which no-one channel of communication has privileged status with regard to accountability or ownership. Language changes all of that. With its emergence, infants become estranged from direct contact with their own personal experience. Language forces a space between interpersonal experience: as lived and as represented. And it is exactly across this space that the connections and associations that constitute neurotic behaviour may form. But also with language, infants for the first time can share their personal experience of the world with others, including 'being with' others in intimacy, isolation, loneliness, fear, awe, and love.
>
> (Stern 1985: 182)

Thus language has a dimension that can betray experience and a dimension that can give a voice to experience. In my work, emphasis is given to inner phantasy life as well as external experiences. The influences on my development as an art therapist began with the experience of working with Edward Adamson, a studio-based model; to be followed by work with Diana Halliday and Michael Edwards which gave a Jungian perspective. Later, training as a child psychotherapist in the Kleinian/British Independent tradition, helped me to think about the inner and outer world of the child, and the formation of states of mind, that we may meet in therapy. In child psychotherapy training, shared subjectivity (outside the dynamics around the image) was the main focus, working within the transference/countertransference dynamic.

The children whose clinical work is drawn upon (except Chapter five) were all referred because of my dual qualification, and were considered to be hard to reach. It was hoped that working with images and play might enable them to find a voice of their own, and it is these explorations which form the basis of the book. In the world of therapy organisations, where the boundaries are hard fought, as to who is in and who is out of the moral circle, a plural approach may seem provocative, and arouses anxiety. Britton, writing about publication anxiety, mentions anxieties about affiliation, and ancestral figures, as well as a need for affirmation of shared ideas and declarations of shared origins (Britton 1997). When confronted with a hard to reach child, in distress to themselves and their family, we need to think, what is it that might work here, or be a catalyst for change. This led to an adaptation of technique.

Art therapists work in many different settings, some of which have been described in a previous publication (Case and Dalley 1992). Here, a traditional studio setting will be contrasted with a traditional child psychotherapy room. A traditional studio setting is a working art studio in that, art materials, work in progress from different clients, sometimes the art therapist's own work may be visible; one enters a workshop which is visually stimulating and sensuously engaging in terms of what can be seen, smelt and touched. Clients will each have a storage folder, but work may also be on display on the walls. A traditional child psychotherapy room will have a couch, table and chairs, it may or may not have a sink, doll's house or sand tray, but it will have a box of age-appropriate toys for each child, that are for their sole use. The furnishings and walls are kept very plain with no personal items of the therapist with the intention not to excite curiosity or because items may need protection (Hartnup 1999). Some therapists prefer a bare room so that the child can structure the interaction with greater freedom. The two disciplines share a similar understanding of therapeutic boundaries but are contrasted, with the former giving an invitation to use art materials (within a relationship) and the latter an invitation towards interaction personally or through play (the box of materials). The combined approach was to take art materials and play materials for the child's individual use; with a shared sand tray, and sink for water. This helped to reach neglected deprived children, in that these materials were for their sole use. The art materials frequently worked on a sensual level, to engage the child, where there had been deprivation. The outbursts of aggression from children who had been physically abused in the past and from children struggling with separation rage meant that if they destroyed play or art materials, then, as long as they and the therapist were kept safe, then no one else would be affected. The child enters into the therapist's space in the therapy room. Personal items of the therapist are better left outside but it is important that a receptive environment which is warm and visually stimulating even to a small degree is available, so that a colourful rug, tissues, a blanket, clock and pictures on the walls give a visual communication of warm containment. Some children are able to work very well within a traditional art therapy studio or room, or within a traditional child psychotherapy room. Others, I suggest, benefit from a combined approach. Their own box of toys and box of art materials correspond to the inner core of the self, and are for their own use, and I resist temptations to be drawn into doing the work for them by painting or drawing; at the same time offering every support to their taking these first steps on their own.

Before outlining the chapters a brief excursion will be made into the impact of neurological research on our understanding of the development of the brain and the implications for therapy, followed by a consideration of psychodynamic theory and primitive states of mind.

THE FINDINGS OF NEUROLOGICAL RESEARCH AND OUR UNDERSTANDING OF TRAUMA, NEGLECT AND MATERNAL DEPRESSION

In the last fifteen years, since *Working with Children in Art Therapy* was first published, there has been a blossoming of research, by neurobiologists, into the workings of the brain and the way that it is formed through early experiences (Case and Dalley 1990). Pally (2000), gives an accessible overview in *The Mind-Brain Relationship*. Balbernie (2001) writes: 'A baby's developing brain is damaged when exposed to neglect, trauma, and abuse, and prolonged maternal depression' (2001: 249). First of all, neglect, has been seen to cause actual damage to the developing brain by the failure of the needed stimulus at the right time, so that neural pathways atrophy. Further, actual trauma, which initiates primitive flight/fight or freezing responses, fosters these patterns of response over the more elaborate reflective processes, where thought takes precedence over action. Child abuse and neglect can directly shape the way that the brain is programmed during crucial early years when there is intense synapse production (Schore 2001a; Glaser 2000), and have negative long-term effects (Nelson and Bosquet 2000). The very malleability of the mind, an adaptability which aids our survival, means that it will adapt to the conditions it finds itself in, and then keep responding in these ways, as neural pathways have developed, even when no longer in the neglectful situation. This means, in adverse attachments for example, that a foster child will continue to respond as if they are with an abusive parent, even when with caring foster parents.

The quality of the baby's emotional relationship with its mother/caregiver is crucial: 'Research suggests that emotion operates as a central organising process within the brain. In this way, an individual's ability to organise emotions – a product in part of earlier attachment relationships – directly shapes the ability of the mind to integrate experience and to adapt to future stressors' (Seigal 1999: 4, in Balbernie 2001). An infant's brain is shaped by emotional interactions with the mature brain of the caregiver (Seigal 1999), so that 'for the developing infant the mother essentially *is* the environment' (Schore 1994: 78). The brain starts life with multi-potentialities in development. The early use of the brain within the co-created environment between mother and child and the wider circle about them will foster the growth of use-dependant pathways (Perry *et al.* 1995). Reflections and understandings of the baby's emotional life by the mother will be mirrored in mind development in the baby. In this way the orbital cortex which is the place of reflective thought will develop in the child: 'The orbitofrontal cortex is known to play an essential role in the processing of interpersonal signals necessary for the initiation of social interactions between individuals' (Schore 2001b: 36).

The orbitofrontal cortex mediates empathic and emotional relatedness; or attuned communication. It contributes to generating self-awareness, personal identity, episodic memory and the ability to imagine oneself in the future or to remember oneself in the past (Balbernie 2001). Particularly in the right hemisphere, functions develop which control emotion, and appraise incoming stimuli and interpersonal communications: in fact it is here that the emotions are managed.

However in adverse circumstances of neglect, abuse and trauma, there will be a failure in such development. This will lead to a huge range of problems and presentations such as withdrawnness and dissociation, or distractibility and poor impulse control (Perry *et al.* 1995). Neglect leads to a lack of sensory stimulus, whereas trauma, the overactivation of important neural systems during sensitive periods of development, leads to hyperarousal (which initially may bring help), but changes to immobility, freezing, dissociation, or fainting: a 'surrender' response. 'Traumatised children use a variety of dissociative techniques. Children report going to a "different place", *assuming persona of heroes or animals*, "a sense of watching a movie that I was in" or "just floating" – classic depersonalisation or derealisation reponses' (Perry *et al.* 1995: 281; emphasis added).

Maternal depression is a form of unintended neglect (Zeanah *et al.* 1997). It is thought that babies exposed to short-term depression may recover but prolonged depression is damaging to the left frontal region of the cortex associated with outwardly directed emotions (Nelson and Bosquet 2000). Depressed mothers find it difficult to respond to the baby. For infants between the ages of six and eighteen months, having a depressed mother can lead to persisting emotional and cognitive difficulties for these infants (Murray 1997; Sinclair and Murray 1998; Balbernie 2001). Maternal depression affects mother–infant communication which plays a crucial role in protecting the child against mental or emotional disorders: 'this position of communication is based on the specific adaptive relevance of communication in human evolution' (Papousek and Papousek 1997: 38).

Mothers support the child's development of symbolic capacities, and acquisition of language and this is adversely affected by maternal depression. Tronick and Weinberg (1997) posit the toxic effect of maternal depression on a child's social and emotional functioning and development: 'the human brain is inherently dyadic and is created through interactive exchanges' (Tronick and Weinberg 1997: 73). A healthy mother and infant develop a model of mutual regulation which, if successful, allows the creation of dyadic states of consciousness allowing error and repair. Infants become aware of mother's depression and become hypervigilant of mother's emotional state in order to protect themselves; causing them to become emotionally restricted. In the dyadic mother–infant system, during maternal depression, the infant is deprived of the experience of expanding his or her states of consciousness in collaboration with mother. Instead they may take on elements of the mother's depressed state, e.g. sadness, hostility, withdrawnness, and disengagement in order to form a larger dyadic system. In the service of growth the infant incorporates the mother's depressed states of consciousness.

This research highlights the need for early intervention programmes. However, it is not too late for older children, which is the area of work encompassed in this book. It is possible for neural pathways to connect where previously there have been none; and it is possible for reflective thinking processes to develop in therapy but it is a slow and uphill task. Schore has emphasised that human learning takes place throughout the life-cycle; although a complete cure is unrealistic it is possible to repair some damage and improve the quality of relationship and therefore the future life of the child and their children. He maintains that '[T]he patient–therapist relationship acts as a growth promoting environment that supports the experience-dependant maturation of the right brain, especially those areas that have connections with the subcortical limbic structures that mediate emotional arousal' (Schore 1994: 473, in Balbernie 2001).

Fonagy and Target (1998) suggest that there has been a shift in emphasis in psychoanalytic practice from a focus on the retrieval of forgotten experience to the creation of a meaningful narrative being considered as mutative. This echoes a move towards the interactional and interpersonal aspects of the work, working towards the development of a reflective function (Fonagy and Target 1997). Schore suggests that in therapy:

> ... nonverbal transference–countertransference interactions that take place at pre-conscious-unconscious levels represent right hemisphere to right hemisphere communications of fast-acting, automatic, regulated and dysregulated emotional states between patient and therapist. Transference events clearly occur during moments of emotional arousal, and recent neurobiological studies indicate that 'attention is altered during emotional arousal such that there is a heightened sensitivity to cues related to the current emotional state'
> (Lane *et al.* 1999: 986, in Schore 2001c: 315)

Resonance between the analyst and the patient's unconscious then becomes of prime importance as they attune empathically. This suggests that the patient must have a vivid affective experience of the therapist (Amini *et al.* 1996, in Schore 2001c). In cases where there has been acute terror, neglect or depression, the natural environment, nature and the animal world, may act as a catalyst for the creation of images. The creation of images through art mediums can act as mediators, allowing movements towards a person to person relationship.

PSYCHODYNAMIC THEORY AND PRIMITIVE STATES OF MIND

In order for healthy emotional development to take place the baby needs a carer who is physically, emotionally and mentally receptive. Psychodynamic theory has made a huge contribution to understanding what happens when there is a failure of environment around the child in terms of unconscious primitive states of mind being uncontained. These then impact on all relationships and are shown in the ways that the child relates towards the therapist. If these primitive states of mind can be understood and contained, a new way of relating will develop towards the therapist and then, in relations in the external world. At this stage, three useful concepts will be highlighted for the reader: Bion's 'container/contained'; Fordham's 'self and deintegration', and Meltzer's 'claustrum'. A theoretical overview follows in Chapter six.

Bion and 'container/contained'

The idea of 'containing' is central in analytic psychotherapy. Klein described the ego developing through projection and introjection. Engaged emotional contact between mother and baby is essential to this process. Klein's description of projective identification is one in which one person contains a part of another. The baby projects anxieties and fears into the mother, where they will hopefully be understood and returned to the baby in a modified way. However, if the baby has intense anxieties and fears that the mother is unable to contain, the child splits off this part of the self with the accompanying feelings into the mother through the mechanism of projective identification. The mother may shut herself off from these feelings, not allowing them to enter, or to become prey to these anxieties herself.

Projective identification was explored particularly by Rosenfeld (1952) and Bion (1959) with very disturbed patients who projected disturbed parts of the self on to the analyst and then had problems in introjective processes as they became fearful as to what might be put back into them. Bion thought that the mother needed to be able to be receptive to the infant's terror through a state of mind he called reverie. In this way, 'beta elements' are transformed by 'alpha function', that is, extreme anxiety is made bearable and given meaning.

Later, Meltzer *et al.* (1986) distinguished between projective identification which is characterised by a need to communicate and a wish for containment, with 'intrusive identification' which is more of an invasion of the object in order to evacuate anxieties or to control the object from inside in phantasy. One can think about this container/contained relationship in different ways. For instance, in Chapter three, one can see Lucy searching for containment by creating chaos in the therapy room. Sally, in the case study, is a child who used projective identification in order to evacuate anxieties and to control, as described by Meltzer.

Fordham and 'the self and deintegration'

Two children, Henry and Colin, had difficulty in 'letting anything out' and with children in this state of mind Fordham's theories about the self are helpful.

Fordham developed Jung's work in describing a theory of the self, based on Jung's model of the psyche, to see if he could make sense of the primitive states of mind in childhood psychosis. Jung, in his work with children, had had a sense of the limitless quality of the child's unconscious and of the power of the parent's unconscious processes, as the principal cause of neurosis in the child. Jung's conception of the child's mind was similar to the ideas of Levy-Bruhl on participation mystique. He envisioned it as unconscious, like the mind of primitive tribal people in their relationship to certain objects and the environment. Fordham developed ideas about the self of the child, emphasising that the child had an individual life. Through his observations of children he realised that they did develop a boundary to the self, for example, he saw an instance of ego development in a two year old, arising from actions of the self: 'the scribble became a circle and she integrated the realisation that there was a boundary between fantasy and reality' (Astor 1995: 46).

Fordham developed Jung's two different concepts of the self (as the whole personality, as a central archetype), to include a primary or original state of integration. He conceived of the self not as an archetype, but as beyond archetypes and ego, which are then seen as arising out of, or deintegrating from, the self. He thought that this primal self gave rise to structures from interaction with the environment which it in part created. He called the dynamic of the self, deintegration and reintegration. A deintegrate is a part of the self; Astor gives examples of a baby's cry, as an objectively manifested deintegrate, for biological adaptation; or a creation of an image with potentially symbolic meaning as a subjectively manifesting deintegrate. In thinking about images it is possible to understand the difficulty that some clients have in reflecting on a picture with the therapist after they have made it, as it is not possible to get a third perspective on it until it has been reintegrated. Fordham understood the process of deintegration, as energy from the self to objects, and returning as a reintegration, energy to the self.

Fordham thought that the self gave the 'underlying potential structure' for the baby's response to the world around them. As the ego develops the personality takes on further structuring and subject and object become more distinct. A boundary begins to be formed and the separating out of 'me' and 'not me' (Astor 1995). Fordham thought of this as the beginning of the individuation process. Fordham had followed Jung in believing there to be an original state of primitive identity (via participation mystique). He had thought that the infant and mother were in a fused state but observation studies revealed these to be periodic. 'What was more important was the mother's capacity to receive and make sense of the baby's communications such that the baby took from its mother's attention an experience of the world, usually of safety and of being understood' (Astor 1995: 56).

Jung had conceptualised psychosis as an extreme form of a disorder of the self, from his work with adult patients. He had understood psychotic symptoms as the psyche's way of restoring itself to health. Jung had allowed unconscious spontaneous expression with play with stones and water to heal him (Jung 1963: 168). He had seen that through play he could integrate childhood memories and personal conflicts from his inner and outer world. In thinking about autistic children, Fordham questioned whether an inner world was being defended from impingement or whether the self was failing to engage with the world, failing to deintegrate, because there was a fear of the ego disintegrating. This would be a different barrier to development. Fordham pictured in this case not a world of inner objects but a world of self–objects, acting to destroy anything that was not a self–object. His work was to discover if children could have a similar experience to Jung through play and the making of images which would touch the core of their psychosis and facilitate healing. He worked with a child called Alan who lived in a phantasy world, described in *The Self and Autism* (Fordham 1976). Astor describes the essential core of Fordham's technique and interpretative method which 'was to refer to Alan's world as he experienced it, namely outside of himself. He spoke of it as if it was in projection only and not inner to him . . . In other words he analysed the projective identificatory content, in projection' (Astor 1985: 89–90). It was also characteristic of him to respect the child's defences, because he thought that they are of value to the individual and it is their 'irreversibility and rigidity' which give rise to the difficulties. In the treatment, Alan, began to bring back to his body/mind, what he had split off from it. Fordham understood these to be deintegrating parts of the self being held in a split-off and projected world in the service of defence. They were exteriorised and not treated as part of the self. He had failures in reintegration in that he did not acknowledge interpretation which referred these experiences to his inner world. Fordham's work with another patient, James, explored the failure of the deintegrative process (Fordham 1976).

Meltzer: the 'claustrum'

The third concept is that of the claustrum which can aid thinking about children who have a massive use of projective identification. In projective identification the patient's characteristics can be attributed to others, or they can take on characteristics of others to themselves. The work of Meltzer and Rosenfeld has demonstrated how projective identification can be to an internal object (Rosenfeld 1952; Meltzer 1967, 1992).

Meltzer defined the 'claustrum' as a phantasy of the inside of the mother's body divided into three parts: 'the head, as the seat of omniscience, or alternatively, the breast with its promise of ease and satiation, the genitals where erotic activity constantly takes place, the bottom compartment where relationships are degraded to an unmitigated striving for power' (Dubinsky 1997: 19). Dubinsky describes claustrum phantasies as often evoking a sense of place, and that there is an overlap with oedipal and sibling rivalry:

> The phantasy of intruding in the claustrum may be induced by difficulties in the early relationship, as the child may want to intrude omnipotently inside a mother experienced as inaccessible. The child may indeed feel that there is no place in the mother's mind or heart, because the mother is depressed or preoccupied, or because the child's jealousy portrays the mother as wholly absorbed with his father and siblings.
>
> (Dubinsky 1997: 20–21).

Claustrum phantasies are evident in children's behaviour in the room with the therapist and also in their pictures (see Chapter five pp. 104–8). In the case study, Sally moves between the different 'compartments' described by Meltzer, often entering in phantasy by diving under the therapist's chair in an intrusive way.

Children in these states of mind try to get rid of unbearable feelings. A relationship of container/contained needs to be introjected for thought to develop but when this has not happened unbearable thoughts are felt as concrete 'things-in-themselves' to be got rid of by projection or acting out, in the absence of symbolic capacities (Bion 1962a). At such times the therapy room can feel like a battleground. Verbal interpretation is very risky; to a vulnerable child (or adult) in these states of mind words can feel like being attacked. Acting out occurs to avoid tension, frustration and inner conflicts. Internal relationships are also acted out as we saw above in claustrum phantasies. The therapy moves towards becoming a 'playful battleground' as our understanding of the child grows. Play with the projected relationships in the transference/countertransference dynamic can aid understanding and in this an attitude of curiosity is helpful. Firm boundaries are needed as children can come in states of fear and terror disguised in omnipotent behaviour. Acting out/acting in becomes a form of tangible engagement with these states of mind. Moving from psychodynamic theory to the world of art, Langer's theory around discursive and presentational symbolism can be helpful in thinking about the way that children present material as a way of communication:

> The symbolism of the secondary process is discursive; conscious rational thinking is symbolised through words which have a linear, discrete successive order. The symbolism of the primary process is non-discursive, expressed in visual and auditory imagery rather than in words. It presents its constituents simultaneously not successively, it operates imaginatively but cannot generalise.
>
> (Case and Dalley 1992: 143)

Langer (1963) thought that language is the only means of articulating thought, everything which is not thought is 'the inexpressible world of feeling'; that is 'not symbols of thought but symptoms of inner life' (Langer 1963: 85). She discusses pictures and images as being examples of 'non-discursive symbolism', with units that do not have independent meanings like a language. There is no fixed meaning apart from content. 'It is first and foremost a direct *presentation* of an individual object' (Langer 1963: 85). When children are acting out/acting in I find it useful to try to step back from what is often a fraught situation to think what image is being presented here, but I sometimes have to continue in the part that the child-director has given me until I can reach this point. The clinical material in the book presents primitive states of mind to the reader. These are difficult to describe in language which is discursive, so that a combined approach has been chosen which uses stories, images and poetry that will hopefully engage the reader in the states of mind under consideration.

In this book the following links will be made: we are animals, and have a contradictory relationship to the rest of the animal world; animals, animal images, and the natural world outside the therapy room can act as a catalyst for a deeper use of materials, or for a coming into relationship with the therapist. Traumatised children can take on an animal persona, in situations where supportive emotional human to human contact has not been available.

THE CHAPTERS

Chapter one, An Animal Alphabet, introduces our contradictory and ambivalent relationship to animals. We both 'see ourselves' and want to 'distance ourselves' from them, so that we fluctuate in mental and emotional distance towards our fellow animals. In this way they can offer a mirror of the human condition. In Chapter two, I explore how the emergence of animal images in therapy can assist communication and engage patient and child in the work. This will be concerned particularly with the three-dimensional anthropomorphic animal image that has a presence in therapy that can be related to 'body to body'. It is suggested here and in Chapter four that transitional animal toys appearing in images may represent an infant part of the older child. The presence of live animals in therapy may give a concrete and symbolic representation of part of the self that is coming on stage in therapy. In Chapters two and three, the concepts of participation mystique and duality-unity allow a different perspective on three-dimensional images that are 'out there' but also 'part of me'. This way of thinking gives a particular engagement and investment in the things that we make and builds on the work of Schaverien to do with transactional objects and the scapegoat transference with adults. Chapter three concentrates on nature seen through the therapy room window as a catalyst in the patient's search for an object relationship. It is suggested that it may be easier for children to relate 'out there', finding an image to match an inner state and thus the beginnings of an emotional language. In cases where there has been severe neglect, children do not feel safe enough to relate person to person or to have imaginative interactions. The window allows the experience to be safely framed and to be seen as an extension of the therapy room. Such aesthetic encounters can allow experience of the beautiful or the sublime, fostering both the first use of materials but also a coming into relationship with the therapist. This is especially important when there has been a failure of the 'environment mother' (Winnicott 1971).

In Part two, the theme of 'duality-unity' is continued in the different context of mother–baby relationship, undoubtedly our first experience of at-oneness. The introduction explores the closeness and separation inherent in personality development. It begins by considering the parent's experience of pregnancy and some of the factors which contribute to the parent's imaginings of the expected baby. The Introduction to Part two looks at some of the concepts developed by Klein, Bion, Winnicott and Bick (pp. 73–7). Winnicott's ideas about 'psychosomatic unity for healthy living' and 'environmental impingement' are of particular interest in the backgrounds of the children discussed in this book who were 'hard to reach'. Bick developed some interesting concepts in relation to children who lack containment 'second skin formation' and 'adhesive identification', which are taken up further in Chapters five and six.

Chapter four explores separation and sleeplessness in the older child, building on the pioneering work of Daws with sleepless infants and their mothers. Clinical work with families, parents, and individual children in both child psychotherapy and art therapy focuses on 'helpful images' from dream and art work, as well as mental images from the parents and those evoked in the therapist's mind. The making of images in art therapy can give a form to those imagined phantoms of the night that haunt the sleep of sensitive children. Animal images may emerge in child therapy to represent and symbolise the traumatised younger self that is frozen in fear. The child's favourite toy, that has usually been a transitional object, signals the coming on to the scene of the infant within the child.

Chapter five introduces the taking on of an animal persona by children in therapy. Children who have been traumatised may take on an animal persona in order to protect the core self which is under threat inside. Where this core self is frozen in fear they are able to interact with the environment, which includes the therapist, through the senses. This defence protects the self from harm when the strain of 'being human' becomes too great. Defences, where maternal containment has been inadequate, particularly Bick's concepts of adhesive identification and second skin formation are considered in this context. The chapter follows with an excursion into literature to consider two kinds of 'becoming an animal', one of which is related to empathy and the other to a more intrusive identification to escape the pain of human existence. Clinical material follows to look at the projective processes in the use of animal puppets, and the taking on of an animal persona by an abused and traumatised child. Finally, some ideas about pet–human interaction and the positive gains in children turning to animals are considered.

Chapter six describes some of the main contributors to psychoanalytic understanding of autistic and psychotic states of mind, looking at the work of Meltzer and Tustin as well as more recent developments from Tavistock Workshops. This chapter concludes with extracts from two firsthand accounts, one of Aspergers, one of autism, to contribute to understanding the taking on of an animal persona.

In Chapters seven, eight and nine, the previous themes are united into a clinical narrative. The story of part of the work with my patient, Sally, attempts to look at the dynamics inherent in work with children emerging from a confusional state with mother, focusing on paintings, clay-work, play/stories, and language development. Case histories interweave life history, words (and images) of the patient, with words (and mental images) of the therapist, addressed to an imaginary reader. Case studies can make us feel guilty because of the breaking of confidentiality, even when we have permission. However, there is a need in therapists who work mainly alone, to share their work, to test out ideas, and to create a community of work. There are some pitfalls in such story-making; Spence (1997) suggests that for every compelling interpretation there are others equally valid, which are obscured by the presentation. He also suggests that in the classic narrative of psychoanalysis the therapist is presented as the hero or heroine. Ward quotes Bion, saying that through the fiction of the narrative, '[T]he reader is prepared for the triumph of psychoanalysis in contrast with the patients previous misfortunes . . .' (Bion 1967: 120, quoted in Ward 1997: 7). The positive in case history is that it shares experience; and the reader may be able to engage with the narrative, even if it inevitably 'smooths over rough edges' (Ward 1997). Near the beginning of work with Sally, another professional asked: 'Why are you wasting your time with Sally when you could make a real difference with other children?' This was a comment on the bewildering number of symp-toms and the lack of hope for a successful outcome. Working with the com-plex and difficult is necessary, as these children will go on to have children and the intergenerational dynamics will go yet another round. Families like Sally's need early intervention; as by the time they were referred, they had become isolated and stuck. The special school environment had scope for a wide variety of interventions with the whole family, providing a first link to a community. Edwards, writing in support of the case study as a form of research, says: 'Image-making, story-telling, therapy and research are each, in their own way, concerned with joining together actions, intentions, emo-tions, perceptions and events into meaningful narratives, though these narratives may take different forms' (Edwards 1999: 7).

Case studies are on a cusp of the private and the public; Borossa comments: 'Clinical writing is simultaneously called to function as a narrative representa-tion of the *private interaction* between patient and analyst and as a regula-tor of psychoanalysis as a discipline and an institution, therefore very much part of the *public domain*' (Borossa 1997: 47). Spurling (1997) also comments on the case study in its role of 'gate-keeping', in line with requirements for entry into the various therapy professions. Despite its pitfalls and drawbacks, the possibility for identification with patient and therapist, leading to discus-sion, make it a relevant method of research. Hillman writes: 'we are all in this field of psychotherapy, not medical empiricists, but workers in story' (Hillman 1983: 9). In the case study in Part three, the family, and Sally in particular, start therapy without a story, and with muddled characters. Sally took on an animal persona, as a way of being animated with the therapist, emerging into this way of being as she came out of autistic defences. The animal personas could be seen as the creation of characters that gradually developed story-line and plot; becoming a way that Sally could imagine her own history and future. Finally, Chapter ten, ends the case history, and offers some conclusions.

Chapter I

An animal alphabet of our actual and symbolic relationship to animals

> Animal species differ at their peripheries, and resemble each other at their centres; they are connected by the inaccessible, and separated by the apparent.
>
> (Foucault 1970: 267)

Apes

'The genetic relationship of the other great apes to humans is quite close, such that Diamond (1992) has argued that, according to the principles of scientific taxonomy applied to all other animals, humans should be labelled "the third chimpanzee", along with chimpanzees and bonobos [pygmy chimpanzees]' (Waldau 2002: 60). Waldau goes on to discuss the extraordinary similarity of the genetic material as follows: 98.4 per cent for human–chimpanzee similarity and 97.7 per cent for human–gorilla similarity. 'The identity is, so to speak, more than skin deep. For example chimpanzees and humans, though different in appearance, are closer genetically than are the two species of elephants (Fouts 1997: 94–5, in Waldau 2002: 61).

Bears

A brief report on bear parks around the world on *Newsround*, a BBC children's programme (7 December 1999) reported that: the bears are kept in circumstances utterly unlike their normal environmental conditions. They live in crowded surroundings with many other bears and are kept hungry so that they beg for food and fight for it, to amuse and entertain tourists. Bears are nomadic and live a solitary existence, avoiding contact, so that these are quite tortuous conditions for them. Many of the bears showed autistic and institutional defences such as rocking, self-mutilation, pacing, and bizarre repetitive movements. The news item lasted a minute or two, but the images left a feeling of horror for the sake of the bears in tortuous captivity; not only do they bring images of damaged children to mind, but also, it feels as if little people are trapped in those bear skins. They look human. Objectively, I think that this is because they stand on two legs, like me. I became more open to feeling what it would be like to be a captive, either an animal in a zoo, or a human in a prison. Looking at the bears, gave a moment of insight where I was less defended and felt the pain anew. Is it because their response cannot be articulated in our languages, that, we have an empathic feeling response to animals distress, recognising their physical response as one that would be our own, if we were in that situation? In this way do they bring us in touch with our humanity? When suffering is stripped of words, do we see in animals our human selves more clearly?

Chimpanzees

The tourists seemed to be captivated by the dressing up of baby bears in costumes. This was similar to chimpanzee tea parties that I was taken to as a child. To 'be an animal', as a term of abuse, is to be ruled by natural passions and urges. In aping ourselves the chimpanzees allowed us to look at ourselves with laughter as they did the things that we were not allowed to do. We were delighted when they did not pour out the tea 'properly'. They let us see our animal selves that are confined by social restraint. Animals offer up a mirror to us of our human condition. This is set in motion as we learn to understand our own emotions through attributing them to anthropomorphic animal characters of our childhood. Douglas comments that: 'Animals are natural objects which help determine what it is to be a human social subject' (Douglas 1966).

Dog

When animal images appear in art therapy, they frequently assist communication and material is presented in a way more acceptable to the patient, it engages them in the work; and may offer a channel for putting thoughts and feelings into words. This may be so particularly for children who lack words for mental states. Images of pets and transitional object toy animals and young animal characters from book, television, film and video frequently make appearance in the images of children trying to communicate. One elective mute child drew her pet dog 'in the picture' with a lead, but only her hand was visible at the picture edge. In this way her dog stood in for her at the beginning of therapy, eager and tail wagging, but at the other end of the lead 'out of the picture' was a much more reluctant part of her. It could be thought that her instinct was to make contact, but all the complex reasons that had led to her symptom of elective muteness were off stage. In this picture she also presented an acceptable side of her self, wanting the therapist to like her and to see her attractiveness. Towards the end of therapy she drew herself and her dog fully in the picture, unconsciously having come full circle and linking back to the start. In this way, the animal image acted to engage the therapist, by mute means, at the start of therapy. Animal images can be a sign of hope that parts of the self, hidden or not yet given recognition, will be seen, put forward in a palatable form.

Elephant

In South-East Asia white elephants are seen as descendants of the original winged elephants that roamed the cloudscapes above earth and as avatars of the Buddha. Chadwick describes a captive white elephant, Pra Barom Nakkot, who because of his colour was imprisoned and chained in a pavilion, unable to move and never let out (Chadwick 1994). Worship and ill-treatment intertwine: an example of the way that we can hold two contradictory views towards animals in our minds. 'It has however been known since time immemorial that human ownership of an elephant makes it unsocial and a psychological misfit' (Chadwick 1994: 311). There is not space here to look at the complexity of elephant life, their matriarchal culture and social system, long adolescence, and elaborate and varied communication. For instance only one-third of elephant calls are audible to the human ear, the remainder are subsonic. The trunk gives them a range of expression to equal the expression of a primate's face. Little is known of their body language communication. Of the elephant's confinement and solitary captivity, Chadwick says: 'Forever alone. Colossal. And very likely insane' (Chadwick 1994: 353).

Fox

Our ambivalence towards animals can be encapsulated by this story. Sitting with a group of persons covering several generations, someone spoke of a friend who had a fox's den at the bottom of their garden. There were several different responses. Some felt it as an almost magical occurrence of nature overlapping with human contact, with awe that nature would reveal herself. Some commented on the prevalence of foxes living in towns and their urban occurrence, as an interesting phenomenon. Some expressed worries about domestic pets if should they fall prey to the fox's appetite. Others expressed horror of dirty vermin living in one's garden and thought they would communicate diseases and fleas at the very least. The town person's separation from the country and nature creates the possibility of two extremes, mystical awe and horror of the visceral. There is a complex argument, taking place in Britain, about the countryside, between town and country. Having been bought up in the town with expeditions to the country I retain an element of joy and surprise about contacts with nature: remembering the day we saw a toad blown up to prevent it being swallowed by a snake. If I come across a deer in a field or a fox crosses the road I still feel delight. But for those living in the country a fox or badger can be a predator and thieve the chickens, creating mayhem and then one thinks of the brave cockerel who died trying to protect the chickens: here nature is one's adversary.

Gods

Lovejoy (1960) used the term 'anthropocentric teleology' to describe and criticise the claim that the physical world, including other animals, had been designed by a Creator to serve humanity, a view he called 'one of the most curious monuments of human imbecility' (1960: 186). Western perceptions of animals stem from the Judaeo/Christian religion where animals and plants are understood to be put on earth to serve the interests of humanity (Thomas 1983). This anthropocentric view of the world with man at the centre with absolute mastery over other life forms is hard to shift and has led to the physical side of life and nature being seen as a source of impurity and evil. Seeing animals as inferior and subordinate was given more credence by the earlier rationalist philosophers of ancient Greece: Plato and Aristotle. There are other views, of animals possessing equal dignity, and souls, like humans; of reincarnation and the transmigration of souls. This view has been held in the west, by Cathars as well as in eastern religions (Hamilton 1981). There are two quite opposing views, of animals as soulless, a Cartesian view of them as being insensate machines which allowed one to do what one liked: or the view that gives them equal status (Thomas 1983). The view that animals are inferior has enabled man to exploit them. In order to do this a natural tendency to see ourselves in animals has to be overcome. Animals, especially in captivity, will begin to treat other animals of different species as members of their own (Hediger 1965).

Human animals

Gray writes:

> For much of their history and all of pre-history, humans did not see themselves as being any different from the other animals among which they lived. Hunter-gatherers saw their prey as equals, if not superiors, and animals were worshipped as divinities in many cultures. The humanist sense of a gulf between ourselves and other animals is an aberration. It is the animist feeling of belonging with the rest of the world that is normal. Feeble as it may be today, the feeling of sharing a common destiny with other living things is embedded in the human psyche. Those who struggle to conserve what is left of the environment are moved by the love of living things, *biophilia*, the frail bond of feeling that ties humankind to the Earth.
>
> (Gray 2002: 17)

Intelligence, Illness and Institutions

Companion animals offer fairly constant, non-judgemental, often uncon-
ditional love and respect to individuals who may not have this relationship
with other humans. Pets have the capacity to make us feel needed and in
doing this they can boost our self-esteem. Pets that are relaxed and at ease
may enable us to relax:

> . . . .the presence of undisturbed living organisms exerts a calming effect
> because the sight and sound of undisturbed animals and plants have
> been a useful sign of safety for most, if not all, of man's evolutionary
> history . . . like other primates we use the flight behaviour of other animals
> with more acute senses as signals of danger.
>
> (Katcher *et al.* 1984: 178)

Another important area is that of tactile stimulation. Pet owning is significant in predicting survival in the elderly after illness, stroking relieves stress
and reduces blood pressure. In a curious way animals have the ability to
'humanise' and 'normalise' environments which are institutional and cus-
todial. This is curious because at other times we are anxious to distance
ourselves from animals. We are humans, above you other animals and separated by our particular intelligence. We look down and distance ourselves
from these different intelligences of the animal world.

Jo-fi

The function of pets as surrogates has been noted by several writers on
human–pet interaction. They are usually thought to be stand-ins for displaced love to a child, or other member of the family. However it has also
been noted that pet owning runs in families and that if your family has pets
then you are likely to have pets for your children (Veevers 1985). It may also
be a culture. Freud, on his pet Chow Chow, Jo-fi:

> Affectionate without ambivalence, the simplicity of a life free from the
> almost unbearable conflicts of civilisation, the beauty of existence com-
> plete in itself and yet, despite all divergences in organic development
> [there is] that feeling of intimate affinity, of an undisputed solidarity . . . a
> bond of friendship unites us both . . . .
>
> (Freud 1975: 434)

This quote, rich in feeling, epitomises the depth of attachment between man
and animal.

Kanzi

A young language trained chimpanzee learnt to use a system of abstract symbols because he had been exposed to the abstract symbols at a time when he was peculiarly ripe for learning, demonstrating the same facility as a young child to learn 'any language' (Savage-Rumbaugh and Lewin 1994). Waldau discusses how the search for language competence in apes has been anthropocentric – a search for human dimensions in other animals rather than looking at the realities of other animals: 'Great emphasis has been given to the possession of language abilities as an indicator of intelligence in other animals, reflecting the centrality of emphasis on "language", in the classical arguments for the distinctive place of humans relative to other animals. For example, the Stoics and Augustine were Descartes' intellectual predecessors in advancing the thesis that membership in humans' language community is the critical factor for moral considerability' (Waldau 2002: 69). This, also Christian view, can be seen in the *Narnia* children's books of C. S. Lewis (1950–56). In these it is perfectly all right to kill ordinary animals but a horror to kill 'talking animals'.

Live animals in therapy

Children sometimes bring live animals into a therapy session. Their presence can suggest the older part of the child coming into relationship with a younger part: given concrete presence in animal form. Dorothy, age eleven, had been referred for art therapy to a community clinic. She had dyspraxia: with the accompanying symptoms of poor coordination, and short-term memory difficulties but added to this a hate of change and a lack of visual imagination. Her mother suffered from depression which further complicated the picture. At the start of therapy she had got stuck, not knowing what to do, but during the first year she had moved to being able to engage with her own ideas for drawing, painting, or modelling, and was able to initiate brief areas in conversation. She thought that she could not visualise, i.e. have a picture in her head, but I found that this developed while we worked together. Dorothy played ball with me each session before starting anything else. It felt like touching base with the therapist's liveliness and the stimulus of what this generated between us, then, she could draw. It was as if she arrived with something quite passive inside and had to work up to something more lively. A year into therapy she drew 'a black chick'. The chick is half red robin (a red breast) and half a blackbird. It had an open beak, ready to feed. The image both expressed and allowed reflection on Dorothy's experience of being parented. Her mother (the blackbird) had fought a long battle with depression. It was difficult for her to have an active model of parenting, different from her own background. In this way father had come to be the source of energy and vitality in the family (red robin), although he could also be overwhelmed at times.

The following session Dorothy bought in three hybrid shrimps in a tiny two-inch bottle with a cork in the top. They are called 'sea monkeys' and are very lively, in fact they were in constant movement up, down and around the bottle. They were almost transparent and were entrancing to watch because they almost fired off in movement, presumably by jets of water. Dorothy showed me that the male is bigger and that the female has tiny egg sacs. They were bought from a supermarket in a packet and are just added to water. Dorothy had bought them in to show me because her mother had thought that I would like to see them. She told me that she and her mum had been clearing out the attic together last week and had found a tank and had decided to use it again. They had found bags of baby clothes from when she was little, and old, favourite toys.

The clearing out of the attic was a healthy sign of psychic contents in movement. Dorothy and her mother were engaged together in re-visiting her babyhood and the shrimps suggested a lively baby with two lively parents. Dorothy's parents were seeing another therapist and talking about how the past might be affecting the present relationships in the family. Dorothy was engaging in therapy in a lively way and taking what she learnt from this relationship back into family life. The shrimps suggested the stirring of both a lively new part of mother and Dorothy that had been ossified: but that could, like the dried shrimps, come to life when put into fresh water (the therapy situations). The tank in the attic suggested symbolically that the family could nurture the baby parts of each other. The shrimps in their rapid movements were mesmerising, and engaged together in animal watching, we stirred inside in response. Animals that are connected with water, and hence with 'primal waters', often 'stand as symbols of the origin of things, and of the powers of rebirth' (Cirlot 1962: 11). At the next parent review, mum told me that Dorothy had bought a hairy dog cuddly toy, the first in which she had shown an interest; a transitional object allowing play and development around separation (Winnicott 1971).

Mole

Animal stories help us to discover and understand ourselves in the world; some stories are especially good at illustrating a particular stage of life. Children identify with the animals they find in fairy stories and other childhood narratives and in this way work out many of the psychological problems associated with growth and maturation (Bettelheim 1978). *The Wind in the Willows* is a classic children's book that has delighted generations (Grahame 1927). It works on many levels and is satisfying for adults and children alike. It is essentially a book about transition, moving to the next stage and the loops back that we make, as part of normal development. We meet the Mole when he is an innocent abroad and it is his learning about life with which we identify. The Water Rat is able to reflect, he is a poet, and to do that you have to have lived life and have something to reflect upon. The appeal of the Mole is that he has become emancipated from his hole, underground, and is learning about the world above with the Water Rat as his guide. We sympathise with his wish to try out new things and empathise with his misadventures. Mole defies the Water Rat's advice and goes alone to the Wild Wood.

The description of Mole alone in the Wild Wood is a brilliant evocation of being lost as a small child and will resonate in the memory of the older reader, and with thrilling currency in the mind of the younger. It is beautifully written with a build up of effect. 'There was nothing to alarm him at first entry.' As the Mole goes further into the Wild Wood and begins to get lost, it changes. At first it is fun and exciting. '[f]unguses on stumps resembled caricatures, and startled him for a moment by their likeness to something familiar and far away.' 'Then the faces began.' Mole sees faces in every hole but they all seem to be the same one. 'Then the whistling began.' Whichever way the Mole turns the whistling changes direction. 'Then the pattering began.' Mole thinks it is only falling leaves at first but it multiplies and becomes regular. Eventually as this all builds up the Mole panics and begins to run anyway and is totally lost (Grahame 1927: 43–5).

The continuing popularity of this book is partly its masterful story-telling but also its encapsulation of latency themes into adolescence; while being in touch with early life experiences, it understands what growing up is about. In this way children's literature can act as a transitional phenonemenon in that it allows imaginative play with the next stages of life, through identification with the characters.

> Children's fiction is replete with moments of horror, awe, fascination and suspense. Self and environment are mutually transformative as if something of the child's sense of ontogenetic metamorphosis is registered in the fiction he reads. Often, as in *The Wind in the Willows*, the tale is about a journey, a picaresque adventure that is faithful to the child's appreciation of his own psycho-somatic transformations.
>
> (Bollas 1987: 38)

Nature

Animals are huge parts of people's lives as family pets or on a different scale, part of our living world. We cohabit as part of the earth's ecology. Savishinsky suggests that family pets may be a bridge between culture and nature:

> The contrast between culture and nature is recognised in all societies, but the gap between them is emphasised more by some people than others. Totems, rituals and myths mediate between culture and nature and cultural categories keep these two ideas distinct and in their place.

But pets actually bridge and embody both of these realms. My pet theory about pets is that their ambiguity as cultured, non-human creatures who share our intimate lives allows them to mediate in this manner. In keeping pets, we combine the conscious and the unconscious in the same way that we do when observing rituals, telling myths, and respecting categories. The bonding and reconciliation of culture with nature that pets symbolise is one of the most important of these meanings, and it is not less effective for the way it works on us. We are not only the sole species that makes symbols: we are also the only creatures who keep other animals as pets.

(Savishinsky 1983: 129)

Other self: the dragon with two heads

The natural world and the mythical world offer a huge range of images that may be drawn upon to find a match for an internal state. Colin, age nine, would sometimes bring pre-drawn pictures from colouring books into the therapy session which he would proceed to colour in. It felt safer than using materials in the therapy room. He was fearful of contact, traumatised through domestic violence, now living in a foster family. The content of the images was meaningful and an unconscious communication to the therapist. In this session, it is possible to see that Colin was becoming aware of having needs and a wish to be in relationship to the therapist.

We had just returned after a holiday break, and Colin had responded to the separation by bringing in a newspaper, pretending to read, and almost hiding his head in it. This had the effect of leaving me feeling left out of his interesting activity and in this way he let me know what it had felt like to be excluded during the holiday (Case 2000b). He had also brought a picture that was partially coloured in. It was of a dragon, from the Disney film *The Sword and the Stone*. The dragon has two heads that look like they are arguing or thinking and feeling different things. After we had talked about some possible feelings about the holiday gap, he was able to abandon the newspaper. While he set to work busily colouring in, I sat with him, both trying out some ideas, but also thinking to myself about the different layers of meaning. What he brings is usually useful material to be worked with: Colin said that the dragon heads were arguing and that they were stuck together.

The mythical dragon was able to give expression to a sense of two people in one skin. Colin had for some time anxiously checked the clock through the session. This had felt both like anxiety that the session would go on too long, when is the end, but also how much is left, if only there were more. The two fluctuated through the session. In a similar way the two dragon heads in one skin gave expression to a wish to be safely inside one skin with me but also a fear of being trapped in one skin with me. Another aspect was that they also felt like different points of view beginning to emerge in Colin: the familiar way that he had learnt to deal with life and the possibility of a new voice inside as things began to be able to be felt inside that were previously defended against (Case 2002). It was interesting to think about the form taken by this expression. The dragon suggests fire and strength if angered, although appearing in a rather comic form. There was a real base to this in that one of his disturbing symptoms had been fire-raising. There was a part of him that could feel on fire with inexpressible rage, a reaction to the neglect he had suffered.

Pets

Our instinct to nurture and care for the young of our own species spills over to include those animal young that we can relate to either as pets, domestic animals or the exotic. We tend to relate better to those animals that are most like us or who come to symbolise some aspect of our lives. A child's first relationship with a live animal is likely to be with a family pet. At the same time they may also be eating animals. Midgley comments: 'the symbolism of meat-eating is never neutral. To himself the meat-eater seems to be eating life. To the vegetarian, he seems to be eating death. There is a kind of gestalt-shift between the two positions which makes it hard to change, and hard to raise questions on this matter at all without becoming embattled' (Midgley 1984: 27). There is an enormous split between our treatment of pets and our treatment of domestic animals reared for human consumption. Most pets are domesticated species. They have no significant practical purpose. We do not eat them or use their skin, or work them. They have the run of the house, personal names and are honorary members of the family. Children's books present life on the farm as a happy family only enviably larger with more animals, looking as if they were pets. The reality is very different, in that with factory farming, animals become objects and are subjected to a lifetime of continual deprivation, distress and discomfort (Serpell 1986).

Quakers

The first recorded use of animals as institutional adjuncts was in 1792 at William Tuke's Quaker Retreat in York, where animals were part of the living environment and patients were encouraged to care for them, because they were seen to have a humanising influence (McCulloch 1983). Animal Assisted Therapy (AAT), the actual and deliberate presence of animals as a medium in therapy, is not the subject of this book but the theories that underlie such work, have related interest. Here I can only offer a very brief account of the range of AAT available, not counting the well established guide dogs for the blind or deaf, but concentrating on the more clearly mental health issues. There is an accessible and popular overview in *Creature Comfort: Animals that Heal* (Graham 1999). Some earlier pioneers from the United States give a historical perspective on man's changing relationship to animals as well as chapters on a variety of pet therapy programmes (Levinson 1969, 1972; Corson and Corson 1980; Arkow 1984; Cusack 1988). There are good overviews of the animal/human bond from a variety of perspectives in Anderson (1975), Fogle (1981), Katcher and Beck (1983) and Anderson et al. (1984). In pet-facilitated therapy the animal mediates therapy under the guidance of the human therapist. The animal can: act as a link between therapist and human; draw out verbal and emotional responsiveness; facilitate social interaction for the client; provide a source of tactile comfort; build upon the client's inner resources and generally enhance the quality of life of the client (Brickell 1986). There are established programmes in the use of dolphins to promote communication in autistic children as well as sufferers of mental health problems (Dobbs 1991; Nathanson et al. 1997; Smith 1983; Cochrane and Callan 1992). There are well established programmes using horse-riding with disabled people and for children with language disorders (De Pauw 1984; Dismuke 1984; Hama et al. 1996). These projects take the patient to the animal's environment. Other projects take the animal to the institutional or home setting of the patient; dogs and cats, as well as other small and furry animals (Allen and Budson 1982; Baun et al. 1984; Beck et al. 1986; Brickell 1986; Corson et al. 1977; Whyam 1997; Yates 1987). One use of animal therapists is to help restore the spirits of those who are depressed through mental health; mental handicap or disability-related causes, another, to relieve the loneliness of the elderly.

Reflexive consciousness

The tendency to attribute human characteristics to animals is called anthropomorphism. Children find it harder than adults to make a distinction between humans and non-humans, and treat family pets as persons. They may find it easier to talk to their pet about intimate feelings, because there is no fear of ridicule or lack of understanding.

For this reason, children's literature uses anthropomorphic animal characters, rather then more realistic images, as a medium for conveying social values and rules (Sharefkin and Ruchlis 1974). Possibly children relate more clearly to animals because they are similarly dependant and are not so socialised or encultured as adults, which enables them to identify with the needs, feelings, motives and desires of animals. Serpell suggests that the human tendency to humanise or personify animals is part of our 'reflexive consciousness' (Serpell 1986: 139). Our ability to introspect and reflect on our motives and reasons for doing things is the nub of our social adaptation. We use self-knowledge to predict how others will behave, and use it on animals too. In doing this we transcend the species barrier. Our guilt about killing 'animal kin', has led us to develop many myths, rituals, beliefs, in order to assuage our guilt.

Speciesism

Waldau defines speciesism as the 'inclusion of all human animals within, and the exclusion of all other animals from, the moral circle' (Waldau 2002: 38). To understand the moral circle one need only think about a subject such as fox-hunting, and the violent emotions it engenders on both sides, for and against, to see that it is to do with where we draw a boundary, which animals are in or out. Richard Ryder (1992) first used the term 'speciesism' in relation to the selfishness of medical experiments – the mistreatment of other species justified by the 'benefits for our own species'. The *Oxford Dictionary of Philosophy* defines it in relation to racism and sexism, and indeed it grew out of the Liberation movements of the sixties and seventies. 'By analogy with racism and sexism, the improper stance of refusing respect to the lives, dignity, rights or needs of animals or other human species' (Blackburn 1994: 358).

Transitional objects

One of the primary ways that animals become part of children's lives is in the form of toys, which may be taken everywhere with them, from early on, as transitional objects (Winnicott 1951). Winnicott defined transitional objects and phenomena when he was exploring the beginnings of the ability to symbolise. He summarised the special qualities of the child to their transitional object, their first 'not me' possession: the infant has rights over the object which the adults agree to; it is affectionately cuddled as well as mutilated; it must never change, unless by the infant; it must survive loving and hating; and it must be seen to have a vital reality of its own. It is also crucial that it is in an 'intermediate area of experiencing', it doesn't come from within or without: it is between inner and outer realities, in a space between mother and child.

Transitional objects, in our culture, have importance in the early stages of object-relating and also in symbol-formation. Winnicott, thought that it was the fate of the transitional object to lose meaning, because the phenomena 'widens out into that of play, and of artistic creativity and appreciation, and of religious feeling, and of dreaming, and also of fetishism, lying and stealing, the origin and loss of affectionate feeling, drug addiction, the talisman of obsessional rituals, etc.' (Winnicott 1971: 5). Transitional phenomena presage the possibility of being able to accept difference and similarity, but also, with adverse circumstances can clearly lead to difficulties in later life. Looking at these ideas from a western point of view we put a value on separation, individuality, and possession. Infants are given small representations of cuddly animals or blankets and these come to act as separators from human contact. This is rather curious.

U

... are an animal. Tester comments that 'culture attempts to order the world logically in a way which makes every part of external reality intelligible and assigns it a place in taxonomy. As Douglas (1966) and Leach (1964) point out, the places where these logical orders overlap, or where an object can be allocated to more than one category, become sites of danger or taboo. The interstices are places where the 'fictive reality' (Douglas's phrase) maintaining social life is threatened with dissolution' (Tester 1991: 43).

This true story is amusing and touching, because it plays with these borders: A kangaroo with one eye, who had been brought up on a farm, and thought it was a dog, raised the alarm when a farmer became unconscious by knocking on the farmhouse door (News Report, BBC Radio Four, 23 September 2003).

Victoria

Victoria, age nine, had been referred to a mixed art therapy group at an ordinary primary school by her teacher. The group was for children with special needs or circumstances. Victoria was the eldest child from a large family and held responsibility for her younger siblings, co-parenting with her mother. In the group she was encouraged to use the space and time for herself but found this difficult, either wanting to assist other children or to make presents for her large family. In this session she had decided to make something for herself for the first time. Victoria chose clay and started to make a rabbit. Victoria is West Indian and is very aware in this multi-ethnic school of what colour people are and what racial group they belong to. She is in the majority, as 66 per cent of children in the school are West Indian. She had been staying with a friend's granny who is white and talked about this, while she decided to paint her rabbit white: pink nose, yellow mouth, brown whiskers and blue eyes.

Next session she began to make a pig money-box from clay by putting two thumb pots together. She was painting the body of the pig with brown paint while the clay was still wet and it went very smeary, it became 'dirty pig', but when she put the ears and face on she decided it was a dog, 'Dirty Dog', with much laughter and fun. She was very pleased with it. The following session she painted Dirty Dog and then placed the two animals together and talked about them (Illustration 1.1). Three-dimensional animals have a special presence: 'I like doing things made out of clay ... my dog is called Dirty Dog, because he is very dirty. He don't like having a bath and he always goes after cats, but the cats chase him back. He starts to run. When I call him in to have a wash, he is filled with dirty mud, all round him. My rabbit is called "Bright" 'cos he's so lovely and bright. He's got nice bright eyes and he's nice to me. My rabbit could read and write. That's why I call

Illustration 1.1 Victoria: Bright Eye and Dirty Dog.

him "Bright Eye" '. The two animals represent different parts of her and her struggle with school and the multi-cultural context in which she lives, but within a predominantly wider white culture. There is in the animal contrast the pull towards play and pre-school life, more to do with the senses, and the pull towards being successful at school and achieving well, more to do with intellectual development, and the three Rs. Dirty Dog lives in his senses, chasing, and does not like civilised washing, so that he represents instinctual life. He is the freer, fun loving, playful, pre-school part of Victoria. The white rabbit represents the expectations on her from school and home, to be gentle and biddable, 'a little mother', but also to achieve well. Looked at in a race and cultural context she has painted her pre-school self brown-skinned and her school self white-skinned. This reflected her West Indian home culture and the external world white culture. Some of the racial issues which were bought up in therapy in this group are discussed in another publication (Case 1999).

WXYZ: are at the end of the book pp. 208–10.

Chapter 2

Animals on stage in therapy: anthropomorphic animal objects

> Animism and autism seem to be opposite modes of operation of the primitive mind. Animism consists of endowing objects with life; pathological autism is a death-dealing process which blocks out things with body stuff to make them non-existent. It also reduces alive people to the state of inanimate things.
>
> (Tustin 1972: 83)

INTRODUCTION

This chapter will consider how animals form part of our imaginal world and how their appearance in art therapy can symbolise a particular kind of engagement in the therapy. The animal alphabet gave a kaleidoscopic view of our complex and contradictory relationship to nature and the animal world of which we form a part. Animal images can encompass the ambivalence we hold to our own desires and appear when the conflict between heart and head, passion and thought, nature and civilisation, conscious and unconscious is raging. Conversely, animals can also appear as an image of spirit, when the will to live has been low and an anthropomorphic animal guide from within needs to be externalised to give tangible form to a faint impulse. Animals are ubiquitous in art therapy with children; making their presence felt in pictures, coming to life in sand play or becoming a physical presence in clay. In this chapter the focus will be on the latter, sand and clay, on three-dimensional animal images, and their particular physical presence. Anthropomorphic animal objects, particularly three-dimensional ones, appear at a point in therapy when our animal instincts are becoming humanised. They come on to the stage in therapy in a preverbal form and catch our attention in a precise way because we relate to them body to body. In a peculiar way we become more aware of our humanity through our engagement with animal form. It has characteristics of being both like us, and not like us, which allows the child to accept this as part of themselves at their own pace; distance and closeness to the feelings embodied in the image can be played with in this way.

This dynamic can be seen in speech when we tend to use characteristics of animals to describe different human traits. So that we say someone is slothful, busy as a bee, brave as a lion, greedy as a pig, playful as a kitten, scared as a mouse, proud as a peacock. One of the difficulties of our raiding the animal world for similes, metaphors and symbols, as we have seen in the alphabet, is that we then tend to see the animals through that rather tunnel vision. If it becomes painful to see certain characteristics in ourselves then we can project them on to the animal world, and disparage them. At the same time we can admire them for other qualities. We can stereotype them and then be shocked when they turn out to have other instinctual characteristics that do not fit our view of them, for instance when a 'cuddly rabbit' has teeth and claws. As we saw in the alphabet, the way that we use and abuse the animal world has much in common with colonisation and racism, in that we can move from a fascination with the exotic, and a wish to own that beauty, to entrapment and captivity, to cruelty and a despising of 'inferior' species. The recent decision of child protection services, the RSPCA, and the police to work together highlights the common abuse of children and animals by the same people; a family that abuses animals is likely to abuse children. At the same time that we can project on to the animal world characteristics that we want to disown, we can also locate there characteristics that we want to protect, develop, or to emulate.

ANIMAL SYMBOLISM

Animals play an important and varied role in symbolism. They are important to us because they can represent the natural environment from which we feel cut off. For adults they may express our more primitive self from which we feel estranged and may represent in dreams, fantasy and images a wish to be more spontaneous, free, less restricted, and natural. Children are more likely to identify with the animal:

> There is a great deal of resemblance between the relations of children and of primitive men towards animals. Children show no trace of the arrogance which urges civilised men to draw a hard and fast line between their own nature and that of all other animals. Children have no scruples over allowing animals to rank as their full equals. Uninhibited as they are in the avowal of their bodily needs, they no doubt feel themselves more akin to animals than to their elders, who may well be a puzzle to them.
>
> (Freud 1913: 126–7)

Many children and adults feel an affinity towards particular animals, they are drawn towards a distinguishing feature or set of characteristics and as such they become part of material to be discussed in therapy. Cirlot (1962) links the origins of animal symbolism with totemism and animal worship. Frazer (1890) gives examples of two forms of animal worship. Animals may be respected, commonly revered and neither killed nor eaten; but they may also be worshipped because they are killed and eaten. In both kinds they are worshipped because the worshipper hopes for some benefit or quality from the animal, i.e. protection, advice, help, or the use of its flesh or skin. Frazer suggests that earlier than the totemistic worship described is the way that 'man endeavours to adapt the agencies of nature to his needs', through sympathetic magic (Frazer 1890: 134). In sympathetic magic the person may imitate what he wants to happen, e.g. act an animal being killed, or draw a successful hunt, or there may be a resemblance of qualities, wearing the skin of a ferocious animal to be successful in war. In these beliefs the relationship of man, animal and nature is very close and seen to be able to influence each other. Remnants of these primitive beliefs are still very persuasive and take serious form in superstition, e.g. a black cat crossing your path bringing good luck, or seeing magpies, 'one for sorrow, two for joy, three for a girl and four for a boy, etc.'.

The use of sympathetic magic may be easier for us to see in another 'primitive' culture. In fact, a visit to the Pitt Rivers Museum at Oxford shows in one cabinet: fish-shaped mascots used by fishermen of Great Yarmouth who would never go fishing without them, like attracting like; and prey god fetishes from New Mexico, tiny stone carvings of animal predators, carried while hunting. It was supposed that the hearts of animals of prey were infused with a spirit that has influence over the hearts of the animals they prey upon. If you make a stone model of the animal his heart still lives although he is changed into stone and this will aid you. In the same cabinet are more gruesome findings from Somerset to do with witchcraft: moles' feet as a charm against the toothache, taken from a live mole that is left to get away (how it could, without feet is a mystery); presumably it (symbolically) carries toothache away. There were also the hearts of different animals with nails in them, found hidden in Somerset chimneys, to bring about another's death or to break an evil spell.

Anima means life and soul. Animism is the belief that 'the phenomena of animal life are produced by an immaterial *anima*, soul, or vital principal, distinct from matter' (*Oxford English Dictionary*). Animism is the attribution of a living soul to inanimate objects and natural phenomena; thereby the belief in the existence of soul and spirit apart from matter. If one links our tendency to see ourselves in the world about us, so that animals, trees, and mountains can easily be given human form, personified, named; then the next step is to imagine them alive, with a soul and having power to affect our lives. Adults look at animals with a mixture of emotions, because in our relationship to them we see ourselves as battling between our higher, civilised behaviour and our bestial instincts; we may envy the fact that the animal is true to itself, it cannot be any other way, its qualities remaining constant.

Animals can appear as representatives of the unconscious, sometimes darkly, expressing a shadow side of the personality, sometimes more lightly, as a source of energy and vitality (Chetwynd 1982: 14). We may feel that in our relationship to pets we reconnect to our own nature and make ourselves more complete, or we may fight against our animal self and wish to subdue it (Savishinsky 1983).

Nature as adversary, against civilisation, is ritualised in fox-hunting. Our own animal natures and appetites that we fear may surface aslant our more socialised selves are ritually slain in the bull-fight. There must be a need in some, for whom the struggle between the two is a bitter hard-fought one, internally, to see the fight externalised. With the inevitable violence that accompanies these activities there is much room and opportunity for the interplay of cruel and sadomasochistic traits. The audiences to these pursuits can delight in the idea of pain/danger without actually being in it. This is epitomised in the bull-fight where the human animal fights another animal mammal. The victory of man over bull symbolises the victory of civilisation over the beast within us as well as over nature. It also holds elements of day over night, light over dark and good over evil. In this way whenever two animals are in battle, there may be a battle of 'higher' and 'lower' instincts.

A sense of identification with an animal, suggests a wish to come into relationship with an aspect of the unconscious, symbolised by the animal. This sense of them, as holding the possibility of renewal from the unconscious gives them a positive aspect: 'Animals in general seem to represent the lower instinctive forces in man which often know the way when our conscious is entirely at sea' (Hannah 1992: 127). Each animal can be thought of as an aspect of instinct. For instance, the dog, which appears very frequently in Part three, has lived so long with humans that it has become partly humanised, an instinct between animal and man. He has the capacity to relate. Hannah (1992: 91) gives examples of aspects of the dog in opposite pairs, loyal friend/betrayer, guide/trickster, watchdog/thief, healer/devourer of corpses.

TRANSITIONAL OBJECT AND TRANSACTIONAL OBJECT

Before discussing particular examples of case material where anthropomorphic animal objects make their appearance it will be helpful to clarify two related terms, that is: transitional object and transactional object. We saw in the animal alphabet that many transitional objects are in fact animals. Like family pets, transitional objects often have a special name so that there is considerable overlap between them in that both have a vital reality of their own: to the child. Although a family pet is alive and a transitional object is not, it is 'as if' alive; for instance if an older sibling is threatening to throw a younger sibling's teddy out of a window the response will be *as if* it will be hurt, because of the huge investment of self qualities and child/mother relationship in the object. A transitional object is in an in-between area – an 'intermediate area of experiencing', between inner and outer reality, between mother and child (Winnicott 1971). Its presence as 'stand in' for mother allows the sense of continuing presence of mother in her absence. The appearance of a child's transitional object in an image in therapy is usually poignant, and can express the first contact with a wounded infant within (Case 2003).

In the therapy room it is possible to see how art objects made, can be in an intermediate area of experiencing between child and art therapist, between inner and outer reality. When an object that has been made has an ongoing life in the therapy it takes on some of the qualities of a transitional object, fetish or talisman. In her writing, Schaverien, has made a huge contribution to explicating this complex area with adult patients (1987, 1992, 1994; Killick and Schaverien 1997). She suggests that the picture can act as a transactional object (a term borrowed from anthropology) through which unconscious transactions may be channelled and acted out. In the animal alphabet we saw how a mute child unconsciously used an image of her dog in the picture, to stand in for her, to greet the therapist. Schaverien (1994, 1995a) has discussed the art object mediating as a transactional object in anorexia, where it can take the place of food and when acknowledgement of interpersonal relationships is too threatening, it can hold the transference. She has discussed two further ways that the picture can mediate in psychosis, as a fetish and as a talisman (Schaverien 1992; Killick and Schaverien 1997). The scapegoat transference is a form of unconscious transference of attributes and states, through which an art object may come to embody otherwise intolerable affect (Schaverien 1987, 1992, 1998). Looked at in this way, the making of an art object and identification with it through magical thinking, can offer a route for a conscious attitude to develop. The route taken is from an undifferentiated state, towards the development of a symbolic attitude. Art objects may become transactional objects in the therapy. 'Such objects may be regarded as talismans in the therapeutic relationship because they are experienced as carriers or containers of magical significance' (Schaverien 1994). The magical investment of art works could be thought about in terms of projective processes initially between object, maker and therapist in the interactional field of the therapy. The image is invested with significance by the maker. It is then treated in the therapy as if it is imbued with the invested characteristics, in concrete form, and can take on a life of its own.

In child art therapy, animal images which have an anthropomorphic quality, representing an aspect of the self which is 'coming into being', can be undifferentiated extensions of the self, having qualities of transitional and transactional objects. They may be images of engagement, using the term in both its sense of betrothal and in its sense of interlinking. The making of an engaging animal deepens the therapy, both in terms of relationship to the therapist and in terms of the child's own engagement with the process. Having a three-dimensional model of an animal in the room is like welcoming another little person into the room, because of our tendency to see ourselves in another animal: personification. We respond differently to the three-dimensional; to another with a body like ourselves. It is this concrete aspect of the three-dimensional that is important to children who may be able to interact and respond on this body to body level, part transitional object, part art object, and part transactional object. We saw in the case of Victoria how three-dimensional images can be placed in relation to each other and how links can be made to parts of the self. Clinical material follows to illustrate some aspects of the appearance of three-dimensional anthropomorphic animal objects in therapy. The first was made in sand, an impermanent material, and the second, in clay, which transforms as it dries out, taking on permanency, and tangible presence for the duration of the therapy.

ANIMAL PRESENCE IN SAND PLAY: SIMON

Simon, age ten, was striking to look at with long black hair. He had been referred for therapy from a special school because of enormous difficulties within the family around oedipal issues. He had been born in traumatic circumstances amidst fears that mother and baby might die. The trauma of that time with its accompanying fear, horror and anxieties was still present. Mother and Simon felt stuck in a mother/baby relationship, as if she could never give him enough. In such circumstances parents often feel guilty, because of the child's traumatic entry into the world. Mother could not help him to move on to the next stage, or heal the rift in their bonding caused by the traumatic separation at birth, through illness. Simon dominated life at home, making it impossible for his parents to have a life together as a couple. He had developed a defensive manner which could cause hostility, in response to his critical comments. Father, who might in better circumstances have been able to help mother and son normally separate, felt left out and found it difficult to form a father/son relationship. Simon's struggles were those of a toddler, angry tantrums when he did not get his own way, but in the body of a much bigger boy. Simon's need to have mother's whole attention for himself had been transferred to the school classroom, exacerbated by his teacher's maternity leave and birth of a new baby. It had also been transferred to the therapist and therapy room. He found it unbearable that the therapist also saw other children. This was heightened, as he was seen by a therapist who also saw other children at his special school. This session, eleven months into the therapy, began with nothing feeling right for Simon.

Session

Simon was painfully aware of whom else the therapist saw, and thought that they 'got more of her'. His critical and controlling voice really disguised how agonising it was to share an important person's attention. As he came in he asked questions and made comments about another child that I saw who is away with 'flu. He suspected that this child would not have been able to have their session this morning but an awful suspicion is around that this child might have got more of the therapist because he is ill. These agonising thoughts prevented him from enjoying the time he had for himself. He was very jerky and restless, his long jet-black hair fell in an attractive fringe over his forehead but he kept shaking it back nervously and with irritation. He coughed and took cough sweets to draw attention to the fact that the therapist should be concerned about *him*. I talked about how painful these thoughts were. He picked up some toys he had used last week and as some dry sand fell off them he commented that X had been here; as if someone else had used them, whereas in fact he had used them himself in the sand last week. He began to use the sand and thought that it felt different because X had not been here this morning. He poured water over the sand and toys that he had dumped into the sand tray and began to irritably mix it up. He hated sand on his hands and flicked it off, brushed hair off his forehead, washed his hands, wetted his hair, saying he hated this, all repeated. He was gradually making a mound that was quite big across the sand tray. I talked to his irritation, and that nothing seemed right, and that he did not feel well. As it went on I said it felt as if the ghosts of other children were here which made it hard for him to settle and relax and how X's absence from school and his session was affecting him more than when he was here. There was silence while he went on mixing, building, brushing his hair back, exclaiming and washing.

Then a shape took form across the centre of the sand tray. It felt suddenly as if he were combing the back of an animal's fur with the end of a modelling tool. He carried working on this shape and asked me to guess what it was. I said that I thought it had the feel of an animal. He said he was going to be a sandmaker today, did I know what that was? This was said in a scornful way as if I probably would not. A projection of his great anxiety about inferiority to these ghost rivals in his mind. I talked of this and then wondered if he meant that he was going to make a picture in the sand. He said, 'No, a sandmaker, someone who *makes* things in the sand!' He then carried on making an animal shape in the sand frequently stepping on my toes as he moved round the sand tray although I had moved back. In every way there was only room for two not three, so that he and the sand would work together and I the third, were necessarily to be in the way. This was a clear indication, in the transference, of how difficult it was in this family for every member to have room. Gradually a more working silence developed and all the irritations of his hair, the sand, and my feet gave way to the emerging form.

He formed a tail and then two sets of feet each side and then tentative work began on the head. He made large blobs for eyes but no pupils at this stage. He asked me what I thought it was but in a more reasonable way than his earlier questions and I said that I thought it was a kind of amphibian and did he want to tell me? He said 'Crocodile'. He was anxious about the head. There was not very much room for it in the tray, how could he get it in. He kept building it up trying to fit it in, wiping it out and then trying again. He literally struggled for enough room for thought over action – the crocodile's feet and claws have plenty of room. Then he had the same problem with the teeth. I talked of what a strong image it was and how it filled the sand tray as if there really was not enough room for it. It felt that it had emerged as a guardian of the space. There was to be no room for X here. There was a worry about how could there be room for 'X' and himself in my mind and in my room. Silence while he was doing the teeth. Then there was talk of how his teacher had had her baby now and they had a new teacher. We talked of this and he seemed to like the new teacher and they were getting on well. I said that it was still difficult to think of his teacher not able to be with them because she was with a new baby. The acknowledgement that he liked his replacement teacher was a huge step forward, he had let go of a grievance and also loss about the regular teacher's absence. When he was near finishing he said that he could not bear to break it up and could he not leave it. Clearly he cannot because everything has to be cleared away for the next child and he knew that. He then wanted to show his escort who is a man. To do this would be to go against accepted technique which is to keep to the session boundaries and not to take material out or let anyone else in. We could not find what motivated this wish except that his escort liked to make things. There was a puzzle here that could not be solved by my drawing the image in the sand tray, so that it is preserved in some form, which it sometimes can be. The baby crocodile needed to be bought into the light of day, to the real world. I agreed that this could happen just before the end of the session. It had some element of a little Simon wishing to show a parent what he could do.

Simon went to get his escort and I explained that Simon had wanted to show him something he had made. It then became apparent that his escort was deaf and could not hear, but could lip-read. He went back to wait for Simon, who usually came to the therapy room on his own, so that the escort and I had not met before. In discussion of this Simon said that his escort was deaf, 'like his father'. I said that I thought he would like to show his father what he could make. He said, 'yes', and gave the crocodile eyes.

Discussion

This was a very sad moment. There is a sense here in which Simon feels that his father is deaf and blind to his struggles to find his own place in the family. Part of the struggle to find enough room for the crocodile in the sand tray is his struggle to find enough room for his growing self at home. Simon needs to be mirrored as a son by his father. It was, as if, the visit by his escort gave the baby crocodile sight. Good mirroring by a parent can give us a sense of ourselves and that aids insight. The little crocodile/Simon struggles for living and growing room in the sand tray as he struggles in the house at home, and in the classroom at school. In a sense he has been all teeth and claws in his jibing and critical comments and his wish to take his father's place while feeling inadequate to do so underneath. He also struggles with baby rage of baby at the breast-biting age when there is the realisation that mother is not always there, and indeed has preoccupations with other family members.

The making of the baby crocodile in the sand allowed a form for oral, aggressive, biting, *lebensraum* feelings and enabled connections to surface and be made between Simon's feelings towards his fellow pupils and therapy siblings, his teacher's baby, and his father. The lack of communication in the family was vividly re-enacted by the palpable presence of the male escort in that initially, we openly had to struggle with the fact that he could not hear me and I could not make myself understood. In fact of course, Simon's father is not actually deaf, just metaphorically. In terms of technique I should have been able to make a connection between male escort and father without the escort actually coming into the room. Instead, the dynamic was enacted. The actual situation really bought vividly alive the family dynamic as we all struggled to make ourselves understood. Simon had to go to these lengths to make me understand the depths of his difficulty at home.

Interestingly, as therapy for parents and child progressed and these difficult feelings surfaced and became understood, staff began to comment to me on what a nice boy he was and what a pleasure to be with. He began to make friends and as his own social life took off he was more able to let his parents have a relationship. They were also greatly helped by parental work going on at the same time. We associate the crocodile with biting power, quite a destructive force and appropriate for the depth of emotional turmoil and destruction that can be aroused in families when everyone is out of place. This family had been torn apart by the trauma of near death of mother and child at birth. Mother had not been able to aid Simon to grow up and separate and neither had his father been able to express any enjoyment in having a son, and aid his development, so that everyone had remained stuck in painful positions. Work with this family had involved not only individual therapy for Simon but also extensive family work and support and special schooling, but Simon was eventually successfully reintegrated into normal school. There is an element of sympathetic magic in Simon's wish to leave his large biting crocodile in the sand tray to guard against the sand tray's use by the next child, but there is also a wish for his father to see his son's difficulties and achievement as a 'sandmaker'. The animal image worked on several levels. In his identity as 'sandmaker' he showed a wish to master these oedipal conflicts. It was a step forward in maturity to be able to enjoy his new teacher and allow the old teacher to be with her new baby. In being able to give shape to the baby crocodile, Simon gained a perspective on his own difficulty, as the two of us could look on it and discuss it. We related to its animal presence. This anthropomorphic animal object had a live presence in the room. It also acted as a transactional object that transgressed the therapy boundaries, needing to be seen by a man that could represent a father, someone who also made things and would appreciate Simon's achievement.

ANIMAL PRESENCE IN CLAY: HENRY

Henry, age ten, was referred for art therapy from a special school when there was a great deal of concern about him and his future. He had delinquent behaviour of a daredevil type, taking enormous risks with his life. He presented an unhappy picture of having no friends of his own age, only playing with much younger children, and had terrible rages and temper tantrums at home. When he was fifteen months old his father had died tragically in a fatal road accident. His mother had been left with Henry and his older brother, age three, to care for, when quite numbed by the tragedy. She described her complete depression and loss, just sitting, staring, not able to respond to the children for months afterwards. Whereas the older child had language and possibly more resilience in contacting his out of reach mother; Henry, had smashed his playpen to pieces in trying to reach her and communicate with her. He could be seen to have lost not only his father but also his lively, responsive mother. She described knowing this was happening but being unable to respond. In Klein's understanding of the child's inner world it can be seen that he lost both outer and inner 'good objects' and that the work of the therapy would be to rebuild his inner world, his outer world had been repaired and waited for him, in that mother had eventually recovered and had a new partner, but Henry was unable to accept him and his behaviour became increasingly unmanageable (Klein 1940).

He presented as an attractive boy, with curly brown hair, and brown eyes, but who felt distant and out of reach. Our relationship had an understated quality; one of treating each other very carefully as if nothing more robust could get established. Observation and 'being with' were the key paradigms. It seemed that being with a depressed and bereaved mother had caused him to dampen down any vitality when with a responsive adult. It was as if, if he were too boisterous, the person would collapse, not sustain anything too lively. It was a case where I needed to stand far back and talk to different parts of him to give them recognition and wait for him to come closer and reveal himself to me as we developed more robustness in being together. He had the air of being with an object very carefully, making no ripples, keeping separate of liveliness. I found that I sometimes had to struggle to think about him, as if he had slipped out of my mind. This echoed his experience of slipping out of his mother's mind while she was numbed with grief. When he had an outburst at home he expressed the rage of the family for what had happened to them, actively railing about his loss. These two parts of him were in marked contrast, angry and full of rage – the delinquent with no internal sense of the preciousness of his own life, and the cut off dampened down boy who caused no ripples.

Three months into therapy Henry made a bird out of black paper one session and tried to hang it up on the perch of the door-spring. He could not get it to balance, so that it kept falling over. It looked rather sad, hanging by string and Sellotape, and he took it down and put it away in his folder immediately. It had been a try-out for having a perch or place in the room that he could call his own, but was all over in a few seconds. However, we talked about this and his expressed wish to have a place here to talk but his great difficulty in communicating except by nods and sounds.

Sessions

Five months later, eight months into therapy, a tragedy affected us all at the school. One of the members of staff lost a relative in a tragic road accident. Henry was unusually communicative, talking immediately about the tragedy but getting many facts muddled up with the tragic loss of his father in the past. The present communal sense of loss had awakened his past loss. He began to Sellotape over the letter shapes of his name as we talked, and then flicked all colours of paint at the paper so that when he took the Sellotape off he had his name left in white. His talk roamed over all the losses he had ever had in his family. I talked with him about this and about his fears for himself and for others he loved. I talked of his name on the picture and how it came clearly through the chaos of fragmented colours, as he had come through the fragmented feeling produced in him by this sudden death. He began to add shadows to the letters of his name.

The following session he spent the first part of the session completing the shadow effect on his name. We talked about his name standing out, as he does, he is alive, but the shadow both of last week's tragedy and his father's death are present. He then wanted to make a ball out of something, he wanted two containers that would join and hold a ball of string, and the string would come out. Like the image of 'Dirty Dog', described in the Alphabet (pp. 29–30), this was a lovely image of potential attachment. An image of containment by two parent half-circles and the string free to come out or be held inside. It felt very hopeful that two supportive parts coming together, to hold a third, had developed in his mind.

He got clay out and began to make a bowl shape, but after working on it for some time, almost asked permission to make a bird. I talked about the playful sense of being able to go with what the clay suggests to your hands. He made a round body, and head, beak, and face, then a tail to balance it.

It was beautifully balanced (Illustration 2.1) He was very intent and absorbed by it. Then he began to shape a nest with the clay that was left, but to my surprise he made a ring shape. He was working hard and intensely at this. He eventually sat the bird in it so that it was resting on the ring, so that looking at it you would not know that it had no base. Then he took the tiny piece of clay still left from what he had taken originally and he made an egg. He was pleased with this and asked me to guess what it was. He balanced the egg between the bird's body and tail, pleased that the bird fitted in the nest and the egg in the space. He separated them and decorated the sides of the bird and the nest, with some tension and worry that this might spoil it.

I checked out with him that he had intended a ring and was just not getting more clay, but he said very clearly that he wanted it like it was. At first my internal response had been that it was bottomless, not containing, but he was so pleased with it, that I then had a sense of it as a life-belt. He began to

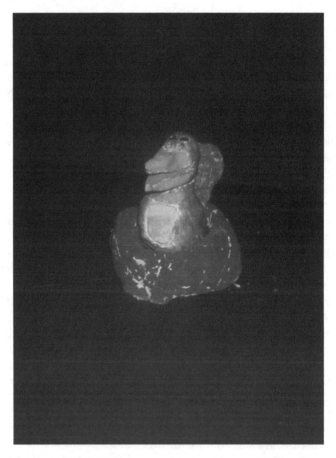

Illustration 2.1   Henry: Bird on nest.

question me about how long we might work together, a new sense of his wish to be here for a long time and enough robustness in the relationship to explore this question.

The following session he spent a large part of the time painting the bird. He was quite relaxed. He painted the front of the bird yellow, the beak orange with red inside. He finally chose a turquoise green for the bird after much deliberation. He began to talk about his older brother and how people usually thought that the things that he made had been made by his brother, not him. It was as if nobody thought that he could 'do anything good'. I talked of how fed up and angry that must make him and he nodded. I talked of how in families one person got associated with certain things and it was hard to get people to notice that you had changed, or had different parts to you: you could get stuck in a role. We talked about how he too could make things creatively.

He then asked what kind of bird liked to find bright things and thinking it over decided a jackdaw or magpie. He told me that a year ago he had found a gold watch in a nest, in the crook of a tree branch. He then painted the egg all colours, and got tissues from the box in the room. He used the tissues to make a soft base for the egg to lie in underneath the bird, after much experiment-ation, as he also wanted to see the egg, but could not be sure whether to have it on the bird's tail/body. He then carefully and proudly carried it to the window sill and cleared up. I talked of the special egg and wondered what might hatch and he said 'A dinosaur!' grinning. He got a deep mauve tissue paper out and rearranged a new base of this for the egg, and a second piece like a protective shawl over the bird. Two sessions later he finished a previously unfinished three-dimensional model out of papier mâché that had a space inside, and put the bird and nest inside, saying that it would be safe there.

Discussion

The bird continued to be important to Henry through the remaining thirteen months of therapy. He often checked that it was still there and safe on coming into therapy, and later placed it in a model house that he had made. In quite a concrete way the fact that it could be looked after and was not harmed or interfered with between sessions meant to Henry that he had a continuing safe and contained space. His image of finding a gold watch – gold time – in the nest of the session was very moving, as it had been a year ago that we had first met for assessment sessions. The session time was a life-buoy to him, in that it helped him weather the birth of step-siblings, as well as helping him keep his place in the family. He had been a looked-after child at the start of therapy but had managed a staged reintegration into the family, during the first weeks. A supportive relationship in therapy enabled him to take in the care offered by mother and stepfather, which had been there for some time, but he had been unable to accept the inevitable changes and developments that had come with mother's new relationship.

Henry had previously played with death in his delinquent activities. The image of the bird on the nest with a precious egg (an image of potential wholeness) suggested that he had been able to internalise a caring mother, both now feeling more contained himself but also being able to be protective to his half-siblings. If the bird represents his spirit that had fled when he had failed to contact his bereaved mother, then it felt as if he had come home to roost, the attachment rejoined. The egg, carefully looked after, also suggests the possibility for new parts of Henry developing. Birds, with eggs on the nest to protect, are vulnerable and appear in children's work in connection with nurture, having mother in place, but also can express aggressive feelings towards siblings, and mother's fertility. This theme will be continued in the case study in Part three. Henry expressed a fear of 'spoiling it' while decorating the nest and bird. There can be wishes to steal the eggs, as in bird nesting; or to protect the eggs; having internalised loving care, one can extend it to others (Kaldegg 1948; Anthony 1973; Case 1987).

Henry's bird had some characteristics of a transitional object in that it was treated as if it were alive. Unconsciously, its continued protected existence kept alive a fragile life force in Henry. It was an image of containment. It was unlike a transitional object in that it was never treated badly. It allowed some imaginative play with the next stage of life through identification. Henry lovingly played with his bird when he took it out of its protective house, rearranging the tissue shawl, checking it, and repositioning the different elements. The tender care had aspects of care for the mother bird, holding aspects of himself, his mother and siblings and of the therapist in the transference. In this way it was reparative but also played out the care for future partner and children. Such an image is transformative in that parts of Henry, previously undeveloped or hidden, were allowed into play. Henry developed his own private ritual of checking on it. It had elements of a talisman. The animal form allowed Henry to develop the latent and hidden wish for loving and nurturing relationships, that were not apparent in the presenting young delinquent; in this way the anthropomorphic form allowed the expression of human qualities.

CONCLUSION

Our likeness and difference from other animals allows an interplay in our minds with parts of the self through anthropomorphic animal images. Their appearance in therapy suggests life stirring in the psyche which can herald a new stage. It may be a new phase in the therapy, as when Victoria began to make images about herself; or a new level of understanding, as Simon had realisations about his need for recognition by his father; or an image of the renewal of a fragile life of relationships, as in Henry's bird on the nest. Our empathic response to see ourselves in others allows a particular engagement with the three-dimensional. It is sometimes more comfortable to talk about part of the self through an animal image than it is to talk more directly, so that it can be an instrumental halfway point to talking about oneself. In this way animal forms created by the child can help them to discover themselves. Animals may represent new life stirring, as is shown by their actual presence in therapy, facilitating contact with the little child inside the older, as we saw with Dorothy, in the Alphabet.

Participation mystique

The puzzling difference in people's responses to a fox in the garden, particularly the mystical sense of encounters with nature; the bringing of live animals into therapy; children's investment in the making of animal images that take on a life of their own; leads us to think about man and society, and the representations of nature that we hold. In western Europe, we are heavily influenced by the Judaeo-Christian religions portrayal/betrayal of animals and nature as there for our own use, to serve our ends, but lying underneath this attitude and response is an older animism. Levy-Bruhl (1966) became interested in Durkheim's formulation of 'collective representations' as a way of explaining our response to nature.

> Collective representations are those intimations of reality which are given to the individual by virtue of his membership in a group; hence they include all elements of his symbolic system. The individual's views of the nature of his universe and of man and of man's relation to nature are given to him, impressed upon his consciousness by ritual and myth and are not subject to question. They are the basic premises according to which he organises his inner and outer worlds. They are sensed rather than thought, experienced emotionally rather than reasoned intellectually. They are not arrived at individually but are apprehended as part of the group experience.
>
> (Blenzel 1966: xii)

Levy-Bruhl was interested, like Freud, in the non-rational; particularly, prelogical or mystical thinking. He originally located this aspect of mental life in 'native peoples', but later revised his thinking to seeing that we all have elements of prelogical or mystical thinking which exist side by side and represent two different ways of structuring perceptions of reality (Levy-Bruhl 1975: 101). The mystical was not restricted to religious transcendent experience but to all experience which apprehends forces and relationships imperceptible to the senses. This has similarity to and differences from Freud's primary process and secondary process thinking modes, in that, the symbolism of the secondary process is discursive, conscious rational thinking, which is symbolised through words which have a linear, discrete successive order. His primary process which is earlier, presents its constituents simultaneously, in non-linear time, it operates imaginatively, but cannot generalise. It is non-discursive and often has visual imagery (dreams, pictures). Its complexity is not limited by what the mind can retain from the beginning of an apperceptive act to the end (Case and Dalley 1992). Freud is describing the individual's mental mechanism which enables the 'mystical thinking' that is described by Levy-Bruhl. One of the things that they had in common was in thinking that the 'unconscious' and that 'participation' were difficult to explain logically; one can only explain using our rational thought processes.

Both Freud and Levy-Bruhl were thinking about the way that man makes a relation to the world about him. Freud looked at the role of the conscious and the unconscious in structuring reality; later, object relation theorists, built on this, understanding the importance of the mechanisms of projection, intro-jection and identification in forming man's relation to the world. Gordon (1965) has an interesting discussion of projective identification which makes links between Klein's concept and Jung's use of the terms, participation mystique, primitive identity, and contamination. Levy-Bruhl looked at logical mentality and mystical thinking (participation mystique) and the way it is suffused with emotion.

Participation is the apprehension of meaning in life, sensed rather than reasoned: 'without identification, without involvement with others and with nature, one has no identity' (Blenzel 1966: xviii). Levy-Bruhl later realised that myths and collective representations on which totemism is based, belief in spirits, separate and external souls, sympathetic magic is in all human minds. Levy-Bruhl called this sense of one person being in two parts and places, 'duality-unity' (Levy-Bruhl 1975: 73). This contributes to our under-standing of the investment that we can have in the things that we make: as we have seen in the children's work.

Chapter 3

Animation through the window: the beautiful and the sublime

Art is the objectification of feeling, and the subjectification of nature.

(Langer 1967: 180)

INTRODUCTION: ANIMATION

In this chapter there will be a focus on nature encountered through the therapy room window. This will be discussed in relation to the development of animation and imaginative activity where there has been previous severe deprivation (Case 2002). Clinical material from work with looked-after children, in foster care, will illustrate how driven play, which has the function of keeping fear and feeling from consciousness, can give way to imaginative interaction with the environment. It may be safer for severely deprived children to see animation outside the window, rather than between therapist and child; this may be a necessary stage before a child can be brought into a state of imaginative play with materials inside the therapy room. The term 'animation' is used in the sense of new imaginative play for each particular child, stimulated by an encounter with nature, an apprehension of beauty, or the sublime. This is contrasted with the more driven play of a manic defence against awareness of self and others. The framing of experience both in therapy and in aesthetic moments is also of relevance in thinking about the extension of the therapy room, in a child's mind, to space outside the window. There are particular moments in child therapy that are mutative, and encounters with nature can sometimes be a catalyst for such a change.

Children's experiences with nature through the therapy room window can have the quality of participation, as I understand it, and can give them a sense of belonging and connectedness to the world outside that begins to move to the person of the therapist, inside. The aesthetic takes place between the subjective and the objective. Our perception of nature is filtered by collective representation and by individual psychology and experience. The aesthetic experience where one feels at the same time part of a picture, or landscape, or relationship but also separate as one comes out of it, has a psychological predecessor in Winnicott's me/not me, of potential space and transitional phenonema and to Bollas's thoughts about the first aesthetic experience being based on mother's form of relating; which he described as a transforming experience (Winnicott 1971; Bollas 1987).

THE BEAUTIFUL AND THE SUBLIME

An interest in children's responses to a picture on the wall of the art therapy room, a drawing by Holbein of Jane Seymour, led to an exploration of beauty in relation to silence, art and inner states of mind (Case 1995, 1996, 2000a). Reid writes of both the importance of the discovery of beauty, and of the physical and psychic environment that the therapist needs to make for damaged children (Reid 1990). Traditionally, beauty has been associated with art and the sublime with nature. In his classic essay, Burke describes the two experiences in the following way:

> Whatever is fitted in any sort to excite the ideas of pain, and danger, that is to say, whatever is in any sort terrible, or is conversant about terrible objects, or operates in a manner analogous to terror, is a source of the sublime, that is, it is productive of the strongest emotion which the mind is capable of feeling.
>
> (Burke 1757: 216)

Qualities of the sublime: astonishment, terror, fear, obscurity, night, power, pain, might or strength, vastness, depth, infinity, privation, solitude and silence.

In contrast to the sublime, beauty is described in social terms, Burke understanding it as a 'social quality' in relation to people and animals:

> 'for where women and men, and not only they, but when other animals give us a sense of joy and pleasure in beholding them . . . they inspire us with sentiments of tenderness and affection towards their persons; we like to have them near us, and we enter willingly into a kind of relation with them . . .
>
> (Burke 1757: 219)

Qualities of the beautiful: small, diminuitive, delicacy, pleasing variation, grace, elegance, clear, light, sweetness.

In thinking in this chapter of children's experiences looking out of the therapy room window at the outside world it is useful to remember that although looking out of the window may be at times a diversion from the work of therapy, it can also be a search for an object relation that cannot yet be expressed to the person of the therapist. Milner writes:

the relationship to oneself and the external world is basically and originally a relationship of one person to another, even though it does eventually become differentiated into relations to living beings and relations to things, inanimate nature. In other words, in the beginning one's mother is, literally, the whole world. Of course, the idea of the first relationship to the outside world being felt as a relationship to persons was one I had frequently met with in discussions of childhood and savage animism.

(Milner 1971: 116)

Fuller has a fruitful discussion of the aesthetic experience, whether it is in relation to art or nature:

What I am saying, however is that aesthetic emotion is involved with this nexus of the submergence of the self into the environment, and the differentiation of self out of it. Here the senses of touch and sight, indeed sensuous activity in its entirety, play a part which seems to be prior to (or at least apart from) conceptual activity. The 'sublime' (romantic, colour) emphasises one aspect of this nexus – that of mergence, and union; 'beauty' (classical, outline) and its derivatives stresses the other – that of separation. In reality, there are a miasma of intermediate positions.

(Fuller 1980: 199)

DISORGANISED/DISORIENTED ATTACHMENT

The two children under discussion in this chapter had backgrounds where there had been severe deprivation and neglect, parental drug use and emotional, physical, and suspected sexual abuse. In attachment terms they had characteristics to be found in category D – disorganised/disoriented: that is, of having had frightened or frightening parents, so that the people to whom they wished to run to for protection were the frightening stimulus, which can result in disorientation or disassociation. Parents may alternatively be found to be abusive or unavailable due to bereavement; or parents who have suffered trauma in their own attachments. This category, was formed after some puzzling exceptions were noted to the three more familiar groupings of, secure attachment, anxious resistant attachment and anxious avoidant attachment. It is understood to be a disorganised version of one of the more familiar patterns, often the anxious resistant (Ainsworth *et al.* 1971; Main and Weston 1981; Crittenden 1985; Main and Solomon 1986, 1990; Bowlby 1988; Main and Hesse 1990). At the beginning of therapy, they were full of fear, defended against any intimate contact of mind that might put them in touch with thoughts or feelings. Black and Newman (1996) give a useful overview of the effects of domestic violence on children. Children with this kind of background who are looked after can suffer a double deprivation: firstly, their experience of neglect, secondly, their crippling defenses make them hard to contact and help (Henry 1974). There were many similarities in background, and both children were diagnosed with ADHD, and taking the drug, Ritalin; however there were also markedly different features, in that the first child, Colin, had been shut in a room, alone for extended periods of time, and had experienced known physical abuse, but the second child, Lucy, had been left roaming and neglected in the presence of adults who were heavy drug users. They presented quite differently in therapy.

ANIMATION AND BEAUTY: COLIN

Colin, blonde, with blue eyes, was referred for therapy when he was eight years old; some part of this work is explored in an earlier paper (Case 2002). He had many symptoms on referral, including unpredictable outbursts of aggression and obsessional patterns of behaviour. Perry (1997) discusses the effects of living with violence on the child's developing brain. Children appear unpredictable to others because their automatic responses to frightening stimuli are triggered frequently to lesser stimuli. The stress reaction has become inbuilt. Colin was undersize for his age and had difficulty in eating with others. He would hide faeces and hoard food. Colin had been living in a secure environment for four years but had been unable to progress or take in the care that was offered, causing much anxiety to his foster family. He often cracked the joints in his fingers which, I understood as the noise of the joints cracking letting him know that he was alive, as well as being a relief of tension.

Being with and thinking about

In the initial stages of work with Colin I felt that he had the most minimal awareness of being with another person. I had to fight with myself to maintain an active state of being with him and thinking about him. If I did not monitor my own attention I could drift off into unfocused inner moods, a countertransference response to Colin's absences. He had, in fact been checked and found not to have epilepsy. The particular feeling that he evoked also put me in touch with his lack of experience of being in relationship to another and therefore his lack of emotional investment in human contact. Words felt like leaves on the surface of his mind. I was aware that they did not reach him and that he needed something deeper, a preverbal holding.

He attempted forays into the world of drawing, playing, and painting but could only put the materials out and sigh tensely before putting them away. To go into any activity beyond the arranging and rearranging of materials, it seemed, would raise the danger of stirring up the murky sediment of feelings.

I had commented on what was happening by saying quiet things such as, 'You got the pencils out and would like to use them but you feel that you cannot'; 'You have sharpened them and put them back. They look ready to use'. This naming or simply verbalising what is happening can make one feel that not enough is being done, but it does seem to be an essential stage of preparation for play (Hopkins 1998). In the silence Colin created I had the thought, 'This is an inanimate silence', and I felt like a piece of furniture. The communication of his experience to me was one of the withdrawal of animated emotional contact. An aspect of mental health is the capacity for animation and imaginative activity. Colin lacked this freedom, humour, or play. The therapy room has the potential to be a 'strongroom of vocabulary', to steal a phrase from Seamus Heaney (Heaney 1996). It can be a place where words, play, sand, art, music and drama can all have expression at different times. It must feel a terrifying place if your inner world is so full of unprocessed overwhelming experiences that you cannot make a mark with a pencil or start a story with the toys. I recalled Winnicott on play:

> Psychotherapy has to do with two people playing together. The corollary of this is that where playing is not possible then work done by the therapist is directed towards bringing the patient from a state of not being able to play into a state of being able to play.
>
> (Winnicott 1971: 38)

In her paper on the development of a potential space, De Astis has written about the 'frozen psychic space where internal objects are not allowed any life of their own and live in suspended animation' (De Astis 1997: 352). In this situation parts of the personality may be lost, under- or un-developed (Alvarez 1996). Fordham's theories about the defences of the self is helpful in work with children like Colin where there has been a catastrophic lack of communication between mother and baby and a resulting lack of capacity to symbolise, it is as if he has 'shut down'. He described it in terms of 'failure of the deintegrative process' as we saw earlier in the Introduction.

Session: first framing

Colin's first use of art materials showed an inner conflict coming to the surface. This happened with drawing, in the shape of football matches and wrestling bouts. He was usually silent while drawing and was not able to enter into conversation about them except for the odd phrase in reply to a question from me. The first picture was of a football match, with the centre of the football pitch dominating in a breast-like shape. This shape was drawn first. There was a player who had kicked the ball, and a large referee, and other less significant players in partially stick-person style. Only the referee had hands. I understood it as a representation of the therapy room, which does have a feeding potential. However he did not yet feel securely contained, as there were no edges to the pitch. The stick-like figures within the central breast-shape suggested that he was aware of other children that I saw. A struggle was emerging, with awareness of potential rivals, of ownership of the feeding, life-giving breast. He had wanted me to help him draw the general players after the main figures were made, and I had said that I would not draw but would be here with him while he drew. This was a knife-edge moment, as to whether he could weather the possible feeling of rejection in order to make something authentically his own. A few weeks later he began to draw wrestling pictures, again of a conflict, but between two wrestlers with a referee present. These pictures had the secure framework of the wrestling ring. After making a wrestling picture he expressed his pleasure by doing forward rolls all the way down a long corridor and then a cartwheel in the foyer. Although this sounds exuberant – and in a way it was – it was also muted and contained. Wordless, it felt like a very young physical expression, as though there were no words to express his excitement, it was all in his body. His drawing went through representational development from stick figures to bodies that had some substance in a few weeks; noting this gave me some pleasure in his development, which was delayed in every aspect.

When one makes a picture, the picture surface already frames experience. In drawing a further frame inside the picture I thought that he was communicating both his unconscious awareness of the secure framework provided by the therapy but also his great need for safety before he could explore any thought or feeling verbally. In writing about the role of illusion in symbol formation and her experiences of painting, Marion Milner comments:

> The frame marks off the different kind of reality that is within it from that which is outside it: but a temporal spatial frame also marks off the special kind of reality of the psychoanalytic session. And in psychoanalysis it is the existence of this frame that makes possible the full development of that creative illusion that analysts call the transference. Also the central idea underlying psychoanalytic technique is that it is by means of this illusion that a better adaptation to the world outside is ultimately developed.
>
> (Milner 1955: 86)

Schaverien, in an art therapy context, also explores 'the picture within the frame' in the sense of the therapeutic frame which is the setting for therapy (Schaverien 1989, 1992). All the arts have a function in society of providing framed experiences in their particular way, whether a picture frame, theatre or concert, poem or novel, within which we can have the illusion of that experience as real. We can have an emotional experience and then come back out of the frame into everyday life. Winnicott, in *Playing and Reality*, has shown how play is the precursor to this cultural activity (Winnicott 1971). Colin's play, however, did not have this symbolic quality.

Wrestling with defences

He did not have the ability to think abstractly or imaginatively. He was obsessed with wrestling, on television and video. Worryingly he did not appear to see it as a framed activity that happens on the stage of the wrestling ring. He could not entertain it as theatre and play. He was identified with the characters as a substitute family. Other children were able to use the wrestlers to play out themes of sibling rivalry and conflict, safely aware that it was play and able to move in and out of playing; he was adamant that it was real.

In his description of 'household matches' between men and women, where household objects were used as implements in the fights, it was clear that he had no identification with a containing and caring object. In his experience, coupling was potentially destructive and he could not move on to allow care from a foster household. He wanted to believe that he was invincible and wanted to be as far away as possible from any soft feelings of vulnerability and helplessness. Colin watched videos with a blinding intensity as if the potential world of real attachments did not exist and so they took the place of that world. They were not used as part of a shared culture, but watched repetitively and alone. They were used to block out real contact with people. The traumatic experiences he had had with his parents were in some way being repeated, though in a more manageable form, through the videos, while they also served to block out any awareness of the actual catastrophe that he had experienced.

One could see that his internal phantasy world was in an imbalance with his external contact with reality. De Astis discusses the overlap between 'disturbed mental space and the space of external reality' (De Astis 1997): Colin's internal objects were more powerful than contact with the current external figures who were trying to care for him. This linked to the problem of how he could be brought into a state of attachment to parental figures, who were there potentially in his domestic situation, and with the therapist, who was available to be made use of in his sessions.

Session: first framing by the window frame

Eight months into the therapy, when we were meeting twice weekly, Colin had begun to emerge from his silences. He was sometimes able to have snatches of conversation with me around an activity, but this alternated with very driven play that did not seem to be playful at all.

Colin turned to the bag of clay that is a new one weighing four and a half kilos, and putting it on the floor began a series of attacks and moves on it. He began jumping from the chair on to the bag soon taking his shoes off and doing wrestling moves on it, smashing it with his elbow, lying flat beside it, or a flat leg smash across it. He seemed to be hurting himself quite a lot but this seemed to increase his doing it more. He rolled up with a hurt foot, then ribs, then jumped deliberately landing on his genitals on the bag and curled up in pain, saying his private parts were hurt. Then more moves, pausing to try to remember if there were special moves of particular wrestlers *in Dynamite, Stonecold, Earthquake*, or *Rock*. I talked of how he seemed to be hurting himself and then felt attacked. I also talked of the clay being like the clay body of an opponent that he felt he had to beat. The moves went on. Clay has a soft body. I thought he was attacking his own soft self that felt like the enemy.

The flight of a blackbird in the tree outside caught his eye and he went to look at the window saying, 'aah, birdy, tweet-tweet'. He pointed to where he thought its nest was.

I said, 'Yes, I think he's feeding from the tree on the berries'. We could see it hopping about.

He said, 'It's not their fault!' His reaction was as if I would be angry at it eating my berries, although I had said it lightly.

I said, 'No, they need to eat to survive. They need the berries to survive the winter'.

He then went back energetically to the wrestling moves. The clay-bag did not burst but left dents, impressions and marks from his attacks.

Discussion

It is possible to see how simply and completely our internal human situation can be transferred on to the animal world. In the session he reacted to the birds eating as if I would be angry with them eating my food. It suggested quite vividly that the mother that he had internalised did not want him to eat and live. Of course, this also shows how internal object relations are trans-ferred on to the therapist in that I became the mother who withholds food that the bird needs to survive just as he identifies with the bird whom he experiences as having to steal food that I want to withhold. I noticed that he has imagined the bird with a nest (home) and I think he is beginning to have some sense that he has a place here in therapy. He had recently begun to react to breaks in therapy (there was something to miss).

The framing of the blackbird by the window stimulated a flow of material from Colin in relation to feeding and transference. In the way that he fre-quently brought his own materials into the room (see pp. 25–6); and in his reaction to the blackbird feeding one can see how he had to provide for himself. He does not eat because he fears that something bad will get into him. His ordinary needs have been rejected so that need feels to him like greed. He imagines that I will be angry at the birds eating 'my berries'. The wish to eat is felt or seen as greed and has to be controlled by his omnipotent side that tells him he can live without. Therapy puts Colin more in touch with need. There is quite often an increase in disturbing symptoms while working with a child. He feels more worried about what will get into him, as my work and presence arouse his needs.

Session: second framing by window frame

Eleven months into therapy, he was becoming more alive and animated in the sessions, albeit briefly. He occasionally smiled and had developed a range of expressions. His first smile was very like a baby's first smile, in that it was almost experimental; and then when I smiled back, clearly delighted by the eye-to-eye contact as much as anything else, his smile became less wavery and firmed up.

One morning we had a stunning moment together. His eye was attracted to something outside the window and he exclaimed, 'A ginger cat! Caroline, there's a ginger cat leaping along the wall. Come and look'. We both looked staring for a moment puzzled. Then he said, 'No, it's not, it's leaves, but it does look like it, doesn't it?' It really did. What we had seen was a gardener throwing up forkfuls of leaves behind a wall. The burnished autumn leaves riffling through the air were shot through with bright sunshine and moment-arily appeared as a ginger cat, running along the top of a wall, which, sud-denly went out of sight – we couldn't see the gardener. Apart from the beauty of the moment that we shared, this experience confirmed my sense that Colin's imagination was beginning to come alive. He could bear something becoming something else. It was interesting that this first sense of the imagin-ation alive and running came in the form of a tom-cat that humans associate with night prowls and independence, caterwauling and sexuality, all aspects of aliveness and instinct that were very missing from this little boy. Hillman (1997) writes that 'Animals wake up the imagination', and in that moment we both felt more alive. It is interesting that he saw this image outside the therapy room, which is less threatening, than seeing something inside, between us. It takes the pressure off the relationship inside the room between child and therapist if one can relate through the medium of the outside world and what nature presents for us to view. Of course, there is always something going on outside. The child needs to be ready for it to happen. The window had acted as a frame enabling him to play imaginatively with what he saw:

> . . . the basic identifications which make it possible to find new objects, to find the familiar in the unfamiliar, require an ability to tolerate a tempor-ary loss of sense of self, a temporary giving up of the discriminating ego which stands apart and tries to see things objectively and rationally and without emotional colouring.
>
> (Milner 1955: 97)

There was a range of movement in this session, from talk of wrestlers in hard-man mode, to animation around the ginger cat. He then went back to wrestlers, but in a different medium. Cutting out the letters of the name of their organisation, he was amazed by the magic of how, when you cut out a letter, the negative shape is left behind and you have another letter! 'It is as if you cut out one and you get two!' He made a concrete discovery that in defining one thing you separate it from another and in this way there are also two. This is the beginning of being able to allow some separation. All the background shapes were carefully kept and any tiny pieces were put in a paper bag that he made. While cutting out, a shape was made that looked to him like a bunny face. He added soft fluffy cheeks and eyes. He turned it around, playing with it, and saw that it looked like a horse's head, but in another way it looked like a man walking. There was excitement with these discoveries and a sense of freer imagination. Further aspects of cutting up and cutting round will be considered in Chapter five and in the case study in Part three.

Discussion

In a concrete way Colin had discovered that there could be more than one point of view: you can look at the same phenomenon from different perspectives and make new discoveries. It was interesting that the experience of seeing outside the room could be brought into the room and continued in a different context. In making the discovery that a fall of leaves can also be seen as a ginger cat he has played with internal and external realities. Shared aesthetic moments between two people recreate early experiences of looking at the world with wonder and enjoyment that was hopefully experienced with parents and is part of the joy of being a parent. Colin's responses made me wonder if some of this experience was happening for the first time, that needs might be met that had not been met before. A sense of safety in the therapy room had led to his being able to entertain softness. I link this with Winnicott's 'pure female element', the propensity 'to be with the other'. This in turn had led towards the developing capacity for symbolisation (Winnicott 1971).

Colin's symptoms gradually eased and I had a sense of a child who was beginning to grow. His personality, which I had felt to be a series of set responses to life, was becoming broader: one instance of this was his smile, and the beginnings of a rudimentary sense of humour. Such moves forward are very fragile and at periods of stress in the external environment old symptoms erupted. Colin had shut down on human emotional contact in order to survive, as it had shut down on him. We were now at a stage when Colin was able to make images and productions that could be talked about and could have new discoveries. We felt on more robust ground, evidenced by him growling a toy towards me and laughing as I pretended to be frightened. We could play together, play with fear for a moment. Now that he could tolerate us 'in relationship' it was possible to look at the relationship and for him to bring in worries and feelings from his life in the foster family.

He had moved through different stages to reach this point. First, there had been the repetitive ordering of materials. Next, he had been able to use the pencils and art materials to make his own productions, but without narrative.

Driven manic play appeared in the place of imaginative activity as a defence against the terrible fear of the therapist as well as fear of the conjunction of thought and feeling which is part of all creative activity. It felt safer for Colin to see and look outside the therapy room before animated imaginative activity could take place between us. Visualisation seems to be one of the building blocks of thinking. It is important in that one looks at things together, sharing perceptions: mother draws attention to an object and baby shows mother something. While he was unable to narrate or draw or talk I drew his attention to what was happening. At first this drawing of attention was all one way. You could say that I was giving him a point of view, or focusing his attention on himself. Later on, I hope to have shown that he then drew my attention to something and in so doing became animated, as we had an experience of a shared vision. We brought two different emotions to the vision of the blackbird eating the berries, but a shared delight over the perception of the ginger cat. One needs, then, to look 'out' before one can internalise, or look 'in'. These are experiences of 'joint attention behaviours', in the descriptive terms of developmental psychologists (Butterworth 1992). We all retain concrete thinking as a base for the abstract thinking which rests upon it. This suggests the importance of seeing before being able to hold on to a good sustaining object inside.

The use of actual space outside the therapy room goes against accepted therapy boundaries but can have a constructive element (Case 1986). Hindle (2000) explores imaginative life needing to be in another realm, outside the therapy room. In a similar way, parts of Colin were split off and experienced outside, which enabled us to look on them almost as if they were taking place on a stage. He identified with the blackbird, a part of him who felt hungry and wanted to eat but was inhibited by an internal object that denied him access to food. The ginger cat was both a shared experience of beauty but also a moment when fragmentary parts could be seen as a whole, perhaps a fleeting perception of integration. He unconsciously made use of the chance encounter with animal life outside the window; it is possible that when he was locked in a room life was experienced, or seen, outside. Having a new experience produces a vitality of being, that quickening of the body when a new idea is thought. Adults may feel a trembling excitement when they think a new thought, but children frequently move. This is an aspect of animated imaginative activity, and was evidenced when Colin first drew within a framework and did forward rolls, and in his excitement in his discoveries about cutting out, where he was jumping with delight about the new.

From being able to bear and enjoy both the beauty and the falling apart of the 'ginger cat/autumn leaves moment', Colin went on to cut out letters and then to play with the shapes left in the paper. He had discovered the interrelationship between figure and ground. Wrestling had been his identity, but in discovering 'bunny shapes' and softness he discovered the reverse of the coin – that which he could not bear to know consciously. It is important that it emerged unconsciously, in a playful and bearable way. It is curious that Colin could bear the falling apart of the ginger cat into leaves; it was a moment of disappointment and loss, which I also felt. It made me give more weight to Houzel's idea that it is the psychic encounter with the beauty of the object that is more important than the beauty of the object *per se* (Houzel 1995; Meltzer and Williams 1988).

ANIMATION AND THE SUBLIME: LUCY

Lucy was referred for therapy when she was eight years old, having been in foster care since she was three. She was chaotic and wild in behaviour, with short bright red hair, and dark eyes. She had had health problems and was a thin stick of a girl with a deprived look. She was in a good foster home and was brought regularly to therapy. Three younger siblings were in different foster situations, taken into care as mother had continued to have further babies. Early in therapy I had to work very hard to establish the most basic ground rules and boundaries to the session. Lucy flitted in and out of the room to check that her foster mother was still there. She was in terror of me but this was hidden by constant activity. Going to the toilet she would rapidly punch the soap dispenser or stuff toilet paper or hand towels somewhere. She would move all the furniture and start to travel around on top of it, throw materials, empty things out and try to spray water around the room. She would be up at the window trying the catches, with rapid talk of death and dying, then off to chuck doll's house furniture around. All psychic contents were in wild flux.

The pace of the session, and leaping from one activity to the other, showed the deep chaos inside and turmoil of feelings that she rushed ahead of; almost trying to outrun them in a manic defence against pain. I have called this the 'roundabout', the creation of discontinuities of experience, when children rush from activity to activity (Case 2000a). She had developed a powerful physical defence against pain, attempting to be an invulnerable tough guy who could not be 'touched' emotionally. As she settled more in therapy she moved from this non-stop activity to slightly more organised gymnastics. Doing bewildering speedy forward and backward rolls, or racing backwards and forwards across the room. To be still, would be to let a feeling come into being, and this was too frightening and too painful.

In a previous paper the creation of a *mise-en-scène* of domestic violence, was discussed, in which the child is both director and actor, leaving the therapist as the 'helpless observer', mirroring the child's situation in the past (Case 1994). When the therapist is in such a situation, when the child cannot make any art work with the materials, but uses the whole room to create representations of past traumatic events it was suggested then, that the therapist's own art work could have a vital role through a 'reflective countertransference': for instance, in understanding one's own angry or helpless feelings, which are aroused in the session, and therefore that of the child. In a later paper, the alternating and fluctuating positions of the 'terrorised' and the 'terrorising', between therapist and client in sessions with physically abused children was discussed (Case 1998). Boronska discusses work with children who are identified with an aggressor, describing sibling work with families who have experienced domestic violence and the difficulty of containing violent outbursts from children (Boronska 2000). The work with Lucy had elements of this in that one could feel helpless to prevent the destruction of toys and materials, as she could show an unusual strength and speed of action. The resulting chaos left it indistinguishable as to what was rubbish and what was good material that might be used constructively, thus mirroring the chaos and disorder and lack of boundary around what was good and healthy and bad and destructive in her early home environment.

One dilemma for the therapist in such a situation is that, if one is firm then the child responds in terror. They may try to rush from the session or create more chaos, to put things between them and you. On the other hand if one is not firm then the chaos and what they see as 'being no boundaries' is also terrifying. It needs very patient, clear communications and attempts to create a middle ground, where child and therapist can be still together for a moment, and then to try to build this moment out in length. Another difficult aspect of the work is how exposed the therapist can feel to colleagues when there is a child so challenging to the boundaries of the session. Children that have been severely abused are going to push the boundaries as far as possible as they desperately seek containment, which highlights the support that the therapist needs from the therapy setting. The way in which trauma enters the consulting room and the resulting technical issues are discussed most fruitfully by Rustin (2001). She argues persuasively that the intense personal anxiety of the therapist about failure and management of the difficulties is linked to the impact of the trauma. In discussion of her patient she also describes furniture moving which she understood as his right to have a part in shaping his world. This was also true of Lucy who moved from creating chaos, to piled-up furniture so that there was space for gymnastic activity, to fruitful rearrangement in the shape of dens, in which she could sit and feel safe. Rustin also discusses the part played by plant-life in the therapy of her patient and how she had to alter her ways of working to accommodate him, taking a risk that a plant he wanted to care for might die and how that might affect the therapy. The plant (nature) carried some of the hopes and anxieties about the therapy. This could be understood as the plant (baby) concretely and symbolically taking the risk to live or die for her patient.

In the following clinical material the emergence of painful feelings will be discussed, focusing on the linkage across several sessions, and the different form of communication at each stage. The part played by nature outside the room window will become apparent.

First session

Lucy came into the session carrying a torn sheet from a pre-school type of colouring book. She thrust it at me saying, 'It's for you'. She then launched into speedy behaviour and furniture moving. I acknowledged her gift and said that I would look after it but she gave no indication that she had heard me and did not refer to it again in the session. The coloured-in picture showed a little girl holding an umbrella in the rain (Illustration 3.1). It was the first image that she had shown me, in any form. It was a communication of needing shelter from the elements. This made me think of Winnicott's 'environment mother', and the failure of this aspect of mothering in her history (Winnicott 1971). There had been failure to protect her from adversity, because of the drug culture, in which she had been living. The little girl could be looked at, at first, as needing shelter from adverse elements – the

Illustration 3.1 Lucy: Girl in the rain.

rain – but also as trying to shelter from the 'rain' of her own tears, as her defences would not allow any feeling to be felt.

Second session

Lucy had been standing at the window, talking of death, and I had been standing near her saying that she would injure herself if she fell but that the window was safely locked and that she was safe in this room. She had then drawn a series of hearts on her arm. There had been excited questions to me about myself. She had had a phantasy that I was married to another therapist she had seen. She had banged on the window and then rushed in and out to the waiting area. She had fiddled with the clock and changed the time. These were attacks on the boundaries of the session, which I had struggled to keep. She had had a moment of terror when the clock alarm went off and she had looked at me as if I had magically produced it. I had talked about this and she had started throwing doll's house furniture across the room. One of the difficulties technically is to find a way of talking that does not feel like sharp objects going into the child – the objects being thrown at me. She had then turned the table upside down and had started using it to try to move across the room. I had tried a moment of play and had said that she looked like she was in a boat, asking her where she was sailing too. She had said 'sailing across the south sea'. I had waved goodbye but she had suddenly panicked and said, 'there might be pirates'. She had leapt out and gone back to the window. I thought from this that she had not experienced the safety necessary for imaginative play. I had tried to introduce a sense of containment by standing by the window 'to keep her safe', catching some of the thrown furniture in the box and encouraging her to stay in the room for the session.

She had turned to the paints and begun mixing purple paint in a sink of water. She had wanted to print a colour off it but, it did not work as it had been too watery. She had ripped some cardboard off a box rather than asking me for some. I had talked about this, of a need for a box to hold things inside. Eventually she had mixed paints on her hand and had done a handprint on black paper. I had talked of it being unique, her handprint. While she had made this and given it to me to keep safe there had been a brief moment of enjoyment and pleasure. Looking at it, bright pinky-red on black paper gave her a momentary sense of herself in the world, her uniqueness, and going on being.

Third session

She had drawn on her hand with the idea of annoying me. I had interpreted this to do with the boundaries and rule about leaving all work here for our work; i.e. if she drew on her hand she could take it with her. She had responded by then tossing the pens everywhere. She had then questioned me, about myself and my family. She had started painting at the sink of water, tearing cardboard into small pieces. She had wanted to paint them and then float them face down. She had left four shapes floating and I had suddenly had a sharp sense of pain and sadness thinking of her and her separated siblings. She had then taken blocks of paint out of a palette and rubbed them on to black paper. I had talked to her about how it was possible to paint on paper. She had ordered me to paint green paint on the paper. She had felt distracted and had played at the doll's house. She returned to the paper to do it herself, but she could not wait to cover the paper, so she had cut the paper smaller. She had begun again with a smaller piece, painting it green and had added footsteps with the paintbrush, a fun, calm moment. She had wanted it stuck to the wall, and then had changed her mind, wanting to show her foster mother, banging her head in her excitement. She had wanted to give her foster mother one of the small cardboard scraps that had been in the water. I had let her do this, feeling that these scraps represented the four children but it was too early to say this. This made me wonder about rent and torn words associated with grief and loss, which I connected to the projection of feelings of sadness from Lucy to me in this session.

Fourth session

It had been a wild, wet and windy day; a day of storm-force gales sweeping the country. On coming into the therapy room Lucy had gone to the window and stood looking out, then sat on the window sill watching the trees move in the wind. There were large ash trees outside the therapy room. They were 60 feet high and were swaying wildly in the gale, like giants with whipping arms. She had commented to me that she did not like rainy, cloudy days and felt sorry for the trees getting wet. We had stayed at the window for some time looking out together. She had felt more settled for the first twenty minutes or so, saying, that she was not going to do anything messy today. She had played at the doll's house, precariously balancing furniture, that had tumbled down. It had been as if she had been trying to find a mental balance but it had kept collapsing as it had done when she had not been held emotionally by anybody. She had suddenly changed activity to using paints.

She had started a black picture, painting black on green card. She had painted red dots on top saying, 'it's black as red'. She had added a yellow sun rising in the black night (Illustration 3.2). She said, 'Rain is falling. It is dark and stormy'. Lucy had been very pleased with the picture and it had felt quite intense and important. She had then carefully added blue footsteps. She was quite calm and engaged with the picture and me, while she painted. Later, she wanted to take it with her and I had talked, as I had at the beginning of therapy, of the importance of keeping all her work together here; reiterating, that I would look after it, until we finished work together. She had got furious at this, had stood on the window sill, had thrown things, had gone to the

Illustration 3.2 Lucy: Rain picture.

toilet and had pretended to be locked in. On a primitive level, my keeping the picture safe had felt as if she was being locked in. I had talked of her anger and upset.

Fifth session

Lucy had brought into the session a photo of herself and one of her separated siblings, and I was able to say how much she missed them and wished they were all living together and how dispersed they were.

Discussion

Painful material forms, collects and takes shape across sessions and in between other defensive behaviour which has the purpose of creating dis-continuities of experience, so that the pain is kept at bay. In a similar way to Colin, Lucy very slowly progressed to her own creations. She was able to identify with the large ash tree outside the window which was being whipped by wind and rain. The framing of this tree by the window gave her an image of something being dwarfed by the elements. The window was important in framing this experience for her in a way, which was bearable. Burke comments on the ash as an image of the sublime: 'oak, ash, elm . . . they are aweful and majestic; they inspire a sort of reverence' (Burke 1757: 275). Some inner aspect of Lucy's experience was located there. In an aesthetic moment there is a phase of union, a matching of experience and also a separating out and appreciation of distinction and separateness. Every act of perception and sensation is imaginative and this is the essence of aesthetic experience, that an exchange takes place.

Lucy was able to paint alone after the experience of matching union with the tree. The sequence of the torn picture of a girl in the rain that she handed to me, the handprint, the footprints on green paper, the scraps of card, and the black on red/desolate tree in the landscape led to the sharing of the painful thoughts about the siblings from whom she was separated. The experience of the sublime seemed to match both experience from the past as well as fear and separation in the present. The tree had vastness, greatness of dimension, and did produce a feeling of awe as one watched it being whipped and moved by the powerful storm. Small children's experience of the greatness and vastness of parental figures may be at the base of our perception of the sublime. Working with children who have had frightening parents I can struggle with the depth of terror that they experience. At the window Lucy was safely able to look out at the tree, framed by the window, and have a matching experience. It is important that we looked out together and shared this, side by side.

CONCLUSIONS

Aesthetic experiences from the therapy room window are important when there has been a failure of the 'environment mother' in keeping the child safe. Bollas (1987) suggests that the uncanny moments of being held by a poem or picture rest on those moments when the infant's internal world would be partly given form by the mother: '. . . each aesthetic experience is transformational and an "aesthetic object" seems to offer an experience where self-fragmentation will be integrated through a processing form' (Bollas 1987: 33).

Children who have had frightening parents, and a failure of emotional holding, may be able to release some memory of that experience, when they have an experience of the sublime. The children's framed experiences at the window acted as a catalyst: 'Sense experience is fundamental; it feeds the imagination which in turn arouses the passions . . . (Burke 1757: 186). They went on to have new experiences with materials in therapy. The experience of beauty, the ginger cat, led to Colin being able to entertain softness, both in being able to accept our link and his own softer feelings. Whereas, the experience of the sublime, the giant tree being whipped by the gale, led to Lucy being able to let herself feel some of the pain of separation of family members. Feeling safe in the present allowed a moment of contact with the lack of protection which she had experienced in the past.

In these aesthetic experiences the children were able to put themselves into a position with a different perspective. Lucy put her self in the place of the other, sympathy and pity for the tree in the gale. Colin was able to lose himself in the ginger cat moment, coming out of the moment refreshed, seeing the world differently. Lucy identified with the aloneness of the tree, its wetness and its relentless buffeting, but also felt some relief that she was now in a safe situation, and protected. Burke describes the sublime as the delight of an idea of pain and danger without actually being in it (Burke 1757: 226). He suggests that darkness is more productive of sublime ideas than light and this relates to her comment on her picture that 'it's black as red'. In his discussion of the facture of painting Maclagan writes:

> This wandering about in a painting has to do with what I shall call our imaginative inhabitation of it, and it is this that gives a depth or resonance of meaning; in other words, our response to its material aesthetic properties has a continuous psychological lining to it.
>
> (Maclagan 2001: 36)

One of the difficulties for looked-after children where there has been abuse is that they may despise softness and yet fear hardness. They are not now in a frightening situation yet can abuse people trying to work with them, despising qualities of relatedness. This is partly identification with the aggressor and fearing their own well hidden terrified self, and partly the development of use-dependent traits in the brain (Perry *et al.* 1995). Children in the 'disorganised' category adapt to the response of their frightening or frightened caregiver by a wholesale internalisation of the caregiver's reaction to them. They then become out of touch with their own emotional state, which becomes an 'alien object' that they then try to externalise, becoming controlling in their attempts to control this part of the self (Fonagy and Target 1998). They are often still held captive internally. This has been explored by Greenwood in relation to art therapy with adult survivors of abuse (Greenwood 2000).

Fuller suggests that some characteristics of the sublime, such as limitlessness, depth of affect aroused, residual terror of the threat of annihilation, are to do with the fact that the environment mother gives both a sense of wellbeing but also of going on being. The sublime may be based on the fear of interruption in 'going on being'. Experiences with children who have had frightened or frightening parents makes me suggest that it may also be based on moments of failure of the maternal environment.

Images as part of ourselves

Lucy found it very difficult to leave her work with the therapist at this stage of the therapy. This is a difficult area for deprived children. It is essential for the development of the therapy that all is gathered into the session and the dynamic is diluted if this does not happen (Meltzer 1967). However, it is difficult if the child believes that they are being separated from part of themselves. If this feels 'a matter of life and death' to the child, because of 'magical thinking', the picture having a sense of duality-unity to the child, I would talk about how I would look after the work and, that it would be here for us to look at, at any time: working *towards* the completion of boundaries. Lucy needed to take the cardboard scrap early in the therapy. Later, she felt angry when I wanted her to keep her painting within the therapy setting, as if locked in herself. Levy-Bruhl discusses Catlin's photography with North American Indians (Catlin 1903, in Levy-Bruhl 1966). The Indians did not want their picture taken as some of 'their life' was seen to be in the picture. 'It would be parting with a portion of their own substance, and placing them at the mercy of anyone who might wish to possess the picture' (Catlin 1903: 122–3). When one paints, there is a period of remaining 'in the picture' which can vary enormously in time, and is not always encompassed by the session. Schaverien has suggested phases of identification, familiarisation, acknowledgement, assimilation, and disposal in the life of the picture (Schaverien 1992).

Children may wish to take a picture because it is part of the session and part of the therapist, as well as being seen as part of themselves, especially when there are separation difficulties. The way that a portrait can be 'materially and psychically identified with the original', can also happen within psychotic episodes, but this is distinguishable from a child's animistic thinking by the transference. Levy-Bruhl writes of pictures: 'every reproduction "participates" in the nature, properties, life of that of which it is the image' (Levy-Bruhl 1966: 64). He describes, prelogical/mystical thinking as 'everywhere it perceives the communications of qualities through transference, contact, projection, contamination, defilement, possession . . .' (Levy-Bruhl 1966: 83). It can be seen vividly at work in Lucy in her fear of the clock and looking in terror at me when the alarm went off unexpectedly after she had tried to change the time (as if I had magically set it off to punish her for touching the clock), as well as in her relation to her picture and other art work.

Part II

Closeness and separation

Introduction: closeness and separation

DUALITY-UNITY

In this introduction, closeness and separation between mother and child, which is essential for personality development, will form a background to Chapters four, five and six focusing on: sleeping difficulties, the location of self in animal personas and psychoanalytical thinking about psychotic and autistic states of mind. It will necessarily offer a brief contribution towards an understanding of personality development. There have been two accessible books recently, on personality development from a psychoanalytic perspective, to which the reader is referred for further, extended reading (Waddell 1998; Hindle and Smith 1999). Waddell offers an overview of the developmental phases across the life-span, from infancy to old age, illustrated with examples from clinical work, but also from literature. Hindle and Smith have edited a similar overview, from infancy to later adolescence.

The psychoanalytic theory of infant development has been built up from observations in a clinical setting, from debate with developmental psychologists working in an experimental setting, and with the observational methods of child psychotherapy training which take place in the home. The work of neurobiologists on the infant's developing brain has also had an influence and impact. Therefore there is not one theory. Present theory is made up of a number of parallel, and developing strands of related ideas about the nature of human personality. Differing clinical interests have illuminated different aspects so that theory of personality development is in a continual process of growth. Each clinical practitioner is likely to use a number of theoretical frameworks that they find useful in elucidating the states of mind of the children and families they meet. There is a good overview to be found in *Our Need for Others and its Roots in Infancy*, which looks at the contributions of different theorists in turn (J. Klein 1987).

It may be useful to take the image of an onion with all its layers and tiny central soft leaves. The baby is at first physically contained within mother's body, and after birth is still physically contained, but within her arms and general care. Mother's thoughts and feelings about her baby and the way she tries to get to know this baby and to understand his communications are also part of the containment. Looking after mother in the next circle out is father, taking care of outer world matters, which enables mother to continue her maternal preoccupation (Winnicott 1956) and to focus on baby. Around father is the circle of the extended families of the parents: grandparents, sisters, brothers, aunts and uncles. The pattern for each family will be culturally determined, with variations within each culture, that would still be considered ordinary and normal. The next ring of the onion would bring us to the community that the family live in that also offer support and contact for new parents, as well as constituting the milieu within which the family live. This way of looking at the-child-in-the-family-in-the-community is a concept developed by Winnicott (1964) and later by Harris and Meltzer (1977).

Raphael-Leff: the parents' experience

Raphael-Leff, a psychoanalyst who has a special practice with pregnancy and early parenthood, has a particular interest in looking at the interwoven subjectivities of carer and infant and unconscious and conscious:

> In pregnancy, there are two bodies, one inside the other. Two people live under one skin – a strange union that recalls gestation of the pregnant woman herself in the uterus of her own mother many years earlier. When so much of life is dedicated to maintaining our integrity as distinct beings, this bodily tandem is an uncanny fact. Two-in-one-body also constitutes a biological enigma, as for reasons we don't quite understand: the mother-to-be's body suppresses her immunological defences to allow the partly foreign body to reside within her. I suggest that psychologically too, in order to make the pregnancy her own she also has to overcome the threats posed by conception. Its meaning flows from the placenta of her emotional reality embedded in the circumstances of her social reality.
>
> (Raphael-Leff, 1993: 8)

The 'two-in-one-body' described above may be the psychological predecessor of the magical thinking of 'duality-unity' described by Levy-Bruhl; in that, there is an earliest experience of this for each one of us, in the unconscious, if not in our conscious awareness. Pregnancy can be understood as the mother serving as a physical container for the growth of the baby, like a living vessel. The placenta both nourishes the foetus and processes the waste products inside her body. Expectant mothers will differ enormously in how much they can enjoy these processes. Their feelings will be affected both by their social reality but also deeply by their unconscious; that is their inner world of psychic reality. With any change ambivalent thoughts are likely to arise. It would be normal for a future mother on having her pregnancy confirmed to feel a whole range of emotions, anticipations, expectations, excitements and anxieties. Being able to tolerate ambivalent thoughts about the baby is a positive sign that a healthy relationship will develop when the baby is born. In her research, Raphael-Leff has shown how more problematic preoccupations lead to difficulties in the mother–child relationship. One possibility is that the mother for many different reasons may idealise herself and the baby in an inner fusion, so that, the baby is not thought about as a future separate person, but as an extension of the mother. Such a mother will therefore find it difficult to let the child grow into independence. A very different inner pattern would be that the mother feels very negatively about the foetus and this pregnancy and phantasises a poisonous attacking baby that threatens her existence. In this situation she is likely to form a barrier about thinking about the baby and to be in fear of it, the monstrous baby. If this is reversed and the mother feels negatively about herself and positively about the baby there will be a fear of harming the baby. This mother will be likely to be plagued with thoughts of not being good enough and fearing that she will be unable to give the baby what it needs as well as fear of being damaging to it:

> The more tolerant a woman is of her own mixed feelings, and those of her own mother, and the more accepting she is of the babyish and child-like aspects of herself, the greater likelihood of her owning these, rather than splitting them off and projecting them into the baby with whom she unconsciously identifies.
>
> (Raphael-Leff 1993: 52)

Motherhood by its very nature demands emotional availability. It is very difficult to be emotionally available if one is preoccupied by anxieties or imaginings about the baby. Every mother brings to each individual pregnancy her own personal feelings, hopes, memories and powerful unconscious mythologies so that an imaginary baby is phantasised on the actual baby she contains. This can sometimes be clear just after a baby is born, when the mother struggles to acknowledge and relate to the baby of reality. Difficulties occur when the imaginary baby has such a strong hold in phantasy that the real baby is supplanted. Each of us contains an inner world full of phantasy, unconscious imagery and internal representations of relationships. Within a parental relationship each partner contributes unresolved issues from across the generations.

Infant observation has helped to highlight the very wide range of experiences that can be encompassed under the umbrella of normal development. Becoming a parent is a great psychic upheaval. The couple undergoes changes in their relationship during the pregnancy so that their relationship together is re-evaluated. Each also re-evaluates their relationship as the child they are to their parents. During the pregnancy there exists an imaginary baby, phantasised in each parent's inner world. When the baby is born there are further changes as the real baby becomes recognised as an individual and hopefully the phantasised baby disperses:

> . . . every parent–child couple involves a 'triple shadow interaction': the re-evolved child a parent conjures up having been with his or her own parents; the desired or detested child he or she fantasises this baby to be in relation to their internal constellation; and the real child whom they are beginning to recognise as an individual.
>
> (Raphael-Leff 1993: 130)

The kind of parent we will become will be influenced by a whole range of factors. Each baby is born into an emotional matrix where entangled threads can blur the perception of this new child and parents can respond to the baby as if they were another, perhaps adored daddy or hated older brother, or loved sister. So that the sex and personality of the baby, and the ante-natal conceptualisation of the baby can be highly significant in influencing how that baby is responded too. Each parent will also have internal models of what kind of parent each will wish to be; as well as a set of beliefs of what babies are like.

Observation

Infant observation was started by Bick and Bowlby at the Tavistock (Bick 1964), with weekly observations of infants in the natural surroundings of their homes by a 'participant observer' trying to fit in as much as possible with the routine and the subculture of the household. It is the mother–infant dyad within the family that is observed. Not only is it fascinating, and a privilege, to be able to have the space to observe a baby over two years, but it is essential in helping the therapist to see the younger child inside the older child that they may be working with in therapy. There is a good introduction to baby observation and the psychoanalytic theory of infant development in *Closely Observed Infants* (Miller *et al.* 1989). Other writers who have contributed to the literature include: Harris 1975a, 1975b; Perez-Sanchez 1990; Reid 1997, and also *The International Journal of Infant Observation and its Applications*. The work of Piontelli, on foetal observation by ultrasound, gives us an extraordinary opportunity to think about the emotional and physical containment of the foetus and to gain more insight into what they might experience; as well as rethinking at what point there is duality-unity and at what point separation: 'One of the most intense debates within the psychoanalytical movement centres on the psychological birth of the human infant; its capacity to live mentally and emotionally in the outside world once out of the narrow boundaries of the womb' (Piontelli 1992: 18).

On the one hand is the point of view that the infant may be physically born but not yet psychologically for the first few months of its postnatal life and we should 'regard it as an ego-less creature still living inside a kind of postnatal womb' (Piontelli 1992: 18). Another point of view is that mental life becomes operative from birth, but only when the newborn infant comes into contact with other people does the infant begin to feel or think.

The establishment of a relationship: the mother–child couple

We have looked at some influences on the parents we become. Now we are going to look at the contribution of various psychoanalysts in thinking about the mother–child couple. The feeding, sleeping and processing of waste products that took place inside the mother's body, now need to happen outside. In order to do this in a good enough way the baby needs to communicate his needs, and the mother to learn this individual baby's moods, upsets, grumbles, and pleasures. The focus will be on the development of the mental and emotional life of the baby, once they are born; the way in which, they come to conceptualise and internalise relationships with their primary caregivers and other members of the family. In the Introduction to Part one we looked at some of the thinking about child development from a neurobiological perspective and at some uncontained primitive states of mind. It is very necessary to keep a foot in the outside world as well as a foot in the inside world when working with children and families. It is therefore a welcome development that there has been a positive meeting of the work of developmental psychologists, who observe the external social relationship of mother and baby, with psychoanalytic theory. Developmental psychologists have mapped the way in which babies are preprogrammed with innate capacities to elicit the care that they need. It is an interactive relationship and involves participation from both so that the crucial needs for survival will be met (Stern 1985).

Object relations theory: Klein, Bion, Bick and Winnicott

Here we will look through the spectacles of object relations theory, that has made a large contribution to considering the mind and how its experiences have affected its development.

Looking at emotional development from the inner world, both Klein, and later Bion, have described what seems to be crucial for the beginning of mental processes. Klein proposed that when the baby's instinctual needs are met by an external object, namely the mother, the infant will have a physically satisfying experience, will start a social relationship with the mother, and will begin to develop mentally. The match between needs and their being met enables this to happen (Klein 1921). Bion (1962a) later described in his terms, the meeting of a preconception, that is, the infant's readiness for certain kinds of experiences, with a realisation, the corresponding external experiences for which the infant is seeking. He saw this as a crucial moment at the start of mental life. Abstract mental life begins or is founded on concrete experiences; an earliest example would be the meeting of mouth and nipple. There is an urge to suck, a need to suck to survive, which is met by the nipple giving a way to access the breast of milk, the warmth and comfort of the mother's body.

Winnicott

Winnicott was interested in the early relationship of mother and infant from a viewpoint of working simultaneously as a paediatrician, child psychiatrist and psychoanalyst. He saw infant development as evolving from the infant–mother unity, generating three main functions, to facilitate healthy development (Winnicott 1960, 1962). The first of these is 'holding/integration'. He saw the infant as unintegrated, as not yet having a mental structure, and that the mother holds the infant both physically and figuratively, giving cohesion to his sensory/motor elements. He thought that she is able to do this through 'primary maternal preoccupation', a state of heightened sensitivity to herself and baby (Winnicott 1956). The mother's sensitive response to the infant's gesture will give him a sense of magical omnipotence which must not be challenged, as this would be an impingement of external environment for which the infant is not yet ready. Successful responses between mother and baby give the infant the experience of 'I am'. This 'feeling real' is a basic component of partial integration states, e.g. being fed, being held, being bathed. This capacity to feel real and alive is one of the qualities of the development of a 'true self'. In between, the baby returns to unintegrated states or periods of rest. If the mother is 'good enough' and has a reliable holding function; the 'rest periods' are the precursors of the adult's ability to relax and for a capacity to be alone (Winnicott 1958).

The second function is 'handling/personalisation'. The mother's handling of the baby facilitates 'personalisation' which is the 'in-dwelling' of self in the body to achieve psychosomatic unity. Later research has shown that each foetus has its own daily pattern of behaviour in the womb, so that there is a potential true-self expression at the beginning of life in the individual pattern of mobility (de Vries et al. 1982; de Vries 1988; Prechtl 1989). Good coordination and muscle tone are the achievement of personalisation. 'Psychosomatic unity' is essential for healthy living, and is a precondition for total involvement with a shared reality, with others in the external world.

The third function is 'object-relating'. Winnicott saw object-relating as evolving from the experience of magical omnipotence. At first objects are not yet differentiated from the self and he called these, self–objects. Aggression plays a healthy role in allowing the development of 'I am' and separateness from mother. The fact that mother can survive these attacks allows her to be seen as a separate person in a shared reality. When mother is seen as a person in her own right then she can be used, 'object usage', rather than treated in an illusionary or omnipotent way. He developed ideas around transitional objects and phenomena to describe play and interaction in a third shared area of me/not me between mother and child. A child needs psychic continuity to allow the growth of a reality sense, of internal and external, self and object. Of the children discussed in Chapters one, two and three, Colin and Lucy had a failure of these functions due to severe neglect, whereas, Henry suffered a lack of continuity through parental bereavement. Winnicott proposed two elements which need to function together in males and females for healthy life: to be able to 'be with' and to be able to 'do with' female and male elements (Winnicott 1971).

A mother needs to hold her child in mind, in her comprehension of the true self of the child, for healthy development. Mothers facilitate their child's ordinary taking of a place and living in the environment. Small failures, where the child is at the limit of what they can manage on their own, allow the development of a reality sense. The child needs mother's support and to be allowed to regress at times. If there is deprivation and the child is not allowed to repair themselves and the environment impinges on the child, then anxieties will overwhelm. The child's sense of continuity and going on being will be broken and this will set in train psychotic defences of the self (see pp. 111–22).

Winnicott's concept of 'primary maternal preoccupation' was a response to observing the infant–mother relationship. He observed that new mothers are in a state of emotional vulnerability but that this played a role in the survival of the infant. The openness to being stirred up emotionally by the baby, allows the mother to be in sympathy with and at times in intense identification with the baby. She is then in touch with his need to be held, feed, suck, sleep, and his anxiety about uncomfortable states of being wet, changed, bathed, etc. We have seen from the work of Raphael-Leff (see pp. 70–72), that mothers will vary enormously, perhaps within themselves at different times, but also each mother with a different baby, in their ability to allow this vulnerability. At times it will be too threatening and the baby can then seem persecuting in its anxiety, need to feed or crying, and can be unbearably overwhelming for the mother in her sense of identity and sense of her own mind.

Bion and Bick

Bion saw that the ability of the mother to be in emotional contact with her baby's state of mind and to be attentive would allow the baby to grow psychologically. He conceptualised the mother's mind acting as a container for the baby. It can be seen as a more abstract form of the containment of foetus by mother in the womb. Bion used this concept or model of 'container/ contained, as a way of thinking about the development of the mind but also as a way of conceptualising other emotional relationships: 'This kind of receptivity to being stirred up emotionally is the basis of our capacity to be responsive in all these occasions throughout life when we are brought into intimate contact with someone else's state of mind' (Shuttleworth 1989: 27).

In this model of container/contained the mother is either consciously or unconsciously processing feelings and states of mind for the baby because at this stage he does not have the capacity to do this for himself. So a fretful baby would need to be held by mother both externally (arms, eyes, voice) but also, internally by her thoughts. If she can stay with the fretful feelings and try several methods of soothing, she may be able to comfort the baby. Her solid response gives him a sense of trust in himself and environment and allows him to let go of mother's external presence and instead to have an internalised image of her. It can be seen as interactive – baby has to arouse feelings in mother – mother needs to be vulnerable to the feelings but not overwhelmed, and needs a secure adult identity. To do this, she needs external support and containment herself when necessary. It is a series of constantly changing states between mother and child in a cognitive/emotional interaction which allows psychological growth of the baby.

Early experiences are probably made up of ordinary concrete experiences of care. That is, the infant's own intense bodily experiences; his perceptions of the external physical world and his emotional and cognitive interactions with his mother. It is thought that the infant actually internalises these experiences as concrete objects/memories. Eventually the baby will have a sense of his own mind but at first he internalises the experience of being held and thought about by someone else's mind. Klein called it 'introjection': a concretely experienced phantasy of taking in the containing mother and feeling her presence within. It can be seen in an infant sucking his thumb and comforting himself with an internalised breast, which he can then recreate. There is a development from a presymbolic stage, to 'transitional objects', which are part me/part not me, to symbolisation: but this arises out of a child's relationship to his internalised mother. This clearly links with the formation of identity. Each person takes in, or internalises, different emotional qualities of early relationships which become part of the self through the process of identification. In terms of attachment theory, each separate relationship the child has in the family will have its own attachment pattern.

In a similar way that experience at this stage seems to be internalised concretely, the infant experiences the splitting off of bad experiences by physical activity, crying, kicking, screaming; ridding himself of these by projection. The mother then contains the experience by providing a receptacle for the distress and in thinking about the baby. This first primitive interpersonal communication is called 'projective identification'. The baby experiences comfort, containment, a receptacle for bad feelings/experiences and internalises a mother with this capacity, giving him an early model of thinking and processing that he will gradually develop after repeated experiences. The baby is able to (a) project his distress into mother and (b) receive back – reintroject – the experiences in a modified form, i.e. mother's understanding of what was upsetting.

This way of thinking about the emotional interaction between mother and baby as container/contained adds its own point of view to a growth of a sense of self. The infant gradually internalises his mother's capacity to think about him and this becomes an emotional resource which he can take to other relationships he makes. A sense of self develops based on identifications with these experiences: 'introjective identification'. This forms the basis of a capacity to learn from the emotional impact of life – to learn from experience (Bion 1962b). Here, in a sense, an ideal is being described, because parents are likely to be more receptive to some aspects of their child's experience than others. Part of the baby's experience may not be thought about and therefore becomes less acceptable to the growing child. These can lead to a split-off existence as a banished part of the self, out of contact with the main personality. It is possible that some art stems psychologically from a desire to find a form for these unrecognised parts of the self.

It can be seen that the process that has been described involves the acceptance of a parent who contains and a child who is actively contained, psychologically dependent on mother. Parents who have been forced themselves to grow up very quickly or who shun dependence because of an unacknowledged longing for it, may find it very difficult to be containing. Winnicott developed a concept of 'environmental impingement' when the baby was left unprotected. When a baby is not sufficiently protected Winnicott saw that the child then has to actively react. Bick (1968, 1986) felt that the experience of being contained/held gave rise to a sense of having a skin or of 'being all of a piece'. She developed work in trying to think about children where maternal containment was inadequate, forcing the baby to rely on herself too early. Children who come to rely on focusing on objects in the environment to hold themselves together in a clinging way rather than depending on human contact, she suggested, acquire a sense of identity by this 'adhesive identification'. She felt that they develop a social appearance of a personality but without any sense of inner mental space or internal resource. Another form of response is to rely on muscular tension or the experience of motion. This way of dealing with the emotional impact of experience she called second-skin formation. Again, this lacks a sense of inner mental space and does not allow permeability of emotional experience. All children are likely to experience some of each at some time but need to experience the containment of another for social and psychological development. In Part two we will consider first, in Chapter four, the impact of separation difficulties on sleeping problems in children, drawing on clinical work as a child psychotherapist, as well as an art therapist. In Chapter five, the focus will be on children who locate themselves in animals, usually a family pet. I would understand this to be a form of adhesive animal identification to protect the self and to hold the self together. The core self of the child is frozen and held protected inside the outer skin of animal identification which allows animation and interaction with the environment. In Chapter six, there will be a theoretical overview of the main contributors of the more complex problems of separation to be seen in autistic and psychotic states of mind.

Chapter 4

Separation and sleeping difficulties: helpful images with sleepless children

> Learning to face the shadows outside helps us to fight the shadows inside.
>
> (Pratchett 2001: 45)

INTRODUCTION

The children and their families discussed in this chapter had all had ongoing sleep problems for several years. Some of the children were referred for therapy only in latency when it was seen that they would not 'just grow out of it'. In all the cases an unhappy child was having difficulties at bedtime: with going to bed, and with going to sleep, but also with waking at night and coming into the parents' bed. This usually meant broken sleep for other members of the household, a parent displaced into the child's bed as their place was taken by the child in the parent's bed, and the parents' relationship suffering. Sleep difficulties in children often lead to tiredness, irritability and consequent deterioration of relationships in the family. Family cultures vary about children sleeping with parents but generally, although this may be thought acceptable for infants, toddlers, and young children, it becomes less easy as a child gets older. There is a practical problem as children grow, about room for three in a bed. The parents' privacy is impinged upon which leads to a lack of a restorative and creative sexual life, and older children normally begin to desire a separation as their own social life develops at school. Developing sexuality in adolescence can bring a sense of excitement, disgust and unease about bodies and their private parts, which further complicates sleeping difficulties in the family, if a young person is unable to settle at night on their own. For this reason, if no other, it is helpful to get these treated in the younger stage of latency. If there is an inner conflict in a child about separation then it is often thrown into relief when there is a question of sleepovers at a friend's house, as children with separation difficulties are likely to be the ones who want to go home late evening and panic about sleeping away from a parent.

In her imaginative exploration of sleepless infants Daws (1989) thoughtfully explores the relationship between parent and infant. She questions how much the baby's sleep is a result of parental care and how much it is to do with being able to 'let go' of the baby, to let them find physiological rhythms of their own. In the form of brief psychoanalytic therapy Daws describes, she links the meaning of not sleeping to deeper problems of separation and individuation between mother and baby. We saw in the Introduction (pp. 70–77) that many factors affect the mother–baby relationship. In latency children, there may still be a similar kind of difficulty, but mixed up with other factors from the child's longer life experience, such as bereavements, or trauma, or a developmental disturbance.

A FAMILY APPROACH IN CHILD PSYCHOTHERAPY

When children are referred with sleep difficulties an approach is taken which looks initially at the whole family history. A family tree would be taken, looking at significant losses and events. We would then think about the referred child particularly and their history in detail and link their development with other events in the family. This work is psychoanalytically based, trying to take in the parents' and children's experiences and to begin to reflect with them, on their own family of origin as well as their present family. Where the parents are presenting quite healthily it is hoped to create a space where they can reflect and begin to suggest connections and come up with solutions. Where there are additional problems, for instance, a depressed mother or passive father, then it can be helpful to make practical suggestions, alongside exploration of the family dynamics. This could be thought of as trying to bring some prosaic common sense, into what has frequently become a very fraught situation. An example of this might be playing a story tape while the child is in bed, so that they transfer to the tape as a transitional object and can manage to be in bed with this instead of needing a parent beside them to fall asleep; or it may help to involve father in bedtime routine, reading bedtime stories, if a mother and child are finding it difficult to separate. A small success is very useful in helping parents to draw on their own inner resources to tackle the next stage of the problem. While parents and child have something tangible to do about the difficulties, other conscious and unconscious processes get going as we start to think about family situations in the past and present.

Sleep difficulties and loss: Ian

Ian, his parents' first child, had been an unplanned pregnancy, but both parents had been pleased at the news. They were young and lived in some financial hardship, so that socially and economically their lives were difficult. During the pregnancy there were many worries about the baby and they were told that they would very likely have a handicapped child and were offered a termination. They decided to go ahead with the pregnancy and although the baby was rushed into intensive care, he was in fact quite normal. Mother had postnatal depression, struggling with bereavement due to the death of a sibling, around the time of giving birth. The couple then had a baby girl who was also expected to be damaged, but again was not, although this baby has had a lot of illness causing much anxiety.

Ian was referred for tantrums and difficulties with bedtime and sleeping. At the first family meeting Ian presented as a bright precocious five year old. There were different kinds of attractive toys to play with and art materials but he ignored these and took part in the conversation in an articulate way but rather as one performing to an audience. Underneath this pseudo-adult behaviour I thought he was actually very anxious and his fingers betrayed him as they were constantly wrung together. Mother described Ian as a kind of monster at home who had tantrums if he did not get his own way. She and father both seemed frightened of him and his tenacity in refusing to be put outside the room if he was naughty. He had trouble going to sleep but when I asked what the difficulties were, it appeared that he would sit up in bed reading to all hours. He would wake with bad nightmares and want to come to bed with his mother who felt exhausted by his need to contact her in the night. Both parents, who had had limited educational opportunities them-selves, felt bewildered by this child who read so avidly. He felt quite alien to them, like a changeling, particularly when they had expected a child with limited educational potential. Ian was liked by his teachers and described as a bright and rewarding child.

In the session he was able to talk about his dreams and fears and proved to be a highly imaginative and sensitive child struggling to reach and make contact with his mother. Part of his precocity had been to engage a mother mourning the loss of a sibling. As his mother had been sunk in depression and felt herself to have little to offer to him he had upped his demands, tantrums becoming an effective way to centre her attention on him. The birth of the next child which had brought further anxieties to the parents had increased this behaviour in Ian. He could be understood to be increasing his attachment behaviour the further she felt out of reach, exacerbated by sibling rivalry to the new baby. She focused her nurturing on her younger child who also clung to her and refused to allow father to have any part in her care. Fearing for this child's health she was desperately trying to keep her alive while Ian tried in vain to be with her. It was possible to help father to make a relationship with the younger child which, therefore took pressure off mother and let her spend some time with Ian. At first nobody thought that this would be possible. The parents stopped threatening Ian that they would give him away or leave and tried to be more emotionally responsive to his nightmares rather than seeing them as being naughty. They began to enjoy some of Ian's success at school. It was interesting that once he began to feel more understood that he stopped taking an adult role in the sessions and was able to play in a way appropriate to his age while still being articulate at what upset him.

Ian's parents still felt quite bewildered, trying to adjust to the expectations they had had of a mentally handicapped baby. His behaviour, which seemed to be partly attempts to reach his mother in her depression, and partly an intense curiosity about the world and need to discuss his feelings and impressions, had been seen as possible evidence of brain damage or madness. Phantasies of a damaged monstrous baby contributed towards this view, which had been aroused when they had first been told to expect a handicapped baby. When the monstrous phantasy could be dispelled, both parents were able to see the child they actually had. Mother was encouraged to allow father into the relationship with the younger child, father was encouraged to be more of an active presence in his older son's life, as well, then the family were able to make good moves forward, particularly as they had supportive sets of grandparents. Ian was able to read in bed in the evening, mother coming to settle him at lights-out time. Once he had more time with mother in the day he was able to stop getting up at night and coming into her, she had more sleep and felt more relaxed with him in the day. The nightmares stopped as relationships eased in the family and the two siblings, no longer in quite so painful competition for mother, were sometimes able to enjoy each other's company. In this situation, family meetings offer the best way forward, so that everyone's point of view in the family can be considered, contained, and reflected upon by the therapist and family working together. In some cases, family work may not be enough, and then individual work can offer a space for the child to explore thoughts and feelings through play and art, while the parents work with another therapist on their own issues.

Helpful images in work with sleepless children

It can be seen from the clinical example above that many images are present both in the parents' mind, the child's, and the therapist's while they are working together. Mother and child, and the way they relate, how they see each other, offer essential clues to the difficulties presented, particularly when these are entrenched. In the above case, mother had an image in her mind of having created a 'monstrous baby', so that Ian felt alien to her and she interpreted his tantrums as 'devilish', rather than as due to high anxiety and a wish for closer contact. In the sessions with them, it was very difficult not to stare and listen to Ian when he precociously held forth in an adult conversation which suggested that it had been formed as a result of a dynamic to hold attention, where there might be little chance of getting any; it was so compulsive. The way that he wrung his hands together suggested that he was not really enjoying the role he had taken, and that it had to do with loss. He had lost a lively mother, when she had lost her sibling.

Dreams and nightmares

Children who have sleep difficulties are sometimes woken at night, like Ian, by dreams or nightmares. An earlier word for nightmare (during the seventeenth to nineteenth centuries) was 'night-hag': a female demon who supposedly abducted people at night on horseback. The horse ridden by the night-hag was stolen from stables at night. 'It was believed that she created bad dreams in her victims by producing a feeling of suffocation' (Kacirk 1997: 45). It is an interesting combined image of spirited libido energy (the horse) with a witch-like figure. Witches usually represent the destructive negative side of a mother image, which needs to be integrated and accepted. For the child they are frequently to do with aspects of the 'bad' mother, all those times where she has not been available to the child, mixed with projected hostility; so a condensed image of the sum of the hated, rather than idealised mother, and the child's own aggression. Nightmare was a term 'generated from mara, an incubus – a disease that troubles one so in sleep that he can scarce fetch his breath' (Blount (1656) in Kacirk 1997: 45–46). This may have derived from anxiety causing tension which tightens the chest and makes breath seem short. The combined image suggests energy or animation in the wrong place, i.e. feelings and emotions not given expression to in the day or anxieties and conflicts, often in relation to the parents, disturbing sleep. These dreams arouse anxieties or fears in the child which precipitate their seeking a parent for comfort. Here, a child may be full of unconscious and unexpressed anxiety, anger and jealousy, like Ian. Children may also wake at night to unconsciously get attention that they cannot have in the day. This can sometimes happen when a parent returns to work having been at home with the children. A night terror is a very different sleep disorder where the child is not dreaming or actually awake although they may be sleep-talking or -walking.

It is helpful to look at the content of dreams, if they can be remembered, in order to help the child and his parent reflect on the meaning and associations. Freud has shown how dreams offer vivid and condensed images of present conflict and anxiety, often mixed with earlier memories. Freud's *The Interpretation of Dreams* (1900) is an accessible and fascinating account of dreams and the development of a method of exploration of them by free association. Daws (1989) has an excellent chapter on dreams and the importance of REM (Rapid Eye Movement) sleep: the part of the night's sleep in which we dream. She quotes Hartmann (1973) on the importance of REM sleep as it aids an ability to maintain an optimistic mood, energy and self-confidence, as well as restoring a focused attention. It is therefore essential when there have been emotional changes, consolidating learning or memory from the day. She goes on to discuss Palombo's (1978) work on dreams, who built on Hartmann's work, and here I quote:

He convincingly suggests that dreaming plays a central function in assimilating memories of the day into settled long-term memory. Thus if dreaming is insufficient or interrupted, the consequences are very serious for child and adult alike – they are left with a jumble of unassimilated memories.

(Daws 1989: 85)

Daws likens the work she does to coordinating dream-work, trying to set an integrative process in action:

Remembered dreams have an additional function for a reflective person of illuminating in symbolic form present conflicts, choices, changes, and connecting these with experiences from the past. The dreamer has a chance to ponder over these images and symbols and the memories they release.

(Daws 1989: 85)

Sleep difficulties and dreams: Rebecca

Rebecca, age seven, was referred because she had very poor sleep, waking almost every night with nightmares. She was a hypersensitive child who could easily become excitable and alert. She lived with her mother and father, and older half-brother by her father's previous marriage. A difficulty that was shared by the whole family was the expressing of angry feelings. This was a family with too much 'niceness', which meant that there was little room for natural ambivalence, and some healthy expression of mixed feelings. Feelings were bottled up and then came out in huge tantrums, the ferocity of which then shocked all those involved. When feelings are bottled up too much, ambivalence and aggression may break through the dream material, waking up the child. Hartmann (1984) suggests that people who suffer from night-mares are those with thin or permeable boundaries. Adult patients who had had lifelong nightmares seem to have been extra sensitive perceptually, e.g. to light or sound, but also interpersonally, emotionally empathic to others' feel-ings. Whereas other people might keep thoughts and feelings firmly in their dreams, these sensitive people are more likely to let anger and fears 'through', and they are experienced vividly. Daws thinks that this is useful to bear in mind when working with child patients, as a common-sense approach to 'universal fears' is helpful in de-sensitising. 'Sensitive' appeared in the refer-rals of all the children in this chapter and in my thoughts about them. In a meeting which only mother had been able to come to she said that she had been woken by a dream of Rebecca's the previous night. She recounted the dream. It was very short but significant: '*Dad had fallen down a hole but Rebecca had gone to get help and rescued him*'.

Mum had got out of her own bed and settled in bed with Rebecca, who had a double bed in her room, as well as her own single bed, to make it easier for mother to soothe her. Mother did not know what to make of this dream but began to talk of her own mixed feelings about Rebecca's sleep. She would like Rebecca to go to sleep early because she liked to have some evening to herself, but she does not mind her waking up later, really. When we thought about 'really', she was able to talk of her own fear of the dark and nightmares when she was a child. It was possible to see that mother was quite comforted herself by sharing a bed with Rebecca, and had a conflict about aiding her maturation to the stage of sleeping happily in her own room. She also had no inner model of comfortably falling asleep herself as a child. The arrangement of beds in Rebecca's room suggested a psychological image of duality-unity or of two-in-one, and the difficulties around separation.

Mother carried on talking and eventually told me that her husband and stepson had gone out last night to play snooker together and had been home very late, well after Rebecca's bedtime. She had felt rather left with the struggle to get Rebecca to bed, as they had left early too. I wondered what Rebecca's feelings were about Dad and half-brother going out without her. We talked about possible jealous feelings in the family, who goes with whom and who gets left out, which are complex in a reconstituted family. Could the dream be about a wish for something bad to happen to Daddy, as punishment for being left out, but also a desire to be the heroine who rescues him? Mother was then able to talk about her complex feelings towards her stepson and his adolescent behaviour. Here, there is a big difference in family mores as to what is expected from an adolescent between father's and mother's families of origin. This has led to feelings of resentment on all sides. In order for Rebecca to grow out of a need for mum, mum also has to grow out of a need for her.

Maturation has to be given the right conditions and consistency, for growth to occur. Mother found it difficult to talk to Rebecca about jealous feelings when she herself felt excluded from the father and son relationship, and yet, clearly father and son need to go out together. In the sessions we were able to talk with mother about creating opportunities for play with Rebecca so that there was a place for feelings to be played out. It is during play that children can assimilate and 'play with' difficult thoughts and feelings. There was a model for this in the sessions that Rebecca attended, where she could play and draw out, as well as talk about the dreams that were disturbing her sleep. We were also able to make a space to talk over the family dynamics, and make some practical suggestions for a staged separation at night until Rebecca was sleeping through. There is enormous relief if dreams can be understood and put into child friendly language.

Dreams are necessary to our good health, but in health go on in the background of sleep and do not disturb us. One aspect of dreams is as wish fulfilment. This was central to Freud's theory (Freud 1900). In the above dream, Rebecca wished to be the heroine, bringing rescue to Daddy, and thereby be the most important child in his eyes. Freud also thought that residues from the dream-day – the day before the night of the dream – formed part of the content of the dream, and were incorporated into it. Ella Sharpe, whose work on art and creativity may be familiar to art therapists, believed that the instigating factors of the dream-day were important in determining the interpretation of a dream (Case and Dalley 1992; Sharpe 1937). Children and parents will often give the therapist enough background to understand the dream in the conversation which follows the telling of it, as in this case where mother was telling me both about her daughter but also about her own small child within who wanted to be centrally in her husband's thoughts, and who could struggle with the relationship he had with his son. As children get older the wish fulfilment of the dream may not be so apparent but the dream may have what Freud distinguished as the manifest content and the latent content. Symington writes:

> Freud's idea is that if the wish was to be clearly seen in the dream it would so disturb the dreamer that he or she would wake up; the dream, then, is the guardian of sleep. It is a compromise formation in that it contains wishes which are unacceptable to the conscious ego and so cannot enter consciousness during the waking day, even in sleep, cannot be allowed lucid expression because the dreamer would wake up. The dream therefore expresses the wish, but in disguise.
>
> (Symington 1986: 94)

INDIVIDUAL WORK IN CHILD PSYCHOTHERAPY

Children in therapy sometimes bring very strong visual images, either in the form of pictures, dreams or toys, or, as in the following case, describe an image that is in their mind; that holds clues to their difficulties.

Sleeping difficulties and verbal imagery: Alice

Alice came into the therapy room and wrote 'Why Wolabe?' on a piece of paper, sticking it to the door of the therapy room. She had discovered a way to use the therapy session that involved posing a question at the start of the session to which I was to find an answer. Alice was ambivalent about seeking help and characteristically then changed the subject, saying that we were going to have a party in the therapy room. This was to put a distance between her question and the anxiety that it provoked and to turn to something excit-ing and distracting. She then took charge of the party preparations, very much in control but leaving me to ponder on the question. Near the end of the session she said that she had been to a market at the weekend and had bought an Australian wallaby with a baby in its pouch for her mother as a present. When I wondered if she had had any thoughts about the present she said that 'Mummy liked Australia'. We both knew, as our eyes met, that this was a real but also surface answer. So the question is 'Why Wallaby?', why was she attracted to this particular animal and what was the nature of her communication to her mother, and to me, in the session?

Alice, who had pale blonde hair and was small for her age, seven, had been referred for therapy because of her sleeping difficulties. During the evening she was constantly up and down the stairs, elaborate bedtime rituals meant that mother was engaged the whole evening with Alice and there was no time for a parental relationship. If she was put to sleep in her own room she would wake and try, usually successfully, to get into bed with mother, and stepfather would go to sleep in the spare room. I had gradually learnt that Alice's difficulties in separation extended to other areas of her life. For instance she refused to accept a baby sitter so mum and stepdad could not go out together. She was consumed with thoughts about her mother, where she was and what she was doing when they were apart, which inhibited her enjoyment of her own activities. Attempts to have friendships of her own and to go to sleep-overs had ended disastrously with Alice having to be fetched home in the middle of the evening. During the initial family work we had learnt that Alice's father had died two years previously and that her mother had lost her own mother when a child. This meant a double difficulty for mother in that first she had no inner model of being put to bed or identification with her mother settling her as a child at night in her own room. Second, she still missed and mourned for her own mother as well as, her first husband. Daws on sleepless babies:

> Sorrow is, indeed, also one of my themes, in particular how parents' losses and traumas, for instance the death of the mother's own mother or a birth experienced as disastrous, go on resounding inside the parent and colour such an apparently simple operation as putting a baby to bed. Separations in a parent's life, felt to have been unbearable, may make, the small separation of putting a baby down in its cot also seem unbearable.
>
> (Daws 1989: 2)

Alice's individual therapy centred on the mourning for her father, the difficulty in expressing ambivalence to her stepfather and the fear of separating from her mother. Losing a parent at an early age naturally leads to fears of losing the remaining parent. One can be absolutely sure they are alive if you are with them all the time. We were able to think together about Alice's wallaby image which expressed a wish to stay in physical contact with mum, a baby in the pouch: a halfway state of being born but not yet born. These losses and fears were very real but were further complicated by having to adjust to a new partner in mother's life and her own. A further reason to stay in mother's physical and mental 'pouch' was to make sure that no new babies arrived to 'take her place'. Alice was bright and fun to be with as well as deeply struggling with loss. While talking about some of her difficulties with separation over not being able to go on a sleepover with schoolfriends, or enjoy going to out-of-school activities because of thinking about what her mother might be doing while she was not there, she recognised something of herself and mum in the wallaby image. I could have interpreted this earlier but it was important that she was able to make the discovery in her own time.

The French psychoanalyst, Rey (1975), has used the image of 'marsupial space' to describe the way in which mental space is structured at birth. He suggests that at birth the infant lives in a space surrounded by mother's care but that psychological birth takes place later. This is when the infant has a defined sense of personal space, separate from maternal space. In her own way, Alice too had arrived at the same image to express her dilemma around separation and independence. The image of the wallaby with her baby in her pouch offers an evocative sense of the child which is born physically, but not yet psychologically in her own space. In 'Winnie the Pooh', (Milne 1926), the characters of Kanga and her baby Roo, play with the borderline between at-oneness and separation. In this case the baby Roo has a name that is actually part of mother's name as they have split 'Kangaroo'. The story starts with the other animals, Rabbit, Pooh Bear and Piglet resenting the new-comers to the forest. There is a very funny sequence when the animals attempt to play a trick on Kanga, and Piglet is substituted for Roo. This sequence plays with the feelings of resentment to the newcomers to the forest and with the wish to be the baby that is present in the older child. Kanga gets her own back by feeding Piglet with Roo's medicine. Piglet, who is older than Roo, suddenly finds it is better to be older and more independent and makes good his escape. In this way the author plays with the jealousy of older siblings at the arrival of new babies in relation to the parent, Christopher Robin. The story ends with a new order of relations in the family as all have adjusted to the new arrivals:

> So Kanga and Roo stayed in the Forest. And every Tuesday Roo spent the day with his great friend Rabbit, and every Tuesday Kanga spent the day with her great friend Pooh teaching him how to jump, and every Tuesday Piglet spent the day with his great friend Christopher Robin. So they were all happy again.

(Milne 1926: 83)

Ghost stories and phantoms of the night

China dolls with their fixedly beautiful expressions form the base of ghost stories, particularly among girls age nine to thirteen. They have to be told with bangs or thumps under the table or on the floor and preferably in candlelight at sleepovers:

There is a girl, and for her birthday her parents buy her a new china doll, in a beautiful dress and with a lovely painted face. She has beautiful red cheeks and sky blue eyes. The girl plays with her all the time. One day she is playing out in the garden. Her father calls her in for dinner. She leaves the doll outside, but while they are eating dinner it starts to rain. When she finishes dinner she goes to bed. When her parents tuck her in, she says that she forgot to bring the doll inside. Her father says they can get the doll tomorrow as it is raining. The girl cannot sleep. She is lying there trying to get to sleep when she hears a voice. 'I'm on the first step' (thumps under the table), *she thinks she is imagining it and tries to get to sleep again. A while later she hears the voice again, 'I'm on the second step* (thumps under the table), *I'm gonna get ya'* (thumps under the table). *She starts to feel really scared. She gets up and opens the door, looking on to the stairs, she sees the doll, soaking wet with all her beautiful make-up smudged and running. She runs to see her Dad and tells him what happened. So they take the doll down stairs and lock it in the cupboard. Feeling much better she gets back into bed and tries to sleep. But then she hears the voice again. 'I'm on the third step'* (thumps under the table). *She remembers there are only five steps until her bedroom so she picks up all her covers and gets into the wardrobe. She hears the voice again, 'I'm on the fourth step* (thumps under the table), *I know where you're hiding* (thumps under the table), *you're in the wardrobe'* (thumps under the table). *She opens the wardrobe door a crack and looks out into the empty room. 'I'm on the fifth step* (thumps under the table), *I'm on the landing* (thumps under the table), *I'm opening the door'* (thumps under the table). *And sure enough she sees the door open. When her parents come in, in the morning to wake her up, all they find is her bloodied sheets and the doll smiling, holding a carving knife!*

(Told by Isobel and Hannah)

The China Doll story is typically about the return of the abandoned and forgotten, to seek revenge. The build-up, with the knocks under the table is especially good and scary. There are many variations such as finding the doll in the daughter's place, often discovered by the child's father, or a murdered child and the doll has disappeared. The story has the rage and murderousness of feeling oneself forgotten. It is typically told at an age when children are beginning to delight in more freedom and coming in later, after going out to play, that is, at a time when they probably care less than they did about parents going out on their own; because they have their own burgeoning social life. At this stage children may be perfectly happy to be with friends and not with parents but want their parents to be still thinking about them. The age that these are told also encompasses the onset of menstruation and the change perhaps from being father's latency princess to being a teenager.

Freud's essay on 'The Uncanny', suggests that one is encountering something previously met with, but forgotten (Freud 1919).

As I was going up a stair
I met a man who wasn't there
He wasn't there again today
Oh how I wish he'd go away.

This children's rhyme is an example of the uncanny; where there may be an old fear or projection of one's own hostility that comes back to haunt.

INDIVIDUAL WORK IN ART THERAPY

Lizzy, age 12, was referred because of ongoing sleeping difficulties. She had anxieties about going to bed and getting to sleep. She woke in the night with anxieties about burglars and intruders, and would sleep frequently in her parents' room. Five years previously, a close school friend had lost her father when they had returned to the family home from an outing and surprised an intruder who had attacked him and inflicted fatal injuries. When we explored the family history we found that her parents had some input into the difficulty around separation. They both felt reluctant to let go, as she approached adolescence. They had both suffered from difficult relationships with their own parents so that they wanted to treat their youngest child very tenderly. This was complicated by a miscarriage before Lizzy was born which had led to fears about her health. Lizzy had a wish to keep everything nice in the family, while being plagued with rather horrible images at night. She had a vivid imagination, and was highly sensitive and in tune with feelings and emotions. Lizzy had tried 'everything' to help her sleep, from cuddlies, to night-lights, dream-catchers, objects of mother's, tapes, and bedtime rituals. She was very anxious and active in her waking at night. She heard noises and feared intruders. One of the ways that making images may help is to give a form and substance to these 'worse because imagined' phantoms of the night. Lizzy had a particular fear of people's faces changing expression and of the faces of china dolls. It is possible that these fears were based on an old memory of seeing strong emotion suddenly take someone over, altering their face.

I had thought that it was possible that Lizzy was in a situation of vicarious trauma. The sleeplessness had started after the death of her friend's father, but it had left her with an ongoing fear of burglars, *as if* it had happened to her. It is becoming more recognised that people can become traumatised by their own imagination, through identifying with an actual incident, and then imagining it happening to them and their family (Terr 1981; Tehrani 2002). Vicarious trauma can be experienced by those in the helping professions because of exposure to disturbing material, which can be traumatic to hear. A small child has less defence when hearing painful material, and imaginative children tend to get left with vivid images in their minds. This is an example of Hartmann's description of children with a thin, permeable boundary who tend to be empathic and easily absorb emotions from others. Lizzy did not have any difficulties in speaking about her patterns of wakefulness at night, in therapy, but did suffer from shyness. She wished to find a more confident 'voice of her own'.

Painting out frightening images

In the first phase of therapy she drew towards the end of sessions, building up a gallery of images from her sleepless nights, some of these were scary images of imagined burglars, but two other images will be discussed here. She would take a small piece of paper and then fold it down to a postcard size before starting which echoed her difficulty in taking a place in the world that was also evident in her difficulty in speaking out. In this phase at least two different Lizzy's arrived at the therapy room door, in that she could appear in pigtails looking terribly frail and young or she could arrive with hair loose, feeling much more like a robust emergent teenager. These two different aspects fluctuated in the session. In the third session there was much more sense of an emergent older girl who wanted to be more independent and to be in her own room at night. These two parts of her were very much in conflict. She talked about last week's drawing which had been of an imagined burglar and told me of all the burglaries that had happened in her street. She then separated from me to go to the table to draw on her own. Technically, it is important to have the space to do this, as it is a mini-separation where one is in one's own thoughts in the presence of another. Here, I am thinking about, 'the capacity to be alone' (Winnicott 1958). Part of the process of separating that we have seen in the Introduction is to be alone in the presence of mother. The child gains a sense of 'I am' from mother's preoccupation with him and his needs. Her enjoyment of his ability to play alone near her is necessary to the next stage of development. His sense of her reliability and continued existence allows him to think 'I am alone'. By this stage the child has internalised 'a good object', that is, a reliable picture of her inside, built up through repeated good experiences. It is helpful to have a space in the therapy room where you can meet together to talk, but also a table that children can withdraw to, to make or paint, choosing when they are ready to return. Normally, I would sit at the art therapy table with a child, but I have found it more aiding of independence to give children with sleep difficulties a space of their own in the therapy room. If children can gradually get used to this space, they are more likely to be able to enjoy the choice of materials, and arrange the table for themselves which is a precursor to enjoying 'a room of one's own', both in the sense of a mental space and a physical one.

Lizzy drew herself sitting, on the edge of the bed, with her back to the viewer; some light from the landing is just visible (Illustration 4.1). She is not able to go to sleep, and is awake, while everyone else is asleep. Lying on the

Illustration 4.1 Lizzy: Self with Blackbird.

bed, head on the pillow, is Blackbird, a cuddly bird that she has had a long time. He is black, feathery and furry. There is a space between them. There is an anxious tense quality to the figure. The charcoal drawing is postcard size and emphasises the sense of being lost and alone at night. Three aspects of Lizzy were present: the older girl, who is drawing and presenting the picture to me; the younger little girl, who sits with her back to the viewer, and faces the door and thin shaft of light, poised to go into mother but trying to stay in her own room; and the prostrate Blackbird, representing a very young part of her struggling with separation. Animal cuddlies and transitional objects appear when there is a mute entreaty, representing feelings that cannot be verbalised or are preverbal. Blackbird, is lying on the bed, and pillow and top cover are shaded giving the appearance of a figure. Blackbird expressed the wish not to be separated from this shaded form of mother. In a sense, these three parts of her needed connecting up, because if they were working together the older girl could look after the younger and the younger look after her blackbird (infant self). We all feel afraid at times, but can speak to ourselves about it, get hold of the fear. Drawing and painting fearful images can be a useful way to achieve ownership of disturbing images, literally 'painted out'; it is then possible to view them as a third person, and to gain a common-sense perspective. This is not to deny the extraordinary in images or the numinous, but in these cases the imagination needs to be given a prosaic form; it is so strong. You need some space before you can create. In not being the parent, the therapist can act as a transitional person, mediated by the forming of a therapeutic alliance with the older child wishing to move on to the next stage.

In the fourth month Lizzy painted an image from a half-remembered dream. It was at night and was painted on black paper. She used colour for the first time. '*She was walking through water, along a river, there were trees on the banks. She didn't know why she was doing this.*' The image on paper was of the river, and bank and trees and the moon. The next session, she was looking at the picture and I asked her if she had had any thoughts about it. She began to talk about a film of The Princess and the Goblin that she used to watch, a favourite video of the Scottish story, in which the dream image appears (Macdonald 1967). In the story the princess has a thread which enables her to find her way out of the caverns in which she has become lost and which, are full of goblins. In the story, she in turn is rescued by a boy miner, Curdie. He defeats the goblins by singing rhymes at them, which they cannot stand and by stamping on their toes. The thread comes from the princess's beloved grandmother, and in a sense it is the umbilical cord, that keeping in touch with an internal link to goodness and support. Curdie offers a different solution; it is a more masculine one of vitality and doing, fun and animation, in that newly made up rhymes insulting the goblins are more efficacious. The story wisely suggests that we need both feminine and masculine elements, working together, to keep away night fears. Lizzy's creative dream life came up with this image at a time when she was both exploring dynamics in therapy but also trying out solutions at home. When she was shy at school, a vigorous part of her was needed, so that she could use her very real talents. Associations to this dream fragment, after it was painted, led us into interesting discussions, and in this way through discussion of dream and picture she was able to begin to know her imagination, which is crucial for children who are in danger of being dominated by powerful images from the unconscious. At the end of therapy, the original scary images of burglars had lost their power, becoming images of the past, bogeymen to frighten children.

CONCLUSION

Sleeping difficulties in older children can be helped by a family approach that explores the dynamics behind the separation problems of parents and child. Parent and child need to be helped to let go of each other at the end of the day so that both can enjoy a restorative sleep. Loss and bereavement are very commonly in the background, often having coincided with the pregnancy or birth. Depression can be present, affecting the parent/child relationship as well as fears of further loss. Many helpful images are produced, in conversation, body language, play, dreams, as well as in using art materials, which can give insight into anxieties. Making images in art therapy can give a form to phantoms of the night which is very helpful with sensitive children who have permeable boundaries that easily absorb emotions from others. In grounding the phantoms, to the surface of the paper, the child can become in control and this allows the development of a common-sense perspective as well as a distance from them. Transitional object animals appear when an infant part of the older child is coming on to stage in therapy. Going apart from the therapist, to use materials at a table, can be a precursor to 'enjoying a space of one's own'.

Chapter 5

The location of self in animals

The body mates with forms no less than the mind does.
(Sewell 1960: 37)

INTRODUCTION

An interest in children's location of self in animal persona began while I was working as a therapist at an assessment centre with children received into care (Case 1987; Case and Dalley 1992). These looked-after children came from very disturbed circumstances, some having had responsibility for younger siblings when they had been living with mentally ill parents, or they were victims of emotional, physical or sexual abuse. When these self-parenting children came into care, and family responsibilities were lifted from them, one of the ways they could react would be to regress, behaving like a much younger child. Curiously, other children would 'become an animal', both in the classroom and the therapy room. At the time I was puzzled as to how this could be 'regression'; when they had not been a young animal previously, why would they unconsciously choose animal form? In order to 'be an animal' in the sense of refusing to do school work and going on all fours under the school desks or 'being an animal' in the therapy room the children showed 'good observation' or were often very accurate in their behaviour of dog or cat. This suggests that they really took on an animal identity of the pet animal they were being. I am not using the word 'play', as it did not usually have a playful quality, but was much more 'driven' by inner need. It seems to appear when the strain of being human has become too much. There is a location of self into animal form to protect something valuable in the personality that will or has been crushed or lost if not so protected. It is the location of self that is important because it is a form of identification or duality-unity. Although children can just be 'an animal', they are often a cat or dog that they have known. These animals are family pets or sometimes pets of neighbours that the children have become close to or have seen looked after very well, so that they would like to be that pet. This is most often seen in children who are being fostered, after previous experience of neglect. Bettelheim (1967) discusses a child identified with dogs because they received better treatment and also explores what he thinks of as the myth of feral children who may in fact be autistic. The reasons that children might jump into an animal skin, when human relationships have failed in some way, will be returned to at the end of the chapter, but first, some alternative processes of emotional containment that can be seen in children will be considered.

PROCESSES OF PROJECTION AND IDENTIFICATION

The work of Bion, on the mother's function of containing the child's emotional experience so that they are not overwhelmed, has been described in the Introductions to Part one and two. This model shows the projection and containment of anxiety, and the taking in of this model by the infant who is consequently able to form an internal mental space. Bick developed work in trying to think about children where maternal containment was inadequate, forcing the baby to rely on himself too early (Bick 1968, 1986). Infants may sometimes focus on objects in the environment, to hold them together, or on their own sensations of muscular tension. These infants rely too much on actively focusing on or clinging to physical parts of their environment, rather than relating to fellow humans. This method of acquiring a sense of identity, she called 'adhesive identification'. Meltzer also discusses adhesive identification/adhesive equation, where there is 'no difference' felt between self and other (Meltzer 1975). Bick felt that they develop a social appearance of a personality but without any sense of inner mental space or internal resource. Another form of response is to rely on muscular tension or the experience of motion. This way of dealing with the emotional impact of experience she called second-skin formation. Again, this lacks a sense of inner mental space and does not allow permeability of emotional experience (Bick 1968).

All children may have to rely on these forms of containment sometimes, but need to experience the containment of another for social and psychological development. Ways of relating to, and managing interactions with the world, through muscular tension, is vividly shown by both Colin in the driven play with the bag of clay and by Lucy's gymnastics in Part one; particularly when they have to be in constant motion to manage anxiety, because they have no way of containing or assimilating emotional experience. In writing about children with this state of mind I have called this 'the roundabout', which is the creation of discontinuities of experience within the refractive transference (Case 2000a). This describes the rushing from activity to activity to keep ahead of painful feelings. It is sometimes possible through painting to create a still moment and to be in touch with feeling or to end where the session began and to be momentarily in touch with whatever had started the activity. When children take on an animal persona it has elements of both of these defences in that the child seems to either project themselves or flatten themselves into an animal form; which also means the taking on of animal-type movement. It has elements of imitation, a taking in on a sensory/perceptive level (Gaddini 1969). The lack of separation between self and other and pull to fusion, losing oneself in another, suggests an adhesive iden-tification/adhesive equation as well as a second-skin type of muscular defence, literally, a jump into an animal skin. In the next section, the location of self in animals in literature will be considered to help distinguish empathy from a more intrusive identification.

THE LOCATION OF SELF IN ANIMALS IN LITERATURE

The taking on of animal identity has some very appealing aspects and is often present in children's books. In two of the most popular series as I write, there are 'animagi', wizards who can change into a particular animal in the Harry Potter books (Rowling 1999), and humans with animal souls in the *Northern Lights* trilogy (Pullman 1995–2000). In this section it will be helpful to look at two contrasting uses of this device and what it means within the books in order to gain a different perspective on clinical material. The first is *The Once and Future King*, in which there is the clean-cut changing of the Wart (the future King Arthur) into different animals, by the wizard Merlyn, in order that he might learn through experience (White 1939). This is a combination of feeling and knowing and is at the base of empathy. The second is *The Farseer Trilogy*, where the magical Wit allows those with the gift to get inside an animal's mind and bond with it (Robb 1995–1997). In this way one can live the animal's life and not live the love and pain of one's own life. There is also another gift in the book which is to have 'the Skill', which is to be able to get inside the mind of another human and affect or control their actions: both forms of intrusive identification are described in the Introduction. In these fantasy novels one can avoid the lack or pain of one's own life by different kinds of bonding with another. Its appeal is that all kind of ordinary separ-ations, being on one's own, can be circumscribed, through the magical Wit and Skill.

The Once and Future King

This narrative is an example of a helpful animal fairy story where the young-est son who does not know that he is to be the king discovers himself. The first of the four books is the one most interesting in our thinking about animals in children's stories. White thinks that it is very important that we and Arthur understand our place in nature. Although this was first published in 1939 the kind of issues that are present are modern, addressing the eternal problem around our animal nature and our humanity. Episodes are scattered in the text of the Wart (the boy Arthur) being changed into different animals, for his education; to become another species in order to learn about being human. As he is changed he learns through experience to become self-reliant in his capacities. These episodes are interesting because they are not then discussed between the Wart and Merlyn in the text but they are the experiences that they are. It is only at the end of the fourth book that King Arthur reflects on them and thinks of the lessons he learnt the night before he will die. As a Perch, the Wart experiences the joy of being in the element of water. He meets the king of the moat, the tyrant Pike and has the opportunity to observe in fear the absolute monarch and to see what limitless power can do to one:

> the great body, shadowy and almost invisible among the stems, ended in a face which had been ravaged by all the passions of an absolute monarch – by cruelty, sorrow, age, pride, selfishness, loneliness and thoughts too strong for individual brains . . . He was remorseless, disillusioned, logical, predatory, fierce, pitiless – but his great jewel of an eye was that of a stricken deer, large, fearful, sensitive and full of griefs.
>
> (White 1939: 47)

The code he lives by is that only Might is Right. Later in the series of books it is this that King Arthur attempts to prevent by drawing up the code of the Round Table. White captures the fear and grief and despair at the heart of the tyrant – that which is defended against, in his description of the Pike. In escaping from the jaws of the Pike, the Wart learns to put his back into things. Next, he is changed into a Merlin and has to brave the other predatory birds in the mews. He learns to stand firm in the face of his fear. All the animals that the Wart has become, during his education, come to aid him at the moment when he tries to draw the sword from the stone reminding him of himself and the qualities he needs for the task. It is a beautiful example of how we grow and develop through our identification and introjection of qualities from experiences with others. It is a clean and clear-cut story in that the Wart experiences each animal's point of view in life, through empathy and experiencing life as they live it. One of the contrasts with *The Farseer Trilogy* is that the Wart is the one who changes in order to become the animal; that is, he does not enter into the mind or body of an animal, in an intrusive way to experience how it is.

The Wart also becomes an ant and a goose and it is in contemplation of these two very different animals that he learns something about boundaries and war. The ants are used to demonstrate a kind of totalitarian state and have the rather wonderful notice 'Everything not Forbidden is Compulsory'. In contrast the wild geese have no boundaries because they fly, and boundaries are seen as only imaginary lines on the earth. The only private place is the nest. At the end of his life Arthur thinks again about his goose companion,

Lyo-lyok. He sees that different kinds of civilisations could live together if they claimed no boundaries. He understands that war is fought about nothing because the lines of the boundaries are invisible, 'frontiers are imaginary lines'.

The last animal that the Wart meets is the Badger and it is in this meeting that the animal reads the Wart his treatise on why man has become the master of the animals. In this device White is able to expound his philosophy which is based on western perceptions of animals from the Judaeo-Christian religion where animals and plants are understood to be put on earth to serve the interests of humanity (see p. 20). The badger really tells the Wart a creation myth in which God makes all the eggs first of every living thing. The embryos are all called before God and can choose a specialisation, changing parts of themselves into useful tools for their later life. On the very last day only the last embryo of Man was left. The man embryo chooses to stay in the image which God has given it, choosing to stay defenceless but will try to fashion all that he needs. God says that the man embryo has solved his riddle and gives him 'the Order of Dominion over the Fowls of the Air, and the Beasts of the Earth, and the Fishes of the Sea'. Man therefore, becomes a naked tool, but a user of tools. 'You will look like an embryo till they bury you, but all the others will be embryos before your might' (White 1939: 196). The Badger and the Wart then discuss the order of man over the other species, the badger suggesting that man is not very blessed as every creature will move out of his way in a way that they do not do for each other. The Badger expounds the terrible nature of man who is almost the only one that wages war (exceptions are a few ants and one termite). By war, he means attacking ones own species, rather than the killing for food of a predator. The chapter has a thoughtful ending as the Wart talks excitedly of the glories of war. The Badger poses the following question: ' "Which did you like best", he asked, "the ants or the wild geese?" ' (White 1939: 197)

The Farseer Trilogy

The Farseer Trilogy is told by the hero Fitz looking back on his life as he is chronicling the history of the Six Duchies; the imaginary country in which the author has set the series. Fitz is a royal bastard, who is adopted into the royal household after being brought and left there by his mother's family at the age of six. He has a unique position, really belonging nowhere and yet becoming a catalyst for events in the royal family and in the country by his existence. From this position of loneliness and not belonging, the story intro-duces two kinds of location of self that are strongly contrasted in this imaginary society. Fitz has the Wit, which is a gift or magical link with animals, allowing access to the web that binds all living creatures together, a sense of kinship with the world. In his early life he survives, gains solace and companionship through being able to enter the minds of animals and to sense what they sense, thereby gaining an at-oneness with them and they with him. The animal bondings that Fitz is able to have through the Wit become the siblings he has never had. Loneliness, the loss of his mother, and the sense that he is an outcast, through being a bastard, is the motivation in his seeking of the animal link.

The second kind of location of self in the book is the use of the Skill. The Skill is a telepathic quality in relation to humans, not animals. It is highly regarded, whereas the Wit is seen to become 'as a beast'; in that it starts out as a blessing, understanding the tongues of animals, but becomes a curse in the eyes of those who are against it; as it brings a bonding with animals and a lessening of the human qualities in the person. In terms of our investigation here, it is interesting, that as the lonely child Fitz bonds with a puppy and they become inseparable companions, so he begins to lose the power of human speech, as he does not use it. He thinks as one with the animal. The Skill, that is, having a quality of telepathy, is the bridging of thought from person to person. People who have the Skill can also influence the untrained minds of other humans, giving them an emotional experience, i.e. causing an enemy to feel fear, doubt or confusion. It can also be used to convey positive feeling. In psychodynamic terms, the Wit is related to adhesive identification and the Skill to projective identification, but they both have an intrusive quality, in that they can have an effect on or control their host.

As the trilogy develops, both forms of 'magical communication' are seen to have addictive qualities. They bridge that essential aloneness that humans inhabit. Once one begins to use Skill regularly one experiences an openness of others' contact that is like no other and it is hard to refrain from doing it. Ordinary communication seems so much lesser by comparison. In using the Wit the person feels the longing to become as one with the animal and to experience the world through enhanced senses, but also to never be alone, but to be bonded with the animal in a mutuality of being. Both offer a total understanding that in ordinary life is recreated within a deeply loving relationship, or might normally be experienced as a small infant with mother. Attachment to anyone will mean that there will be future pain. It is impossible not to love or to be attached and not to also have to endure separation and loss, and eventual mourning. One of the palliatives for experiencing loss is to be bonded through the Wit. Then there is the loss of past, and future and one lives life only in the present, the now. Fitz escapes his torturers at one point in the story by leaving his own body and joining the body of the wolf with which he is bonded. He leaves behind pain by being in the wolf's body and mind but also by living only in the moment, with no painful memories or desires. Near the end of the trilogy Fitz is told that he could know the memories of his mother from whom he was taken away but chooses not to, as it is too painful.

The two series of books contrast some of the reasons why one might want to take on animal identity. In the first, there is the wish to learn about the world through the mirror that nature holds for us, and through which we might learn more about ourselves. In the second, there is the wish to escape from the love and pain of human existence, and to create other magical bonds that transcend loneliness, pain, despair and separation. In chapters two and three, the children were either able to engage with a medium and animal imagery or with nature outside the therapy room window. In both of these incidences they had an empathic identification that allowed a moment of psychic realisation or growth. In the following sections of this chapter, there will be a return to clinical material, considering first, projective processes in the use of puppets and second, the child taking on animal form in the therapy room as well as being an animal in her picture.

LOCATION OF PARTS OF THE SELF IN PUPPETS: WHITE RABBIT AND BLACK DOG

The first example selected shows a child using animal puppets and the way in which the different puppets can represent parts of the self (Case 2000a). Wendy, age four, was referred for therapy while she was at nursery. She had many difficulties including being unable to separate from mother or to make any social contact with her peers. She had had traumatic events around her birth and there had been some expectation that she might be a damaged or handicapped baby. She was a selective mute. This made assessment of her educational capacity difficult but it was seen that she was having great difficulty understanding her letters on move to infant school. She had enormous fears. It was difficult for her to distinguish the fears in her head from events outside which made the world a very frightening place. She was terrified of toilets and both fascinated and horrified by the flushing mechanism that takes things away and 'disappears them'. It was as if a part of herself or contents of her mind might go with the contents in the toilet bowl. In her mind her products were still part of her so that she *was* being flushed away. The problem of fear of leaking or flushing away will be returned to in Chapter six on psychotic thinking processes.

Puppets in the form of animals are useful for allowing expression of difficult feelings that might be hard for the child to communicate directly. Two, at least, enable children to either play one on each hand or we can take a puppet each. For a short time almost every week Wendy had been playing with White Rabbit and Black Dog. In this creative play, she usually took White Rabbit who 'knows things' and was scornful of the other puppet, Black Dog. I was to put on Black Dog who did not know his numbers and letters and could not read or write. At school she had been struggling to understand that letters put together in one way spell a word with meaning and put another way are nonsense – how do you do this, what sort of trick is it? Black Dog usually represented the puzzled, frustrated and degraded self who she felt knew nothing and White Rabbit the superior know-all who was mocking. There was some aspect of this part of her in the child who withheld speech with a slow superior smile that provoked frustration in those trying to help her. We can see that these two parts of her are linked together, the superior one a defence against feelings of inferiority. She was vocal when talking to me in play, as if I was part of her, but at other times she could be silent.

Session

In my room Wendy went straight to the box and found the puppets, saying that she wanted Black Dog and White Rabbit. She handed Black Dog to me saying 'Put it on'. She sat quite composed on top of the table, facing me. We had a puppet each. She began a hiding game immediately, making the rabbit go behind the curtain, peering out of the window that was behind it. Then sidling up the curtain and flying up the wall. All this was to puzzle Black Dog and to giggle with excitement at him. There was an exchange of 'hello's' closer together and then Black Dog was left. Then she was up to say hello and to kiss him with her puppet, with excited giggles, as White Rabbit went behind the curtain and Black Dog was left again. The play had some quality of 'peek-a-boo', about early object constancy. Now you see me, now you do not, but it is still me hiding. You can go away and you can come back and I am still here, it is the same you who returns. This was playing over the separation there had been between us since the last session. She was communicating the puzzle of where I went and how I appeared.

There was only a short time of playfulness though before the quality of interaction felt more intense. It seemed that Black Dog was not to understand. Things happened but they were not explained. There was more laughter and giggling and I wondered whether she sometimes felt like this, not knowing what was going on, left to work things out. She got tougher, squeezing Black Dog's nose and hitting him. She wanted Black Dog/me to have these feelings; they were his problem and were nothing to do with her. She was frightened here and moved away to the sand but wanted me to follow with Black Dog. Here she continued to get excited and tipped sand in the puppet's face. Excitedly, 'He's got it in his eye!' I talked about how Black Dog feels everything happens to him and how nothing seems to go right. She was frightened and moved again.

She took some toy cars out of the box of toys in the room. There was no sympathy for Black Dog and no comfort. She really wanted to get rid of this feeling and moved to a new activity if anything of what I said threatened to touch or reach her. She said to me to, 'Get Black Dog' as I had moved with her to the little cars and left him at the sand tray. I sat with the puppet on my hand, watching the play. Every now and then she paused to giggle at Black Dog. The cars are trying to park in a car park but there is to be no room for one of them. This is repeated in different ways so that always one car is edged out, although there could be room. All the time she watched to make sure that Black Dog was looking on. I talked about the little car that cannot find a space of its own and gets pushed out, thinking about there not being enough space for her to find a place of her own in the family with brothers and sisters. It was noticeable that she did not allow Black Dog out of the unenviable place that she had put him in. He had to stay there and be increasingly abused and ridiculed. The play went on and then anxieties became too great and she had to rush to the toilet, both to use it and to evacuate mental anxieties. This brought its own worries as in wanting to flush her fears away in phantasy, there was also a fear that she would lose other parts, which, might be flushed away. We had to carefully negotiate how the toilet door would be left open so that she could see me and could visually hold on to me, but could also have some necessary privacy.

Discussion

The whole family had difficulties around separation so that there was an unconscious phantasy that if one parent and child did one thing and the other parent and another child did something else that everything would fall apart. There was a difficulty for everybody in the area of boundaries and separation. This had been evident at the beginning of therapy when mother's anxieties about Wendy leaving her to go to the therapy room had almost prevented therapy starting. An unconscious phantasy, that individual members will not survive alone for a while, even though they are robust and older children, inhibits all activities. Wendy had more extreme difficulties with her unfavourable start in life not helping the other phantasies present. She had great difficulty separating what was inside and what was outside. If there was a noise in the building while we were working together was it from the corridor, the garden, from me, or inside her head? With this difficulty it was also possible for her to feel that the inside contents of her mind could drain away. Her sense of self, and boundary between self and the rest of the world, were very weak. Her play with the puppets illustrates two parts of herself that were split but closely tied in relationship, White Rabbit and Black Dog. The mechanisms of projection of unwanted parts of the self are clearly visible. When parts of the self are projected on to the puppets it is useful if the therapist can give voice to the unwanted parts; in this case a part of her that feels puzzled and stupid and cannot understand. There is the possibility of these parts eventually being reintrojected and made bearable for her to accept as part of herself. The superior self will then be less necessary as a defence and she will be in a better position to learn.

The projection of unwanted contents on to Black Dog and superior know-all on to White Rabbit shows the mechanisms at work in both our relationship to the animal world and also some of the mechanisms of racism

(Case 1999). Children are less guarded and defensive in relation to feelings using puppets: it arouses less anxiety. Wendy and her response to Black Dog demonstrates how an animal can represent a particular characteristic or part of oneself, and then one is afraid of it and wants to distance oneself from it. When I attempted to talk about Black Dog's possible feelings and link them to possible feelings of her own, she physically moved away from me in the room to literally create a space, becoming anxious. She then wanted me to follow with Black Dog as she needed the victim of her projection to get rid of fresh anxieties, so that there is always a strong (unconscious) link to the person or object on to whom, one is projecting. In her family there was a big struggle for her to find a place of her own. This was played out very vividly in the car park play. The anxieties over her birth had brought many extra separation difficulties through a wish to protect her, so that it was very difficult for her to know who she was, or where she stood in relation to other family members. A previous paper described her split transference to therapist, art object made and objects in the room, which I have called a refractive transference (Case 2000a).

LOCATION OF SELF IN ANIMALS: KITTEN AND MOUSE

In this section, a child taking on animal form in the therapy room as a defensive protection will be introduced. Anna, age six, had been referred for therapy whilst in foster care. She had experienced severe sexual abuse in the past. She was described as a child who attractively engaged adults in a playful and physical way. In this description there was a hope that she might be adopted in the future. Working with young sexually abused children is such a painful area for professionals that seeing ill health in children can be blurred. It is an internal struggle for those working with them to be open to how damaged they are. Physical play can be not playful, but a way of surviving through a more primitive sensory contact as will be shown in the following sessions.

Sessions

At the first meeting with Anna, she stood by the radiator, just inside the room, her body curled in an anxious twist; her fingers in her mouth. I was sitting on a chair near her and talked of this new situation and of her coming to see me and how anxious she felt. I noticed that her eyes were straying to a blanket on the back of the chair that I was sitting on and I remarked on this and moved across to a different chair. She moved across immediately to the chair on which I had been sitting and curled up on it as if in a lap, resting her face against the blanket. She was looking about and laughing and there was a sense that this situation was to be exciting rather than frightening, which

I felt it actually to be. I asked her about her school as she had a school sweatshirt on and it seemed a safe way to begin to meet her. This led to her telling me about her foster home through talk of a kitten that had not always lived there. They all liked the little kitten that had hidden under a chair when it had first come. Talk went on to other aspects of the foster home and then she slipped off the chair and began to explore the room on all fours. She had become the kitten. She moved from safe place to safe place under tables and chairs, peeking out to check before she moved on, inspecting the room by sniffing, touching, licking, and looking.

The following session she came up the stairs on all fours and curled up on the chair again but added to this was the making of squeaky noises with her shoes that suggested the presence of a little mouse too. She again explored and checked the room in a sensory way, travelling into all its corners and experimented with hiding where she thought I could not see her, all of this accompanied by excited giggling. She was finally able to settle at the table with coloured pens and pencils and to draw and I will now describe her picture before thinking about the animal sensory behaviour. From her hiding place on the floor I had noticed that she was peeking looks at the drawing paper and said this, which enabled her to take some, and walk on her knees to the table. As I moved too, to join her there, she brought felts and coloured pencils; still going back and forth like a little animal. She then sat on a chair and drew a green outline of a human head. She spent some time on one eye. Little areas of colour, orange, blue, pink, gradually emerged. Then a mouse appeared in the head. I wondered where the mouse was but she waved her paper about in a vague way and said, 'I don't remember'. I said how difficult it felt to remember sometimes and she nodded. She said that the mouse cannot move because of the *knife*. I said that that sounded frightening. She then drew the knife saying that it belonged to the eye and would fall on the mouse if she moved (Illustration 5.1).

I asked about the pink lines and she said that this is where the mouse got in and fell down but she is not meant to be in this room but she cannot get out, because of the knife. The knife has blood on the end – the mouse's blood. The rest is coloured pink and yellow, that's not blood. She then added more colours saying that the mouse is safe now but she cannot move. The whole head shape was then cut out and glued on to another piece of paper which had some numbers previously drawn upon it. She said, 'It's all sticky so the mouse cannot move; I don't want it on my face'. I talked of how frightened and trapped the mouse felt.

Discussion

Anna takes a kitten form in order to find a way of being with the therapist, in this new situation, as well as to find a place to be in the room. She first of all climbed on to the chair with her head against the blanket, as if against a

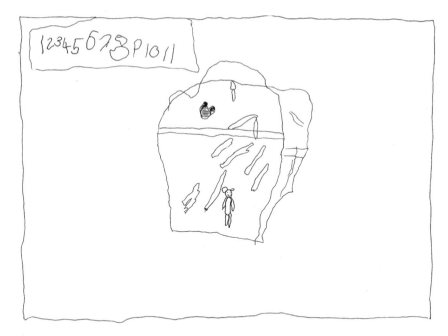

Illustration 5.1 Anna: Mouse in the head.

mummy cat. She was able to explore the room as a kitten and played this exciting and frightening game of being inside/under furniture and peeking out. This is an example of the phantasy of the claustrum offering a shelter, here the breast. Later, while making the picture a different phantasy is presented. Anna's picture, where she described a mouse having fallen in (inside a head) and not able to get out, a knife hanging over it gave a compelling image of her internal state of mind in relation to the abuser. I am aware of being a terrifying object myself in the room and keep quite still in relation to her. Her description of the kitten as 'not always having been there' is an evocative image of being in foster care and presumably covers a whole range of feeling responses to her situation, particularly around loss and change, that cannot be thought or articulated. As a kitten, she undertakes a sensory inspection of the room mainly by smell, touch, licking and looking. In inhabiting an animal form, she has unconsciously side-stepped speech and human communication, and if one did not know this already it would be a sign of damaged object relations. It should be stressed that ordinary play of children as animals is not being described. It is defensive/protective behaviour on a more primitive level of using only the senses. There is a kind of hide-and-seek going on. Can I see her or is she hidden and she is playing this dangerous exciting game of showing herself and hiding.

When she felt safe in the room with me she was able to establish herself at the table and I felt that I could join her there without frightening her. The drawing was interesting on different levels. It communicated something of what it feels like, for her, to be here. The persecuting eye that holds a knife over the mouse who is terrified to move is an image of her first experience of us here. The terror of what this stranger therapist may turn out to be is vividly present. In the drawing she is the mouse inside, but does not know how she got there or where she is. Looking at the drawing on an internal world level it is probable that she does project herself inside her object for safety but then finds herself trapped with no way out. On an internal world level she is projected inside the abuser and has no free volition, she cannot move. In the external world, it is known that she had been abused by adults from a very young age who should have been caring for her with loving parental/adult responsibility. It is known that there was a knife held to her in reality, that is now internalised and paralyses her external relationships.

The knife is like a sword of Damocles held over her. It is not safe to be in the outside world so she has found a place to hide in phantasy, inside an internal object only to discover that she is threatened in phantasy, if she could find a way out. She is persecuted by the eye of the therapy situation and by an internal abuser. There is a paranoid feel to the associations to the image. Internally, she is trapped in the claustrum, a world of projections where she is not able to move, feed, or take in (Meltzer 1992). The animal quality suggests that she is living by her senses. There is a sense that she lives alongside other people, like the kitten, rather than in relationship to them.

When children are traumatised like Anna, there is only room for physical needs to be satisfied at first. Shelter, warmth, food and being alongside other beings all come before relationship with awareness of others, and cultural living. Life is reduced to a sensory quality with antennae out for danger or safety. Such sensory, physical exploration in damaged children can be mistaken for playfulness, especially where one is hoping against hope that they have not been so damaged. Taking the soft kitten animal form is a way of making herself pleasing, which she has learnt to do, in fear of being hurt, but it also shows that life has been reduced to sensory living without language or human culture. She is a stray in our culture as the kitten that was taken into the foster home. In the mouse drawing she is able to unconsciously communicate her inner world of projections and living fear of the abusers. This inner world where she does not know where she is and how she got there and is afraid to move is more real to her than the outside world with adults who are trying to help her in the present. Inhabiting a kitten form in her attempts to explore the external world seems the safest option to her.

Another aspect of this picture was the process of cutting out and sticking down (Case 2005). When she cut the head out and stuck it to a new piece of paper she surrounded it with glue. The picture is so powerful that the significance of the cutting out eluded me initially, because it was shocking to be with her. How can we begin to think about this? One of the feelings it evoked, is of her on an island, which is both a retreat and a prison. She is separated from normal life by her appalling experience. She is cut off from a predictable future that is part of living in security. The experience of sexual abuse and aggression, at knife-point, has left such a scar on her inner world that she is lost somewhere inside in terror. The cutting out and placing of the picture on another sheet surrounded by glue, highlights the isolation, and sense of imprisonment on a sensual world that she was initiated into and is now trapped upon. She is separated out and cut off from the ordinary world of childhood, represented by the numbers on the original page. When she tries to be in the ordinary world something from her past emerges unexpectedly. It is important to stay in touch with her saying that she feels safe. She is now safe, but at the price of being cut off from her natural family of co-victims and abusers.

PETS AND ANIMAL PERSONA

At this stage it is helpful to return to thinking about pets and the use of 'taking on animal personas', which will be explored further in the case study in Part three. One aspect of children becoming pets in the therapy room is that they may be trying to elicit tender loving care from the therapist who they think may find them more attractive in a pet form – you really could not reject, or treat badly, this little kitten or puppy. There were aspects of this in Anna's kitten play, just as there were aspects of 'being treated like a dog' in Wendy's play to the therapist. Pets are the 'other' in the family, they are part of the family but not part of the human family and this gives them a special status. When children become an animal, nearly always a pet, in therapy, they both must gain something and lose something, in order for this transfer to have a meaning. They may escape their human suffering, become appealing to the therapist; they may project dependence and a need to be looked after; they may be diverting the therapist from an aspect of human suffering; they may lose words but gain a nonverbal communication, beseeching looks; they may be able to ask to be put on the therapist's lap which they would not be able to do as a child; they may live in the senses, and thereby feel safer if they are very alert to danger.

Attitudes to pets can arouse just as passionate feelings as other animal issues. People who are disparaging about pet ownership see it as a substitute for normal relationships – a gratuitous perversion of natural behaviour (Midgley 1984). However research into pet owners finds them as being more affectionate and wanting relationships with people *and* animals (Brown *et al.* 1972; Kidd and Feldmann 1981). It has also been suggested that pets allow scope for 'playful domination', a practice which stems from man's inherent insecurity: his need to display his ability to control and subdue the unruly forces of nature (Tuan 1984). This can make pets the repository of any unwanted feeling in the family. Relationship with pets by its often uninhibited physical contact and intimacy has also been construed as essentially sexual in nature (Menninger 1951). Historically, huge quantities of pets, and particularly exotic pets, have been seen as an outward expression of the owner's status and prestige. Serpell gives a fascinating account of Thomas à Becket's entourage of horses and apes, which challenged my previous history book image (Thomas 1983, in Serpell 1986). Similarly, in the present day, Michael Jackson's collection of exotic animals at the Never Land ranch may fulfil status and prestige as well as companionship.

Serpell notes that we have a biological predisposition to respond to infants and young children and that pet features release an innate desire to protect and nurture. This is the so-called 'cute response' (Jolly 1972). People talk to their pets in 'motherese', as if they were young, preverbal children (Hirsh-Pasek and Treiman 1982). When children continually present themselves as a pet it is an indicator of previous communication as a human child having failed to get through to an adult and a sign that either the child has given up trying to communicate normally or thinks from life's experiences that there is more hope in animal form. It may also be a sign that children have turned to pets for comfort and acceptance at a time in their life when human contact has failed. Those putting forward the positive aspects of pet-keeping have stressed that it can enhance emotional development, be a source of companionship, comfort, security in periods of alienation, rejection or crisis (Levinson 1978, 1980). This has been demonstrated in pet psychotherapy, which is particularly useful with children who have difficulty relating or communicating (Levinson 1969; Zahn-Waxler et al. 1984). Davis and Valla (1978) report the finding of a paleolithic burial site 12,500 years old containing the skeleton of a human, resting a hand on the head of a skeleton dog, in an affectionate gesture of attachment. Recently, archaeologists were amazed to find a cat buried next to a human at a neolithic burial site on Cyprus, dated 9,500 years ago (*Guardian*, 9 April 2004). Pets have been a solace to man, since they were first domesticated. Although pets may be valued as emblems of status, for their decorative potential or appeal to collectors, they are most highly regarded as being 'best companions' (Messent and Serpell 1981). It is natural for dogs to be highly attached to individuals and the group. They fit into family life by their eagerness to please, willingness to cooperate and their deference to dominant individuals (Kleimann 1967).

When children have located themselves in a dog form in therapy it has usually had to do with characteristics of expressing attachment needs. The other side of dog behaviour is to act as a wolf and in the case study, in Part three, it can be seen how Sally changes to a wolf to express aggression. This demonstrates our myths and stereotyping of wolves more than it does actual wolf behaviour. Anna chose to be a kitten as a way of exploring the room and finding a way to be in relationship with the therapist. This reflected the way that cats are attached to territory, as well as humans: she needed to make herself at home in the environment, before she could use the materials.

Entangled and confusional children: analytical approaches to psychotic thinking and autistic features in childhood

'Is there any body there?' said the
Traveller,
Knocking on the moonlit door.
(Walter de la Mare 1912)

INTRODUCTION

It can be very disturbing and upsetting to meet a child who has psychotic states of mind or autistic features. That these children may be traumatised, have developmental delay, impairment or neurological damage further complicates the clinical picture and can be confusing for the people working with them as well as those caring for them. For the purposes of this chapter my interest lies with children who are entangled with or in a confusional state with their mother (Tustin 1992). They may show psychotic states of mind at times and/or have autistic features as part of their defensive structure. It is an in-between area and these children and their families pose many technical difficulties. One area is that the parents come, consciously wanting help for their child, but the powerful unconscious processes underlying this wish work against a successful outcome. There may be severe problems around separation for a parent (usually mother) and child, which impact on treatment as we saw with Wendy in the last chapter. Sometimes parents will feel 'driven mad' because they cannot have any time apart from their child but also cannot bear any normal separation, which feels like a death and loss. We saw in Chapter four how underlying loss and experiences of death affect the normal process of separation at bedtime. After birth, we have seen that infants are in an interpersonal relationship with mother and father, but with entangled children, they are confused with mother and lack a separate identity.

In this chapter we will explore the way that thinking has developed about these states of mind and also consider some of the main theoretical contributors. It has not been possible to be comprehensive, due to space, but it has been my intention to look at the contributions of the pioneers in the development of understanding, towards a theoretical base. When I am thinking about these different conditions I find it useful to take a mixed approach. There is primarily the child's experience as they try to communicate it to you and one's own emotional response or countertransference. There is also one's own sense inside of that part of oneself that one might recognise through work with the patient but also through one's own explorations in therapy or analysis. There are increasingly, autobiographical accounts of articulate sufferers of different conditions that enable one to read and reflect on firsthand accounts. Not only are these often informative and moving to read but they also break down barriers about them and us. We may not have the condition that another has but it is helpful to see it on a continuum of human experience. These approaches, together with accounts of clinical experience and theory, offer various ways in to this difficult and complex area. This chapter will pursue a mainly psychoanalytical account of these processes whereas, in the case study to follow in Part three, art therapy literature will be considered together with technical problems for the therapist.

BACKGROUND HISTORY OF THE TERMS PSYCHOTIC, AUTISTIC AND ENTANGLED

Early pioneers

Spensley (1995), in her account of Tustin's life and work, gives a highly readable account of the history. She explains how during the twentieth century a global concept of insanity from which there was no recovery became replaced by a questioning about the aetiology of childhood disorders. There was growing awareness of the immaturity of the child in neurological and psychological development and of the possible contribution of psychological as well as organic factors. Environmental factors such as deprivation and early life experience began to be considered. Looking at the development of thinking about child work it seems that adult work is developed first and then, later, this enables children to be thought about. This is true of adult analysis followed by child psychotherapy and also of art therapy where the pioneering work was with adult populations in mental hospitals. It partly reflects the growth of children being seen as different to adults and of gaining legal rights.

In 1933, Potter defined criteria for diagnosing childhood schizophrenia and its differences from adult presentation. Spensley suggests that although Potter was specifying differences from the adult presentation, the term schizophrenia became an umbrella term for childhood mental illness which, hindered advances in thinking about different manifestations of symptoms. In 1944 Kanner described some defining characteristics in a paper called 'Early infantile autism'. These were formed after studying eleven autistic children who had a combination of: extreme aloneness from the beginning of life, an inability to use language meaningfully, and an anxiously obsessive insistence on the preservation of sameness. The word autism comes from the Greek, *autos* meaning self. It was given because of the defining characteristic of withdrawal, absorption in own internal experience. Following this paper several things seemed to happen. There was a division and separation out of children with these characteristics although some could be seen in combination with other symptoms. There is a continuing bitter controversy about the causation of autism, which is an unfortunate legacy from this era.

There was a split between cognitivists favouring a genetical or organic causation and therefore greater pessimism about the efficacy of treatment, and some dynamicists in the USA understanding autism as a defensive avoidance of 'refrigerator' mothers. This led to guilt for the mothers and a treatment that focused on the children's defences and fears and neglected their genuine disorder and real developmental delays. During this period mothers and parents were blamed for not being warmly emotional in response to these children, as if all they needed was more love. Bettelheim was working with autistic children in the USA at his Orthogenic School. Treatment was based on Bettelheim's understanding of autism as a catastrophic withdrawal from life at a critical point, before the child discovered his essential humanity. Bettelheim (1967) used the term 'empty fortress' to describe 'the ultimate protection from a hell which is inescapable'. One of his thoughts about autistic children was that their mothers unconsciously wished them to be dead. Tischler (1971, 1979) put forward a different point of view, thinking about the consequences for the parents of living with the referred child, and noted how some workers overidentified with the suffering child which could cloud their judgement on the total situation.

There is a medical position that would still today see a totally organic base and which has focused on intellectual impairment and organic brain damage, trying to understand the cognitive deficits of such children, but other workers with children on the autistic spectrum are more likely to see a complicated and mixed aetiology, where many factors will interweave and affect each other. This controversial debate between the organicists and the psychogenecists was probably fuelled by the intense polarisation that develops in such situations, but also because as Tustin points out: the same symptoms can be the result of both an organic deficit but also from psychological factors.

Meltzer

In Britain, Bion wrote a highly influential group of papers between 1950 and 1962, exploring psychotic thought processes with his adult analysands (Bion 1967). His ideas on splitting processes, projective identification, attacks on linking and the development of a theory of thinking have all been essential to later theory. Meltzer and the Tavistock Autism Workshop explored some of the states of mind of autism and hypothesised about their reason for having come into operation (Meltzer *et al.* 1975). Their contribution has been help-ful in three particular areas: first, in the use of the term 'dismantling'; second, in exploration of the impairment of 'spatial and temporal concepts'; and third, in thinking about the employment of 'mindlessness'.

The sense in which there is suspended mental functioning which also suspends the transference relationship, led Meltzer to see that the main qual-ity of the autistic state was its impingement on personality development. Meltzer noted the high intelligence of the autistic children, and an emotional sensibility, a gentleness of disposition. They have an unusual awareness of the mental states of those with whom they are intimately concerned, not the same as identification, but he saw it to be in the nature of a primitive permeability to the emotions of others. This, with their accessibility to the sensory data of the outside world, makes them 'naked to the wind' (Meltzer 1975: 9). They therefore become especially vulnerable to 'catastrophic modes of depressive experience' (Meltzer 1975: 10). He also noted their 'uncompromising posses-siveness of the maternal object' (Meltzer 1975: 10). They have a primitive form of love that is tender and highly sensual; seeking skin to skin intimacy, and the repetition of the joy and triumph of possession.

Meltzer thought that the structure of autism is essentially mindless. The key to this is in the temporary suspension of the recognition of time passing. This is not the same as denial or fragmentation. He differentiates dismantling from splitting processes in the following way: 'Dismantling occurs by a pas-sive device of allowing the various senses, both special and general, internal and external, to attach themselves to the most stimulating object of the moment' (Meltzer *et al.* 1975: 12). In this way attention is suspended and the senses wander, each to the most attractive object of the moment. 'This scat-tering seems to bring about the dismantling of the self as a mental apparatus, but in a very passive, falling to bits way' (Meltzer *et al.* 1975: 12). Splitting is different, in that destructive impulses are employed, in order to make attacks on linking. He thought that the maternal breast acts as an object of high consensual attractiveness in that it could spring together the dismantled self. He suggested that there is an intensity of relationship to the breast of the mothering person which is disturbed by depression or other disturbance and then the dismantled self floats away for longer and longer.

Tustin

Tustin applied her life's work to the emotional component in autism and in trying to think about its treatment through psychotherapy; while allowing that some autism may be organic in origin and that there may be a consti-tutional vulnerability. She was influenced by Mahler *et al.* (1975) who saw that although a child is born into physical separateness they need a period of symbiotic experience with the mother to allow a preparatory time for the

psychological birth of the individual. She envisaged a period of intense physical and emotional holding and nurturing by mother of baby that allowed
and gave a shape and response to the growth of identity of the baby. The
emotional link between mother and child allows the possibility of human
relationship with other minds. From this perspective, autism is seen as a
response to the trauma of failure of a satisfactory symbiotic state with
mother. Tustin later revised her understanding of what was originally
thought of as a 'normal autistic phase'. The work of Stern (1985) and other
observationalists of early infant–mother relationship showed that an interactional theory of emotional life between mother and child superseded these
earlier ideas. 'The essence of these revised understandings is that autism is an
early developmental deviation which occurs in the service of dealing with
unmitigated terror' (Tustin 1992: 10). Interestingly, the work of neurobiologists more recently suggests that the brain does need another brain in interpersonal interaction in order to develop; that 'secure attachment' is an
example of biological symbiosis. The infant's brain needs the intimate relationship of another caregiving human brain to develop, and these interactions bring pleasure and mutual benefit to both, as well as changes to both
brains (Schore 2001c: 25).

Tustin (1992) gave names to two types of state. She used the term 'encapsulated' to describe the state of autistic withdrawal, and the term 'entangled' to
describe psychotic confusion. She saw that both kinds of children shared
submergence in a sensory-dominated world where emotional states were
not apparently felt but the children lost themselves in the sensory quality
of objects in their environment. Cognitive and emotional development
becomes impaired and the world lacks meaning, therefore becoming a very
frightening place. Tustin saw autism as a sensation-dominated state due to
emotional impoverishment and lack of emotional nurturing. That more than
one kind of situation could cause this state of affairs is clear, i.e. an inability
to access care available which is therefore rejected or a lack of offered care
could both cause sensation-dominated experience or a combination of these
factors.

Encapsulated children show the now classical features of autism with early
withdrawal, being mute or echolalic, may have screaming fits, become fascinated by spinning, ordering and arranging objects. These children can have
high intelligence but with areas of impairment because they cannot comprehend anything needing understanding of human relationship. Encapsulated
evokes the sense of them being hidden inside a hard shell and out of reach.
Entangled children mould to others physically and mentally, showing a lack
of separation, and are compliant. There is altogether a lack of separation,
with indistinct speech and a sense of living in a phantasy world. There is
confusion of identity, and a wish not to change this which, Tustin saw, made
them hard to treat. She thought that the encapsulated child suffers from a too
premature awareness of the separateness and otherness of the object.

The entangled child has a similar terror of human attachment and defence against dependency, but it is thought that there has been some kind of awareness of relationship followed by fear of separation and a clinging on to the object as part of oneself. In this case no differentiation of self and other is allowed to exist but the two are blurred into a fusion of self and other as a defence against the reality of separateness. Tustin saw them as having the illusion of being enfolded inside a body other than their own, and they therefore get confused and entangled with other people. Entangled children are fused and confused with the object and can ricochet between warmth and fury, between apparent closeness while locating themselves inside the object and rage at not having the object under their control (Tustin 1992). They are good at attacking the therapist's ability to think because at all costs they do not want any awareness of separateness to impinge on them. They can appear to be in relationship but there is an underlying phantasy of being the same, which they will fight to hold on to. All reality and common sense is perversely twisted to hang on to this delusion and there is a hatred of the reality of a separate object (Spensley 1995). The swift change from a soft invasiveness to hard furious hatred of the object makes for hard work.

An awareness of a bodily separateness is a necessary precursor to the development of a sense of individual identity. In entangled children, the lack of space between mother and child impedes the development of object relations. Tustin (1992) suggests that there is a delusionary state of fusion with mother's body, which increases omnipotence, and these children then have no practice at dealing with life. A mixture of factors may contribute to the illusionary fusion, such as genetic susceptibility and environmental pressure. McDougall describes cases of fusion between mother and child where a child can be used as an object to fill her mother's emptiness and loneliness, that is, a 'cork child' where neither mother nor child have been able to take possession of their own psychic reality or indeed, their body (McDougall 1980, 1986, 1989). The fathers of entangled children may lack a presence in the family. The weakness of father's influence may then contribute to the illusion of fusion with mother in that the oedipus complex, and awareness of mother and father's relationship, gives structure and discipline to the personality.

Two types of children have been delineated but a later writer suggests that there is 'basically one structure with different pictures which are easily interchangeable' (Morra 2002: 301). Tustin found that as treatment progressed, encapsulated children would begin to use entangled defences, as awareness of body separateness began to impinge upon them. Autism can be seen to be a survival mechanism which has a protective and preservative function. With premature and traumatic awareness of bodily separateness the response is to turn away, not to see, not to hear. This blocks the underlying sense of a black hole of psychotic depression which is the sense of the seeming loss of part of the body as a consequence of separateness.

Tustin thought that the endogenous auto-sensuousness was a reaction to an existential terror of existence. 'These children have no internal regulator for the feelings associated with object relation' (Tustin 1992: 21). The infant normally alternates with a natural rhythm towards sensuousness towards the body of other human beings and auto-sensuousness towards the self. She saw this as an alternation or natural ebb and flow between being equated with the breast and identified with the breast. She thought that too much equation meant the development of autism. 'An unhappy mother and baby will cling together to get comfort and support from each other; when this becomes an adhesive fusion with each other, their own identities become lost or confused (Tustin 1992: 22).

Recent developments

Alvarez and Reid

Alvarez and Reid are a new generation of Tavistock Autism Workshops who have built on Meltzer's earlier work. They look at the way that the child's individual and unique personality may interact with autistic symptomatology. They are interested in the way that the: 'non-autistic part of the personality may use, misuse and exploit the autistic symptoms, or it may oppose them and make efforts to reduce their influence' (Alvarez and Reid 1999: 1). This has been tremendously helpful in supporting clinical work. The work of Stern (1985) and the development of an interpersonal view of the life of infant and mother has been very influential:

> They seem to lack a sense of a world in which there are people with minds who could be both interesting and interested in them. This is now known to be essential for the development of a human mind, where thoughts may occur, experiences be remembered, links made and imaginative life develop (Stern 1985). The majority of us have a capacity to judge mental states and some intuition about the feelings and motivation of others – in an ordinary sense to be 'mind readers'. Normally developing children naturally acquire a set of increasingly sophisticated social and communication skills. They can imagine, pretend, interpret, and recognise the feelings of others and detect intentions that are not communicated by speech alone . . . they become emotionally literate.
> (Alvarez and Reid 1999: 1–2)

They go on to explore how children with autism do not develop such a 'rich inner world'. From observations at the Tavistock, they think that this three-dimensional world is rarely absent, but just not fully available or accessible: 'It is as if the three-dimensional space were fragile and unstable: a small breeze might cause it to collapse in on itself like a pack of cards' (Alvarez and Reid 1999: 2).

The cognitive explanation of the core impairment in autism is that people with autism are born without the capacity to form an adequate theory of mind (Leslie 1987; Frith 1989). Alvarez and Reid support the idea of autism as a disorder of intersubjectivity: as a lack of sense of other persons (Hobson 1993; Trevarthen *et al.* 1996). 'We formulate it as an impairment of the normal sense of emotionally based curiosity about, and desire for, interpersonal relationships' (Alvarez and Reid 1999: 2).

Building on the work of Wing and Attwood (1987) who classified autistic children into 'aloof', 'passive', and 'active but odd', Alvarez and Reid have usefully defined various subgroups which can help in the management of cases across the services as well as thinking about future therapy. Alvarez has extended and developed technique in clinical work with the differing presentations (Alvarez 1992; Alvarez and Reid 1999). Passive children can be usefully divided into (a) *un*drawn passive children, and (b) *with*drawn where they are more actively involved in their passivity. Aloof children can be (a) 'thick-skinned' and aloof who are somewhat complacent in their autism and who may or may not go on to develop personality disorder or (b) 'thin-skinned' aloof patients with extreme hypersensitivity. Reid has proposed a new subgroup of children with autism: 'autistic post-traumatic developmental disorder'; she discusses the differences between children having an actual external trauma and the effects of this on an ordinarily sensitive very young infant; and the apparently traumatising effect of quite ordinary life experiences on particularly hypersensitive infants. In psychotherapy some autistic children may progress after treatment to become active but odd, due to the residual effect of developmental delay on normal functioning. Other changes that they mention are that during treatment, the bullish can become vulnerable but hidden behind thick-skinned facades, whereas the hypersensitive child can show an immovable stubborn determination, masked by a delicate presentation (Alvarez and Reid 1999: 9).

Two current concepts, which aid clinical work, are first, 'reclamation' – the need to reclaim the child back into the world of human feeling and communication (Alvarez 1992). Second, the therapist needs to 'demonstrate' – the therapist needs to demonstrate to the child that the world beyond their private autism is interesting (Reid, in Alvarez and Reid 1999). Alvarez stresses the need to get on the right developmental wavelength where there is a communication deficit. The therapist may need to talk differently, or use motherese, sing, tap rhythms, or have a higher and very alive voice. Play may need to be more actively reaching out to the child, building on the slightest and most subtle clue. There needs to be less emphasis on interpretations and more on the here and now, to aid the regaining of lost, split-off, and projected parts of the self:

> Getting a balance between, on the one hand, attempts to focus and engage the child, to turn preconceptions into concepts by being developmentally

attuned and therefore more active; and on the other hand, leaving him space to have his own experience once he is enough *in himself* to be able to do this, is a perpetually difficult task. It is by no means simply a question of playing with the child.

(Alvarez and Reid 1999: 60)

Observation skills are especially important where communication signals are weak, faint or non-existent. They suggest that observation and the use of the countertransference go together.

Rustin, Rhode, Dubinsky and Dubinsky

The editors of *Psychotic States in Children*, point out that the encapsulated classical autistic child has attracted many workers and theories whereas the non-autistic psychosis, the more schizophrenic type illness has attracted less (Rustin *et al.* 1997). There is no doubt that work with the latter kind of child involves enormous wear and tear of the therapist and that although good advances can be made, one is thinking about partial integration of previously unbearable experiences which is perhaps less rewarding, than some of the changes seen in children with other symptomatology. Space in this chapter only allows me to give a flavour of the achievements of these authors in bringing clarity of thought to such a difficult area.

The children they are writing about are often deeply cut off from reality and 'immersed in their private delusory world' (Rustin *et al.* 1997: 1). They live in states of: terror, confusion, panic and madness, and gain relief by trying to rid themselves of these feelings; often projected into others. There is an absence of symbolic capacities, but, in their place: concrete thinking, states of extreme withdrawal, mania, massive confusion, and disorders of thinking. In developing work in this area they follow the path of Klein, Bion, Segal, Rosenfeld and Joseph with child and adult patients. Dubinsky's theoretical overview is extremely helpful in trying to understand psychotic states of mind. Their understanding of psychotic states is that they:

... occur in response to mental pain beyond the endurance of the ego. This can be due to the nature of the emotional experience or to the immaturity of the personality. When these states become the habitual way of coping with mental pain the development of the personality is profoundly affected and mental illness sets in.

(Dubinsky 1997: 5)

In the Introduction to Part two (pp. 69–78) we have seen how emotional experience is given sense and contained by the mother for the baby, transformed and returned in a manageable form. They see the work of therapy to be the giving of emotional comprehension to emotional experience; that is emotions, sense impressions, thoughts, and unconscious phantasies need to be transformed into a form suitable for symbolic thinking. Otherwise these undigested memories are retained as things-in-themselves, to be got rid of by projection or acting out (Bion 1962a). The relationship of container/ contained needs to be introjected for thought to develop. In psychotic children it may have not taken place, or is being attacked by them or denied. Wendy's terrors (see pp. 101–4) give a vivid idea of how concrete thinking and terror combine. She would hear a sound in the building and cower under a chair or whisper about it in terror. Having got rid, through projection, of something that could not be thought about, it would return as a persecutory object. I found that if I talked in a matter of fact manner about the noise and what I thought it was, and that it was outside her, not inside, her fears would subside, though the communication through sound, rather than the actual words was probably most important at this stage, as it is to a baby being soothed.

One of the defences employed by those suffering from psychosis is omnipotence, to keep feelings of helplessness at bay. Rosenfeld has developed theory in this area, describing destructive narcissism (Rosenfeld 1971: 246). Parts of the self are idealised and there is a turning away from parental figures by the phantasy that essential needs can be satisfied by the individual alone. This can be met with in traumatised children, alongside the fragmentation described below, and was apparent at the start of work with Colin and Lucy described in Chapter three. Splitting of parts of the self so that links between emotion and thought cannot be made and painful experience is held separately; it is a further defence:

> Splitting may cause some specific intellectual function, such as memory, or the capacity to think symbolically and to understand metaphor, to be cut off in order to prevent the making of painful emotional links between certain thoughts (Bion 1959). An even more thorough fragmentation leads to the minute splitting of the self described by Bion; or the disintegration described by Rosenfeld (1947: 26–9) and thus cause the cessation of thinking and feeling.
>
> (Dubinsky 1997: 13)

The massive use of projective identification, which is the projection of mental pain into others: 'causes the explosions of aggression and disparagement which mark the therapy of seriously disturbed children' (Dubinsky 1997: 18). In projective identification the patient's characteristics can be attributed to others, or they can take on characteristics of others to themselves. We have seen in the Introduction to Part 1 how projective identification can be to an internal object (Rosenfeld 1952; Meltzer 1967, 1992).

Bion (1957) suggested the joint existence of psychotic and non-psychotic parts of the personality. The psychotic part destroys any contact with reality through the massive use of defence mechanisms, whereas the non-psychotic part is able to bear some contact. This helpless vulnerable part of the personality can remain hidden at times, only showing later in therapy that there was contact with the emotional experience of therapy. This turning away from reality inevitably leads to a restricted mental life which can result in cognitive and developmental delay. In the final part of this chapter, firsthand experiences of autistic states will supplement the theoretical overview.

FIRSTHAND ACCOUNTS

Two first-hand accounts by adults describing their childhood experience of Aspergers and autism contribute towards thinking about defences and ways of relating to others when considering the taking on of an animal persona. Liane Holliday Willey (1999) wrote an autobiographical account of having Aspergers. She realised that she had Aspergers only when her child was also diagnosed. She is evocative of the child living almost on the outside of human experience, observing what it is that humans do socially and what they are. Lacking the communicative abilities to read and understand communications and interactions she shares with autistic children the need to live in a world dominated by sense impressions but has also to beware becoming overloaded when she will need to retreat. Of her observations she writes:

> I was enthralled with the nuances of people's actions. In fact, I often found it desirable to become the other person. Not that I consciously set out to do that, rather it came as something I simply did. As if I had no choice in the matter.
>
> (Holliday Willey 1999: 22)

She would take on other children's look, gait, or actions; or copy their accents, vocal inflections, facial expressions. Or she would become attracted to a part of someone, shape of their nose, colour of their eye or texture of hair. Lacking a way of assimilating information and understanding human relationships, copying, which is part of the process of learning and identification, becomes isolated as a phenomenon. There is a lack of capacity to internalise relationship so that adhesive identification, where there is no difference between self and other, becomes the way to concretely incorporate the other.

Donna Williams (1992) gives an autobiographical account of what it is like to be autistic from the inside. Autistic people seem to lack the capacity to process the ordinary components of emotionally based interaction between themselves and other people. Rather than enjoying a sense of meeting emotionally, it is experienced as overwhelmingly intrusive, invading and threatening. They then need to keep emotional distance, and to relate along-side, rather than directly, or to be with, rather than interact. The world becomes a very frightening place. These difficulties lead them to avoid eye contact and to be apparently emotionally unresponsive. They are likely to lack friends and often have strange speech. The typical stereotyped, repetitive behaviour of autistic children serves to keep the frightening changing world at bay and great distress is felt if this is interfered with. People made Donna feel vulnerable but objects felt safe. Qualities of objects, colour, smell and textures allowed her to get – feel – safe inside them and, if they belonged originally to someone she liked, it would be having a part of that person with you:

> I collected scraps of coloured paper and crocheted bits and would put my fingers through them so that I could fall asleep securely. For me, the people I liked *were* their things, and those things (or things like them) were my protection from the things I didn't like – other people.
>
> (Williams 1992: 5)

This description recalls the duality-unity of participation mystique. It gives us more understanding of the painful invasion of the world into the autistic child to try to understand their hypersensitivity to stimulus:

> Other than the wisps, my bed was surrounded and totally encased by tiny spots which I called stars, like some kind of mystical glass coffin. I have since learned that they are actually air particles yet my vision was so hypersensitive that they would often become a hypnotic foreground with the rest of 'the world' fading away.
>
> (Williams 1992: 9)

Her book gives insight into her constitutional sensitivity and her inability to process the communicative world of human relationships whereby the sensuous world of objects and their qualities comes as a barrier to too much stimulus. It is also possible to see the secondary difficulties that occur given the particular environment that each autistic child is born into as the child interacts with those around them. Donna is quite clear that she is a person with autism who was born into a violent family rather than family circum-stances causing her autism but she also writes, 'it is hard to tell whether I helped shape their situation or they helped to shape mine' (Williams 1992: 31).

Donna describes two personalities that took stage as a way of enabling her to survive in her environment. She located herself into parts of people she had met and became them on the surface with a core of true self hidden from the world, inside. When she met somebody she admired and was attached to, there was no way to identify and internalise the relationship: 'Yet, as all relationships existed within me rather than between myself and others, there was only one way to bring this attachment inescapably into my own world' (Williams 1992: 108). One of her personalities set about becoming this new person. Like all defences it served a purpose of protecting the self, but, at huge cost and damage, in that it was so successful that it took the exceptional person to see that this was the surface only.

Part III

Case study: the heart and the bone

Introduction: the heart and the bone

> ... the art object is closer to the object of play: it objectifies and makes available to the subject the forms of his inner life.
>
> (Wright 1991: 251)

CASE STUDY: A FORM OF RESEARCH THROUGH NARRATIVE

In Part three, previous themes which have been introduced: the making of anthropomorphic animal images and the taking on of animal personas; the impact of nature outside the therapy room as a catalyst for engagement with the therapist and materials; entanglement and separation; as well as the night world of sleeplessness will be united in the form of a case study. Case study as a way of presenting clinical work has a traditional base both in art therapy and psychotherapy. Narrative engages the reader and is an apt way to demonstrate our work to each other, as we learn from our patients in a similar way. They demonstrate to the therapist through their art making and play, preoccupations, feelings, thoughts and states of mind, that may not yet be in verbal articulate form. Children move between art and play, creation, playing out and narrative in order to show, understand, and share inner life. Clinical case studies may engage one imaginatively in the work through intimacy and reflective self-awareness between patient and therapist.

The case study as a form of research is currently unfashionable in the current climate of evidence-based practice, despite its tradition. Hillman writes that: 'Case-history is a fiction in the sense of an invented account of the imagined interior processes of a central character in a narrative story' (Hillman 1983: 12). However, they have been influential on my development as a therapist as they aid emotional knowing, alongside theory, which adds an extra dimension to personal therapy and supervision. Story played an important role in Sally's therapy as at the beginning there was no coherent story. During the therapy, character and image interrelated to gradually build up plot and story-line. This led to both a coherent story of the past as well as the creation of narratives, aiding understanding and emotional comprehension of everyday experiences.

> Our reality is created through our fictions; to be conscious of these fictions is to gain creative access to, and participation in, the poetics or making of our psyche or soul-life; the 'sickness' of our lives has its source in our fictions; our fictions can be 'healed' through willing participation, and, in this atmosphere of healing, they reclaim their intrinsic therapeutic functions.
>
> (Quasha 1983: ix)

Edwards (1999) puts forward a convincing case for the case study having a place alongside other research methodologies. Case study is a subjective method of enquiry, a form of story-telling. It is through stories that meaning is created and shared.

> In my experience, our work is, more often than not, as concerned with feelings, aesthetic sensibilities, moral practices and beliefs as much as it is with objectivity or facts. In practice our work as art therapists embraces both subjective and objective reality.
>
> (Edwards 1999: 4)

The fact that case studies centrally include the therapist's role, make them potentially, an important method of research. The critical subjectivity needed is discussed by Schaverien (1995b), Killick and Greenwood (1995), and Maclagan (1995). Edwards suggests that 'what we take to be the truth' is largely determined by the metaphors, stories, beliefs and doctrines which in any given society shape our ideas about the world and what it is to be human. There are many shorter case studies in chapters in the literature as well as the professional journals, but few longer, extended histories. Among those that have been helpful in terms of the presentation of a story, by which we can both see a process of working, and also a growing relationship are: Freud (1980 [1909]), Axline (1986), Klein (1961), McDougall and Lebovici (1969), Winnicott (1977), in child work, and in adult work: Freud (1980 [1905]; 1980 [1909]; 1981 [1911]; 1981 [1919]), Baynes (1940), Milner (1969, 1971), Schaverien (1992, 1995a, 2002), Dalley *et al.* (1993).

ART THERAPY WITH CHILDREN ON THE AUTISTIC SPECTRUM

The following case study is of work with a child who had an autistic presentation at assessment but who emerged from it in treatment, into an animal persona, together with a very disturbed phase, which has been described by theorists in terms of a psychotic phase, characterised by intrusive identification and a rather destructive symbiosis (Haag 1997). Meltzer (Meltzer *et al.* 1975), comments on post-autistic obssesionality, as a different pathway, but this case followed the former path. Psychoanalytic theory, introduced in the last chapter, has developed ways of thinking about these very primitive states of mind. However, these early preverbal, presymbolic sensual states are difficult to articulate. Spensley comments on the possibility of art therapy being able to illuminate these processes:

> 'In exploring the very processes involved in the development of con-sciousness and the capacity to symbolise, verbal description often proves inadequate to convey meaning or to convince those whose own experi-ence is so remote from these very primitive states. It would, therefore, be of considerable advantage if it proves possible to lend confirmation to some of these concepts through the visual evidence in paintings and drawings'
>
> (Spensley 1984: 6).

It is my intention to elaborate a method of working which uses both art and play in an analytic approach with this hard-to-reach client group. The use of a medium in therapy, creating a triangular interaction, fosters the third perspective of the oedipal triangle as it offers potentially, a situation where child and therapist can view the child's creation (baby) as two parents looking on. For those readers who are not practising art therapists with this client group, it is hoped that the visual images may help one into an understanding of these primitive states of mind and the way art therapists engage with them. In Britain, there is an active subgroup of the British Association of Art Therapists, which meets regularly to discuss work with patients across the autistic spectrum. However, published work has tended to focus either on work with autistic adults or the encapsulated child. The work with children has either a developmental model, or is influenced by the work of Stern (1985) and Alvarez (1992, 1996). Goldsmith (1986) describes work with an adult autistic patient in the context of 'substance and structure' in the art therapy process. This is a thoughtful account of the difficulty with change and the use of painting to maintain the status quo. In this context pictures made can act 'not as containers of meaning but as structures that keep meaning out' (Goldsmith 1986: 20). She writes about her interventions, working alongside or with him, as a force for change. In her recordings of his subsequent speech with its switches and incoherencies, one can see the autistic state acting as a barrier to unbearable feeling. Fox (1998) writes about work with adult autistic patients and the reclamation of symbolic function. She uses the evocative image of 'being lost in space' trying to understand 'what it might be like to be unable to process information into meaning-ful concepts, how frightening and confusing the world might seem, how important is our ability to use symbols' (Fox 1998: 89). There are some similarities between her client, Jason, and the child of the case study in this book. Her approach illustrates the importance of encouraging a feeling that the patient is a separate person and of extending what they are able to attempt: The session 'is structured by the therapist on the edge of a client's needs, so that there is always potentially a little more space to explore' (Fox 1998: 77). She describes, for instance, her patient having 'a clay comforter', a piece of clay repetitively smoothed every week and of change and forward movement needing to be negotiated.

Dubowski (1990) has been instrumental in the furtherance of a developmental model of art therapy with children having learning difficulties, as well as children with encapsulated autism. He has been influenced by Gardner (1985) who put forward persuasive arguments concerning our 'separate intelligences'. Dubowski highlights the importance of development in other modes, e.g. drawing, when language is not available.

'Emerging affective art therapy' is a developmental model of art therapy with the encapsulated autistic child (Evans and Rutten-Saris 1998). This model of art therapy uses concepts, developed by Stern, of exploring vitality affects and their categorical affects in reconstructing infant-based preverbal communication, and the developmental aspects of schemata in the art work. The aim is for preverbal communication to become a shared dialogue when spoken language, and other shared symbols and signs, are not available to the client. This approach emphasises the process of art therapy and the importance of the relationship between therapist and client in the process. Building on the collaborative work of Evans and Rutten-Saris (1998) and Evans (1998), Evans and Dubowski (2001) have constructed a similar model of intervention: 'Interactive art therapy', based on observation of the therapist's and child's experience, using an assessment video as a base for future work.

Dubowski discusses how the ability to communicate with pictures develops through a series of stages which parallel language development and lead to the development of a sense of self (1984, 1990). He stresses the importance of the quality of experience between therapist and child when there is communication deficit or communication sensitivity. Therapeutic interventions in interactive art therapy are based on infant–caregiver interactions such as 'reciprocal cueing' (Brazelton et al. 1974); protoconversations/motherese (Trevarthen and Neisser 1993); helping the child to find some shape or form for meaning. Evans and Dubowski (2001) stress the importance of the earlier stages of drawing development as a foundation for the development of symbolic functioning. They are applying the work of Stern to this specialised form of art therapy, and use his concepts to describe the building blocks of their work with encapsulated children. They aim to develop intersubjectivity between child and therapist as they understand this to be a fundamental part of presymbolic functioning development: 'the early phases of drawing development, the pre-representational drawing activities, are particularly

helpful in engaging autistic children in experiences which provide a foundation for the development of communication skills generally, if these are to
appear'. They suggest that this model of art therapy provides 'a communication scaffolding' which can result in the further use of verbal language (Evans
and Dubowski 2001: 101). Tipple (2003) is developing a particular approach
to the assessment of autistic children in a paediatric disability setting which
recalls gestalt approaches in that it focuses on the here and now of the con-
structs and procedures that shape exchanges in therapy situations, looking at
intersubjectivities and social role and how this influences the art productions.
He sees this approach as a counterpoint to psychodynamic or cognitive
approaches to drawings.

Mannoni's work at the school at Bonneuil, for children with autistic
characteristics, emotional disturbance and learning impairments comes closer
to the post-autistic disturbance which is the subject of the case study. The
school was characterised by having art and theatre studios, a protected space
for creativity, as a form of treatment; together with school/community
life aiding a provisional responsibility. Brenkman (1999) comments on
Mannoni's sense of the two tasks facing these children:

> On the one hand, they must find the means of expressing even their most
> stifled or destructive impulses, their most anti-social urges or most pri-
> vate fears, in an increasingly articulate form, that is, as an expression of
> themselves that can be shared with others without the risk of destroying
> the self or the other; and, on the other hand, they must develop their
> capacity to deal with real-world obligations and dangers without being
> defeated by the outside world's perception of them as ill or retarded.
>
> (Brenkman 1999: xxii)

SALLY: A CASE STUDY

Background

When Sally, age eight, had been referred for assessment it had been difficult
to distinguish different characteristics of developmental delay, learning
difficulties, environmental factors, genetic and emotional factors, as well as
autistic and psychotic traits and trauma. She was a sturdy girl, with curly
bright auburn hair and dark blue eyes. She had been referred to be considered
for individual art therapy/child psychotherapy, because she was a puzzle. In a
previous paper, an interactional mode of assessment using all images available,
both those made, and those in the mind's eye aroused by the narratives of
family and child is described (Case 1998). A large group of professionals were
working with the family, across the three statutory services of Education,
Social Services and the National Health Service. Sally usually presented as a
selective mute, with language only in one specified area to do with animals.

When she spoke it was apparent that she had a language disorder (inter-changeable consonants, distortion, stuttering) as well as delayed language, speaking in a flat monotone out of the home, using only the present tense; but she apparently chattered to her mother at home, not making much sense, more like a stream of consciousness. She had sleeping difficulties, in that she slept very little and slept alongside her parents in their room. She suffered from enuresis and encropresis. There was little sense of her being contained either physically or emotionally, which might link with psychotic anxieties of leaking away. Adding to this picture, was her skin, which bore evidence of her picking at her arms and face, leaving them red and raw. Sally had characteristics of both entangled and encapsulated children, described by Tustin (1992). She was withdrawn, but would occasionally become animated about animals. She had a hard shell kind of exterior body armour, apparently feeling no pain. In other ways she fitted into the entangled picture. She could have a hard, aggressive, distancing stare but at other times felt quite empty. The sense of emptiness with the stare suggests that there is a huge projection out of mental contents. One of her fears was of the toilet flushing, like Wendy in Chapter five (pp. 101–104); a fear of being flushed away, a draining of mental contents that might go with the water. There was a striking sense of lack of containment, both mentally and emotionally, although she seemed to be in a kind of body armour and impenetrable. This might seem contradict-ory at first. The body armour gave an impression of containment, almost imprisoned defence, but the lack of containment was exemplified by the pouring out of body fluids which did not appear to be under her regulation.

Mother and child's relationship

Sally's mother suffered from a deep and prolonged depression and workers with the family found it difficult to keep hope alive for them: as if despair might overtake everyone. At the time of assessment with Sally, mother's mental state and vulnerability had been evident. Within minutes of meeting, tears had come to my eyes, and I had had to struggle with trying to contain my own countertransference responses. Mother had poured out a disjointed history and the different bereavement traumas she had experienced and her own despair about Sally. It was not possible to take a usual history or to gain an impression of a sequence of events. It has been noted by Fonagy *et al.* (1992) in research on attachment disorder that if the parents' generation cannot give a coherent narrative about their own childhood then this is an indicator for disturbed attachment with their own children. Mother moved in a confusing narrative between different periods of time and with confusion of identities in a painful pouring out of distress. Mother's suffering was evident, and it is important not to apportion blame but to try to contain the anxieties and move towards understanding of the complex and interwoven dynamics. The work of Fraiberg *et al.* (1975) on 'ghosts in the nursery', the way that the parent's history impacts on the parent–child relationship is helpful. When parents are preoccupied by dead internal objects it is difficult for them to respond in a lively way to the child: 'Instead, the child comes to identify not with his parent but with his parent's unmourned internal ghost; this prevents him from developing a life and personality of his own' (Barrows 2000: 70).

Being part of a family with an autistic child can be traumatising for family members as their life becomes limited to the demands of the child (Klauber 1998, 1999). Sally was mother's first child and only girl. She was confused when she talked about her, using herself and 'Sally' interchangeably in conversation. They had an entangled relationship with a confused joint identity or overlap, and at a certain point actually changed roles. Mother described how Sally would work mother up to tears and despair, and would then take on a role of comforting her. Father was a silent but supportive presence. He had given up work to help mother with the children. A year later, when I had space and could start work with Sally, there was a big push from all concerned to help the parents to move the children into their own bedrooms. Mother had said that Sally's fear of the dark prevented such a move, but it only now emerged that the children had slept with the parents since birth because mother feared they would die in the night if in a separate room. This move was achieved without anybody dying, to mother's amazement. Traumatic bereavements had led to a situation where it seemed to be necessary to literally 'see the children' to know that they were alive, while under a shadow of grief, that contributed to fear of further family members dying.

Part of the difficulty in clinical work of this nature is to be able to hold in mind not-knowing what has happened to a child. Part of us always wants to say that this or that has happened. There was a question in everyone's minds as to whether constitutional and genetic factors played the major part or if there was the greatest effect of emotional factors. Had there been an outer catastrophe from failure of the environment around Sally or had there been an inner catastrophe? Sally's way of working in the assessment suggested that her mind had massive fragmentation or splitting into compartments had occurred. She would begin an activity with one word in an affectless voice such as 'paint', or 'sand', and abruptly cut off in mid-activity to something else for no observable reason; it seemed to be internal pressure or anxiety to leave something behind. Her voice when she occasionally spoke was one-dimensional, as if from the grave.

Extract from the first assessment session

Sally was with an escort in the waiting room staring at a tank of tropical fish. She stared silently at me. I explained that we would go to the art therapy room and that the escort would stay in the room here. She came into the room with me, staring quite blankly. She had not responded to anything I had said. It is the stare of an empty shell, blank and not engaged but I feel slightly uncomfortable and wonder if she does too. I invited her to take off her coat or put her bag down and talked of the purpose of our meeting. She did not respond so I described the kinds of things in the room and explained that she could choose what she might do. In a flat, dull monotone she said 'off' and shrugged her coat off. She went to the sand tray and made a sweeping gesture in it. Although she was eight and big physically for her age I found myself saying 'sand' as I would to a younger child. I talked of her making a mark and she could see it. She made another mark with a stiff five finger gesture and another looking at me each time. Her body movements are markedly slow and stiff, as if she is encased in armour. I commented on her wanting me to see what she had made and brought chairs over to the sand. We both sat down and she made another mark possibly like a face and I asked what it was. She said 'dog'. Again it was like hearing a voice from the grave. She made another animal kind of shape after I had repeated, 'Yes, dog'. This time she said 'bird'. Then her eye flickered to the paints and she moved to them.

She strongly and awkwardly squeezed out masses of colour at first in separate wells of the palette but then on top of each other trailing across in a mess. She dipped in a brush and did a shape saying 'dog', then another saying 'bird' on a different piece of paper. I asked about the bird picture, did she have a bird? She said with difficulty, it is like listening to someone trying out another language, that she has a bird, 'its inna cage'. She painted bars with emphasis. Her face illumined as she said 'e as a mirra'. I said he likes to see himself and she said 'yes'. It was an enormous effort to have said this and she dropped away to be lost in the pouring and spilling and flicking of paint. The words are often accompanied by stuttering but also sound as if they come through a distorted tube and that external speech is a foreign undertaking. She abruptly came out of this to get into the sand tray where she started scrabbling in it with her hands like dogs' paws. She took off her socks and shoes and buried several toys. She then abruptly changed to crayons and did rough but recognisable little drawings on a divided piece of paper of a dog, bird, cage and rabbit. She named these. Now as it was getting near time to leave she took a toy animal saying 'home' and I had to firmly explain that the toys would stay here for next time and could not go home with her. At the very end she tried to tell me something about her dog, but with enormous effort. It was very hard to understand her but I responded as well as I could to the feeling quality of what she said, more a sense of urgency and said that I would see her next week.

Discussion: play, drawing and clay-work

In the session, the difference between her response when we were engaged around the animal pictures and at other times was marked. Her voice was disconcerting, as if all emotional inflection had been flattened out of it. This changed with the making of the pictures, with a wish to communicate. The mirror suggested that the therapist's concentration and attention and wish to understand gave her some reflection in the session. Her language difficulties indicated a lack of link between parts of herself as well as a problem to do with having no clear sense of another to communicate to, unless the subject was 'animals'. Possibly, Sally had seen something of beauty in her pets, the grace of an animal which is able to effortlessly be itself. Concretely, she wanted to take something from the session to have with her. She fluctuated in age in the session, at times feeling very young, although at the end it was an older child trying to articulate. The attractiveness of the art materials, their strong sensual qualities, and the presence of the therapist, worked together, to pull Sally out of her silent presentation on first meeting. Spensely comments on the art materials fostering 'first attentiveness', and how together with the therapist's skills, a milieu can be created for ego development, initially facilitating the prerequisites for ego development through physical and sensual experiences (Spensely 1984).

It had been noted by school staff that her play in a one-to-one setting could be intimidating. Her play had such a strong quality and she had made physical attacks on staff when playing as an animal. From the account received it was possible that she did not actually play as an animal but *was* the animal in her own mind, as she could become quite aggressive and frightening.

Her drawing using crayon or paintbrush was solely of animals – and had a lyrical and attractive quality. Her name was merged into the animal form. It was engaging to share her wonder and pleasure as an animal emerged in a few strokes. In order to be able to draw in that way there has to be a thinking of oneself into the animal together with observational skill or identification with the thing drawn. In the wish for there not to be the experience of separation, 'entangled children' locate themselves in others by processes of adhesive equation (Tustin 1990). It seemed most probable that the drawings of animals, were in fact drawings of her animal-identified self, not a symbolic act, but rather her *being* the animal (Illustration, P. 3). This is similar to the way that Donna Williams (1992) and Liane Holliday Willey (1999) write of taking on characteristics of other people, actually becoming them so that this persona is the part that interacts with the rest of the world. It is only when she is an animal in play that she is animated and comes out of her rigid body armour. However, working three-dimensionally was not successful or satisfying in that she could not make a three-dimensional shape. She would make bullying attacks on people to get them to make things for her. Once you become a pair of hands for an 'entangled child', your skills are seen as an extension of their own more limited ability, and there is no incentive for them to struggle with the painful reality of their own products. It is another instance of the blurring of 'me' and 'not-me' described by Tustin (1992); it is treating another person as a pencil or pair of scissors, relating to them as an inanimate object rather than as a person with a mind of their own. In a

Illustration P. 3 Sally: Sally/Dog.

similar way she would take people by their clothing to where she wanted them
to be. When she tried to use clay she came up against her two-dimensionality,
which is caused by her flattening herself into another (adhesive equation), her
mother or her pets, and not being able to develop an identity of her own.

Where there has been fragmentation, each medium may enable communication from a particular part of a child and for this reason, a plurality of
approach is useful. This idea led to a decision to have a box of toys; traditional art materials, but for Sally's sole use; and water and sand. This arose
from the assessment where I had seen separate parts of Sally in clay-work,
play, painting, and drawing. In the case study, several themes will be followed
to give some structure to the three years of work with Sally, which was
chaotic over a period of time (Case 2003), in particular, the progress of
Sally's clay-work; her drawing and painting within the developing relationship; her use of animal persona and play as well as the development of her
speech and language. Technical issues in work of this nature will be considered.

Chapter 7

From calm to chaos and rage

> Healing begins when we move out of the audience and on to the stage of the psyche, become characters in a fiction (even the/god-like voice of Truth, a fiction), and as the drama intensifies, the catharsis occurs; we are purged from attachments to literal destinies, find freedom in playing parts, partial, dismembered, Dionysian, never being whole but *participating* in the whole that is a play, remembered by it as actor of it.
>
> (Hillman 1983: 38)

THE CALM BEFORE THE STORM

In this first phase of the work, Sally initially presented in a similar way to the assessment, with drawing, animal play, and attempts at clay-work, without apparent connection, changing from one to the other quite abruptly. She very soon took on an animal persona, usually a dog, for some part of each session and this was in stark contrast to her armoured presentation as a child. She was able to move more freely, and become animated. She fluctuated from presenting autistic/psychotic features, from the claustrum, with its phantasies of being inside mother to inhabiting a dog persona. In the early dog play there was both a rapid change of new themes in the session as well as a repetitive playing over of previous themes. In order to make sense, the emerging themes have been separated to enable the reader to think their own thoughts about them.

Territory, possession, and guarding

Session

When Sally arrived for the session she stared at me. As she looked at me, the look changed, becoming harder and further back, more blank. She knelt down and was a dog. She started just where she had left off last week, getting the blanket in her teeth and putting it on the floor as a bed. She inspected the floor area, sniffing and moving like a dog, lying on her side, back, paws in the air, rolled, sniffing under the table, bringing things like the tissue box in her teeth. I commented on what Sally Dog was doing, and also tried to put some possible feelings into words such as the wish to curl up beside me and be protected, because the idea and feeling grew in me that there began to be things which could be expressed as a dog in dog language that could not be said as a child in human language. She came up to me and put her head on my lap, it was difficult not to pat her. She moved away and turned in circles to lie down. She got up on to a chair and then a tabletop and barked at a picture saying with difficulty, stuttering, 'dog, he bark, he say what he want'. She became more expressive, barking, growling, and whining at different things in the room and at the door after hearing sounds from another room, she emptied and inspected the contents of the wastepaper basket. There was a sense of protecting the space from outside interference and finding evidence of other people being here which I talked about.

Discussion

Sally may look at me to see if I am the same Mrs Case that she saw last time. After staring at me the look changes to having a hard quality, more aggressive, in the sense of being distancing, as if mental contents are being posted in my direction. Whatever feelings are aroused by seeing me, are evacuated. When she becomes blank and kneels down to be a dog, Sally Child is quite out of contact and has been replaced by Sally Dog. It is as if the surface persona that interacts with the world is now the dog. Starting just where she left off last week makes me wonder if the week's gap has been eradicated in her mind and there is to be a seamless quality between the separate sessions. She expresses the idea that dogs can communicate and she is able to communicate, using that language.

Becoming a dog brings with it some freedom of movement and expression. Sally comes out of the rigid body armour and is animated. As a child she needs a bigger distance between us than would be usual. Several defensive mechanisms such as her stare and hard shell body armour seem to impose this on the situation. When she is a dog however she is able to express a wish to be near me and in physical contact by bringing me objects or putting her chin on my knee. One theme that is very apparent is the inspection and territorial guarding of the therapy room. As a dog she is able to show me her growing sense of this space as her space that no one else is to be allowed into. Noises from outside such as musical instruments and people's voices from other therapy rooms are vigorously responded to and the room is often inspected for evidence of other children's presence in a way that she is not able to put into words. Talking about them as feelings which Sally Dog has is one stage removed from talking about them as Sally Child's feelings and is acceptable. I wonder if these emotions and feelings have never been named before. Children with autistic-type features are so sensitive to direct communication one has to tread a line between entering their world in a way that allows them to communicate successfully, but also not to get lost in their world, so that your difference is expunged and you become a figment of their world. This would have happened if I had patted her. These countertransference impulses could be very strong.

Session

Sally said that I was to hear a noise in the night and to go down and calm the dog. I acted this, she had howled and then whimpered and then growled, as if there was something there, rushing forwards and backwards. I talked of the Baby Sally Dog who was frightened by noises in the night and who worried here about the safety of the session. She started making odd movements, very agitated and I found I'd said, 'Sit'. I could not believe I had done this. She had immediately sat quietly like a good dog.

Discussion

In the countertransference one can see that she evokes powerful feelings to contain her. 'Sit' is a containing response to an actual anxious puppy. I had related to her *as an anxious puppy* and she had responded immediately looking relieved and relaxed. It is a technical problem as to how much to enter children's play. Entering it but saying, 'I am just going to think about what we have been playing', is a useful way of keeping one's thoughts going in a reflective way and also communicates and models a reflective state of mind. Responding to her as a dog is indicative of the excellence of her 'being a dog'. It is very complete. The child that stares at me at the door moves further back inside to defend against human to human contact and whatever it is that is aroused by that contact: the dog persona interacts with the outside world. Hope and creativity are apparent in the emergence of new themes, but it is also a possible prison for the child inside. An interface needed to be created between the child within the dog persona and the therapist. For instance I could say in a stage whisper to Sally 'What is the dog doing?' or, 'What shall I do next in the play?', so that although she is a dog she can choose whether to come out of it for a moment to reply and sometimes these exchanges could be lengthened. Sally is able to communicate a range of simple feelings and needs in dog language and in a sense is more flowingly expressive than she is in human language. She whines to show need and utters puppy-type yelps, excited barks, etc.

Language, 'going to the vet' and 'hide-and-seek'

Simple narratives that have a start, middle and end begin to be formed by Sally. These were a response to the regular sessions which also have a start, middle and end. There was an enormous effort to get the words of the simple story-line articulated. She started the sentence with an articulation of sounds to get the first word out, which was not understandable at first. The later words of the sentence would come out in a rush behind. I would then repeat what I thought she had said and she would correct me if I was wrong, and we went on like that, until we had it correctly between us. This could seem laborious to one or other of us if I could not understand or she could not articulate. It sometimes ended with deep frustration but it seemed important to persevere. If one does not persevere through the difficulties that are caused by saying 'I did not understand that, let's try it again', then something is fudged. It allowed the dog/baby to develop in her own time. The shared language that we both understood brought a shared and common reality.

The early themes in the play might usually be expressed by children in question form, such as: 'Who else comes here? Who do you see? Do you see any younger children or babies? Where do you live? Do you have children?' The dog's wish to guard the room and bark at noises outside expressed thoughts that the therapist was her therapist and a natural extension of this thought to a wish that the therapist did not see anybody else. The therapist and therapy room need to be guarded because they are a safe place, in which she has set up her own territory – the dog's bed, usually under a table next to me or under my chair.

Session

Sally Dog held her paw up and I pretended to be a vet, as instructed, coming up to the table that she had jumped up on and inspecting her paw. I pretended to rub some cream into it. I had noticed when she had arrived that her hands were freshly picked and looked very sore. As I was rubbing the pretend cream in, not actually touching her, I commented on her scarred hands and said that Sally had been hurting herself and I was wondering about this. Had she been feeling anxious or worrying about things? I did not expect to get any answer from her as a child; her responses were through the play. At this stage, I was thinking about her, trying to understand what it was that I was seeing. It is important to keep one's own thoughts going in human language and to communicate to the child, as part of her could be listening. She got off the table with some difficulty, pretending to limp, wanting to be carried. I suggested how she could get down to the ground and I went to sit on my usual chair. She came and lay down underneath it, trying to secretly peer up at me. She lay quietly for some time and I commented on her wish to rest near me. She then went off down the room and bought back a toy telephone, which she put on my lap, then took away. Then, she jumped up on to my lap. I commented on her wish for a safe secure place to be. She was then off and around the room and managed to make clear a very incoherent and inarticulate wish 'that the dog wanted to play hide-and-seek'.

Discussion

The vet play suggested her growing understanding that the therapy situation had a healing potential. She could present physical hurts to the 'vet', often a somatic expression of psychic pain, at one further step removed from human feeling, in dog form.

Hide-and-seek was played over and over again in a ritual way as one might with a little child as in fact she could almost always be seen, behind a chair, under the table, crouched in the sand tray, or beside a cupboard. What seemed most important was the delight in being found. There is a need to be held in the boundary of mother's love which is thwarted when mother suffers from prolonged depression as was seen in work with Henry in Chapter two. Children can become lost and withdrawn to contact. This toddler activity, of play running away, paralleled family events and the withdrawal of mother's attention earlier in her history. Hide-and-seek allows the child to be lost and found symbolically (Case 1986, 1990a). The chasing, hide-and-seek and tag games brought with them a lot of warmth and laughter. She was always an animal, usually a dog, but occasionally a cougar when she would express shades of aggression, growling and wanting to frighten me. This was a hint of things to come.

Training and the lead

Session

Sally expressed feelings about one of the first breaks in a fast changing medley of animal noises. She became a dog, cougar, screeching parrot, cow, cat, and lamb. The different animals suggested a range of different feelings that might be present. She tried with great difficulty to tell me something as a dog. Words choked on guttural sounds, as if the true speech could not get out. It felt as if it was twisted round something, 'ee,'ee wants you to train 'im'. What she wanted was for me to throw the toy up the room and for her to fetch it. When I did this the dog shook hands with me by putting a 'paw' out.

Later in the session she became a puppy that wanted to be chased. She pulled the furniture out about the room so that she could be chased around things and when I lightly touched her she chased me and so on. In a pause in this I was able to talk of the gap and how I had gone away and come back. How much she had wanted me to come looking for her and find her during the break.

Discussion

It can be seen that the game of 'training' the dog is about losing and retriev-ing. This game and 'hide-and-seek' are both about losing and finding and related to playing over the feelings aroused by the gaps between the sessions and the holiday breaks. One potentially tricky area to negotiate technically is how emotion could have got lost when she wanted me to train her. It is possible that in obeying orders, 'fetch, bring, sit', the owner's superego could take over and the dog become an animal that obeys without thought or feeling. It could be one way to make emotion vanish, by not having it. It can be a relief to obey orders for those who do not want the responsibility of thinking or feeling. However, training could also be a form for containment. 'Training' brings aspects of the dog into a working relationship with the human, not necessarily to do with compliance. Looked at in this way, Sally's primitive dog/baby states were seeking containment from the dog trainer/mother therapist in order that they could be integrated, humanised, and personalised within our relationship.

There are things that the Child Sally can say but with enormous difficulty. Really she only speaks to tell me what the dog is saying. Sally Dog can 'say' or express other things. She really presents the dog to me to pay attention to. One difficulty is the relation between these two parts, for instance could the child be envious of my responses to the dog? Here, writing about it in retrospect it is much clearer than it was at the time. It needed constant review to get the relationship between what she was presenting and how I responded, good enough. As a child she has distorted communication, needs distance and I wonder if I am totally overwhelming; but as a dog she seems to expect that I am friendly and positive to her and is able to get physically close and freely expressive within dog language. What is it that inhibits this kind of relationship with the child? One tactic I developed was to try to extend the moment of her entering the therapy room as a child before she became a dog. It was sometimes possible to have two or three exchanges and then she would begin to fade away.

A further theme was that she wanted a collar and lead, saying 'Ee go to shops we you'. I compromised saying that it was dangerous to put something around her neck and that I would put the string around her arm. This 'lead' became a string length with a loop at the end, which she held in her hand. We were now in an attached relationship in a very concrete way, an umbilical cord. The play to the shops became a frequently returned to theme. Characteristically we go to the shops together. (The shop is always the sand tray.) I tether her to the leg of the table and as I buy food she lets herself off the lead and hides in the room. I am then to experience the loss of her. In the present this reverses the feelings she has when I am not there between sessions. There had also been a disjointed account from parents at assessment that Sally had once been lost and had said, that a 'bad man' had taken her away; this came to my mind as a possible repetitive playing over of a trauma.

Wetting, soiling, puppies and babies

It will be remembered that one of Sally's referring symptoms was her enuresis and her soiling. She frequently needed to go to the toilet in the session in a way that suggested an evacuation of anxieties aroused in the session. She did not have a mechanism for processing thoughts and feelings in that she had not internalised a 'container/contained relationship' (Bion 1962a). In connection with toileting: another theme that emerged in this first phase was of a puppy that does ' 'is toilet in th' 'ouse'. This was explored by Sally playing different scenarios. My role in the play was to give the puppy a telling off. The combination of lead/umbilical cord and wetting in the house, suggested the wetting took place in the mother's womb, in phantasy.

Session

One session, when I tried to explore the puppy play she sat on the wastepaper basket in the room and nearly squashed it. It emerged that the puppy wanted a basket. We made one out of paper but then other connected themes followed fast as once in the basket, she was a mother dog having pups. This dog has ten puppies and also does its toilet everywhere over the house. There is a connection with the need for a basket with the need for safe containment. Do things, including faeces, spill out, if there is no safe place of containment, which might be some link as yet far off, to her own making of messes or/and is there also tremendous confusion between faeces and babies? Sally had arrived for this session in new clothes, hairstyle, and wearing a piece of mother's jewellery. She had looked momentarily grown up as she stood not speaking but then had quickly dropped to all fours. On arrival she inhabited a mother skin and then there was a divided pull towards being mother, dog or baby. She went out to the toilet in the session and I found that she had peed on the towel and in the bath.

It is possible to see what intense other confusions arise from entanglement. There was possibly a basic confusion between the infant–mother couple and the mother–father couple. There is the play of a puppy doing its toilet in the room, which does not know any better, and there is Sally doing the toilet in the wrong place. Does she know any better? How much is this angry spoiling communication, possibly at my pausing in the play to speak? There is a difference between what Sally Dog can let me know and what Sally Child can let me know. After I had tried to talk about some of these issues in particular about what could be expressed as a dog and what as a child she said 'draw' and got paper. She drew two dogs. One is her pet dog and one is she. She was showing me that it is her pet dog whose persona she takes on. A confusing conversation about pups followed. I could not understand if a dog was expecting pups, or if Sally wanted a puppy. This is a good example of the confusion of thoughts when someone is entangled with another. I did not know whether Sally was identified with her mother's capacity to have babies or her dog's capacity to have puppies, or, if she was telling me that she is about to have a puppy in reality. Person to person relationships are confused and so are phantasy, play and reality.

After this sequence she wanted to play at being a dog on a lead and as it was time to leave at the end of the session she cut the string lead (umbilical cord) in two wanting us each to have half. This was poignant in its recreation of the first symbol, but I also knew that if she took it, she would triumphantly feel that she had part of me/the therapy with her, so I encouraged her to leave it with me. I spoke of her wish to be joined to me by string that could tie up again next week. She left it reluctantly inside a little teapot in her box and I said that I would keep it safe. It was difficult for her to leave it. This may seem harsh to the part of us identified with the child but it is a necessary boundary that enables the therapy material to be gathered in and understood, rather than elements being diluted or lost. Concretely, the little piece of string (baby thread) is contained inside the teapot (mother womb). Struggling with the feelings aroused by separation at the end of the session will generate attempts to think about the session; whereas, if she takes something from the session she feels that she has the session/me with her. Absence can bring a developmental move for the child, because it brings the reality of dependence, separation and loss (O'Shaughnessy 1964).

Clay-work and painting

The potential of art therapy was demonstrated when Sally came out of dog-persona to use materials, as it was possible to make contact with the child. My thoughts on it not being very helpful in the long term to be bullied into making things for Sally made me decide to take a firm stance with clay-work; not to actually make things for Sally, although I would offer assistance if required and it felt appropriate. The importance of 'staying with the image' in art therapy has been stressed by McNiff (1990: 28). With confusional children one needs to 'stay with the image that cannot be made', rather than be seduced into making it for them. At the same time there needs to be an arena for 'interactive play' which eventually will contribute to create the conditions for the image to be made.

Imprint and bluebird

Session

During an early session she had got the clay out and had dumped it in front of me, saying 'Make'. She had got some animals from the box to show me what I was to do. There had been a tussle of wills as I had said that I would be with her while she tried to make it herself. She had kept repeating 'Just start it', pushing it at me, putting my hands on it, and telling me of other people who did, but I had held firm.

Eventually she had tried to make a dolphin but had kept pushing it at me to do, which had effectively spoilt any shape she had started. As I had been talking of what was happening and how frustrating it was for her she had pushed a horse toy into the clay, making an imprint, and kept this (Illustration 7.1). She had been repetitively forceful in trying to get her own way so that I had experienced some of the mental battering her mother experiences. I had talked of how angry she might be feeling about the restrictions but she had responded that, 'Her dog is angry'. The dog persona contained her projected emotions. In a similar situation the next session she had responded by painting a black and dark bluebird, and when I had asked if this was her pet bird that she had painted before she had said 'No, it was a blue tit' (Illustration 7.2). The blue tit painting had been an unconscious response to my not being prepared to be her hands for her; her experience of an ungiving cold breast, the punning, creative response of the unconscious. This had been the first time that she had painted or drawn an animal that was not a pet, so that I had felt that this was a new departure, though with an unconscious play on words.

Illustration 7.1 Sally: Animal imprints.

Illustration 7.2 Sally: Blue tit.

Discussion

The imprinted animals had made me wonder whether they had been a response to the impression made on her by the therapist. There was a refusal or inability to struggle with making something herself, so in this way they had been a semi-defiant response in that she *would* make an animal without me. In some way, this had been a solution to the problem that she could not use the clay without making it go wrong. It was not totally satisfying, because they did not stand up or sit, which is what she would have liked them to do. She had wanted them to look real. The imprinting feels like a move towards a three-dimensional image in reverse, an implosion rather than an explosion, a relief in reverse. I had wondered whether she experienced holding oneself separate, rather than being an extension of herself, as an impingement or intrusion: like the concave shape, it made a dent in the armour that she put around herself. It challenged the illusion of sameness of things and people. When she tried to use clay, she was brought up against her two-dimensionality. This was caused by her flattening herself into mother, or her pets, and the consequent lack of her own identity in relation to the outside world.

Sally's lack of containment made me consider the impact of family trauma upon her as a toddler. This would have had a huge impact on a young mind and could be thought about as: 'the shadow of the object falling upon the ego' (Freud 1917); or as an unassimilable object (Heimann 1942; K. Barrows 2000; P. Barrows 2003). The concave shape could be a response to unintentional projection of mental pain; the outpouring of mental contents into the child as a receptacle, described by Williams, as the introjection of an object that hinders development (G. Williams 1997). This would be the reverse of containing the child's anxieties. I had begun to speak to her about the coming increase of sessions to two a week as I was able to offer her another session. There were severe concerns about Sally and a sense of hopelessness around the family problems at this time. As the boundaries were established, so the transference relationship became fully visible in the dynamic enacted between us.

FROM CHAOS TO RAGE

> I distrust the incommunicable: it is the source of all violence.
>
> (Sartre 1999: 145)

The second phase of the therapy became characterised by a spiral downward into chaos and rage, a descent into a hell of emotions. The increase of sessions to two a week brought a more intense relationship and more awareness of comings and goings and separations. I soon found myself experiencing the change from soft invasiveness to hate previously described in Chapter six. As the autistic features receded, Sally felt the impact of her otherness from the therapist:

> These horrors that could not be put into words always seemed to involve unthinkable separation anxiety. When every separation is experienced as annihilation, all the child can do is construct for himself a world in which he tries hard to live without affects in order to keep himself safe from the threat of destruction.
>
> (Mannoni, quoted in Brenkman 1999: xxiii)

Transference relationship

Session: from softness to hate

I had been aware that she had begun to enter the room with a softened look, loving and possessive. This had been extremely intense. She had stared at me, a look suffused with love, which had felt naked and intimate. I had said that I thought she was thinking about me. She had said 'No'. Again, she had looked, with an almost unbearable, naked, soft look. She had said, stuttering and with a distorted first sound, 'What's your other name?' I had said that my name was Caroline Case and that I thought she had missed me in the gap since last session. She had said, 'Yes'. I had said that it had felt like a long week. She had nodded slightly and then changed looks in the way she did when she was about to become a dog. The dog play that had followed was first of all about chasing. I had to chase her but not to catch her and there had been a different quality to this, a grim and hard satisfaction with suppressed enjoyment. This had then changed to play at night of various disturbances that woke us up. During this, while I had been talking of what feelings I thought were present, she had suddenly come under my chair and had tipped me out, sitting in it.

The play had begun to spiral into something more intrusive, possessive and aggressive, so that it had been hard to keep thinking on my feet. She had begun to jump at me like an excited dog, crushed the wastepaper basket beyond repair, clawing at me, spitting and growling as different animals. There had been a division of dogs for the first time: a Collie that is friendly, an Alsatian that guards me at night, and a wild Terrier that attacks me. When I had talked of these different dogs as parts of her and as different feelings, she had become more aggressive: there had been farting attacks, and also increased attacks on the room, shredding the wastepaper basket and clawing at my clothes and beads. I had felt myself getting angry, and a moment had come when she knew I was angry and let go (the Alsatian part of her guarding me from the Terrier). She had then laid down by the radiator and I had had a flood of feeling. I had felt tearful and shaken, rather shredded like the wastepaper basket. This had been very powerful and I had felt loved, hated, and violated for the rest of the morning. I had recalled one of the comments on referral: that Sally would work her mother up to tears and then they would cry together. It had been time to clear up so I had talked of this and of the gaps between the sessions. She had got herself together also and had been able to say the time of the next session before leaving.

Discussion

The three separate dogs that Sally became suggest the conflicting emotions aroused by the relationship with the therapist. The Collie is a dog that works with man as a sheep-dog, suggesting a therapeutic alliance, being in relationship. The Alsatian guards against intruders and is a police dog, suggesting a policing of my other imagined relationships at work and home, as well as guarding me from the intrusiveness of the Terrier. Terriers work as hunting dogs, they are ratters and rabbit hunters, renowned for not letting go, but this one is wild and attacks the therapist. The therapist's separate identity was being seen and this aroused very painful feelings. The Terrier suggested that her oral-aggressive devouring (loving) impulses had been split off and projected out, as a defence against her fear of abandonment by mother/therapist. These returned via an intrusive identification which provoked the therapist to anger, confirming her conviction that she cannot come alive with mother/therapist. There had been a very powerful attack on words and thinking going on; it had been unbearable to hear me talk because it had confronted her with my separateness. She wanted me to *just play* (i.e. be the giving breast), under her orders, as if an extension of her. In this state of mind thought is really attacked and denuded and one is left exposed to the power of these emotions. In a sense this all follows from an awareness of time.

It had been a recent development to say the day and time of the next session. She would say, '9.30!' with a stammer. This had been a tremendous achievement and was said with some triumph. She had not had any capacity to tell the time previously and solely used the present tense in speech. In conversation with her teacher we discovered that this began as the boundaries of the therapy were established which included not being able to come at other times. To exist in a timeless world is much safer. The timeless world is a world of no boundaries. A sense of time brings with it a sense of comings and goings and separation. It may have been a shock to her, to have heard that I had a different name. She had been confronted with my difference from herself. As she had taken control in my seat, there had been a massive use of projective identification (with an intrusive quality) and I had felt the floods of feeling, between her and her mother, in the countertransference.

Children and adults who are in a state of mind where they wish to remain stuck to mother can experience words and speech as violently intrusive. There are various methods to try to stop speech and thinking. Sally would sometimes speak over me like a demonic Donald Duck. It suggested that everything the therapist was saying was nonsense and by its speedy and manic performance was quite cleverly blotting out further thoughts I might have. It is not really possible to use sentences with children in this state of mind. It seemed better and more useful to use just one word at a time. So that I might say, angry, frightened, sad or whatever other feeling I felt as present rather than a phrase or sentence. At this stage of huge outburst it was too soon to link what was being played to the child directly, instead it needed to be talked about within the play, less directly, or held in the therapist thoughts. At the same time she would push me to the limits of what was containable. It is like an internal explosion to have a link or connection made, and this can increase aggressive behaviour. The return of a projection is felt as violent on its return: as it was first violently made. Gordon (1965) suggests that children who are massively using projective identification need a good womb in which a rebirth may be prepared, and need to involve a real person in the inner drama so that he might then help to disentangle one's confused identity. In trying to avoid separation they seek to control others from inside.

Messy painting – engulfment

The next phase brought with it a very different use of art materials. At the beginning of this phase with Sally there were some attempts to paint that usually resulted in paint flooding on to the picture-surface. Painting messes have been mentioned by several authors: 'painting out' with mentally handicapped clients as destroying and repairing being used as a transitional object to help against actual and felt loss (Hughes 1984); Fox, similarly (1998) refers to 'savage acts of vandalism and blind rage' in work with autistic adults suggesting that the work functioned as transitional objects which the client created and destroyed. Stack mentions phases of self-mutilating and acting-out destructive behaviour in encapsulated autistic adults (Stack 1998). Hallam discusses 'destructive room wrecking outbursts' and how contact with his mentally handicapped client group is made through narrative, 'talking about what the therapist is doing, then what the client is doing, then this leads towards stories' (Hallam 1984: 12). Pearson in relation to adults, and Rabiger in relation to children, discuss aggressive/destructive behaviour within the same client group (Pearson 1984; Rabiger 1984).

Art messes with non-autistic clients include: the function of a 'messy area' when working with bereaved children (Case 1986); externalising a 'bad, rejected baby' in work with looked-after children (Case 1990a). Working with adolescent sex offenders, Aulich describes, 'splattering, pouring, and smearing paint on the paper', and how one client described this as shit and wanted to wrap this around her (Aulich 1994). Aldridge discusses the fluctuation and change from perceiving art material messes as shit to chocolate where there has been significant loss and neglect (Aldridge 1998). In cases of sexual abuse Sagar, and Hanes have written about messy packages representing 'the secret' that the child had to keep (Sagar 1990; Hanes 1997). Murphy reported a positive aspect to mess-making from her research. Therapists see at times that it can be an attack on the therapist and room but it also permits exploration of boundaries in a physical way; making a mess 'allowed for the sense of internal damage to be conveyed and for an acceptable reawakening of sensory experience' (Murphy 1998: 15).

Session: engulfment

Sally had said 'Paint', then, 'Paper', then 'Get brush'. She had got the paints and palette herself. She had begun to squeeze the paints out with tremendous force. The first colour had gone into the first well but the successive colours had gone on top of all the preceding ones before getting to an empty well. In this way the first wells in the palette had soon been brimming over the edge and pouring on to the table. There had been an inexorable force about her in this process. I had talked about the need to keep paint in the wells or on the paper and commented on the loss of the bright individual colours. She had begun to tip the palette up on to the paper but with a twist so that it had flicked up on to the wall, floor and therapist. The spilling and splashing had continued and she had rubbed it in, squashing the paper and folding it and opening it. She showed me a white shape appearing and said it was a ghost. It did look just like this and I agreed. She said it was a ghost at night. She then kept folding and smoothing and the ghost was gone with a charcoal grey mess left. She held it up and said it was frightening at night. I said that it was, and wondered where the ghost was gone? She said that he was hiding in the night. I said how frightening that was to think about. She had then tried to flop it on to the table and then on to the chair so that heavy drips of paint had been going everywhere and I had said that we needed to try to keep this on the table. As I had been trying to help her to contain it safely she had begun to try to wrap me in it. I had eventually got it on to the table but the room had become covered in paint and impossible to work in. I had felt that I was to be engulfed in her mental state, as mother and Sally engulfed each other; the painting was being used quite concretely in this way.

Discussion

The painting had become a space for the child Sally to express her fears and anxieties that utterly engulfed her, and then they are almost simultaneously to be projected into the therapist, mentally as well as physically engulfing, but it is a communication of the frightening aspect of night-time from a child, not a dog. The ghost could be an expression of intergenerational trauma, as it was a family with traumatic bereavements. It could also be her projected out anger and aggression, coming back to haunt her, and making it difficult for her to sleep at night.

The pouring out and flooding of paint over all boundaries of wells, palette, paper, table to floor, walls and over ourselves provides a mirror of emotional flooding, and of feeding and toileting difficulties. The spirals of mess and chaos that the sessions became for several months were difficult for us both to survive. A large part of the work was to focus on containment of anxieties. It was not possible to use words very much, as these were experienced as attacking and would escalate the spiralling down into destructive behaviours. Sally's behaviour showed her struggle with wanting to control me and having me as part of her, to be intrusively identified. This means really wanting not to be separate and to control me by being inside me in phantasy, described by Meltzer in elucidating his theory of the claustrum (Meltzer 1992). Any sense of separateness would provoke her to attack my containing capacities, either directly by leaping at me, or by attacks on the room. There was a lot of shredding of materials to pieces and wrecking, so that for both our safeties some materials and objects had to be removed, although I made it clear that they would be returned if they could be used appropriately. At times she seemed to be searching desperately for something bigger to contain her, trying to get into her art folder or her emptied box of toys, under tables or under my chair and into me. The mess in a room has been thought about as a search for a container for those parts that have never had one (Houzel 1995). Another part of her tried to destroy anything that was whole, pretty, beautiful, wanting to downgrade, destroy, break, fragment, or shred, soil, or smear. The struggles of the confused and entangled child can be seen clearly in this alternation between wanting to be inside and part of the object and the ensuing rage as reality intrudes on this phantasy. The main feeling seems then to be to spoil and destroy in rage, because she feels destroyed by separateness.

Attacks on the therapist arouse great anxiety, so that children enter the next session in great fear of what they will find. During this time she would enter uncertainly. Looking at me and realising I was whole and had survived the last session, she would become a dog, which enabled her freely to inspect the room, often the areas where she had attacked most last session. She was also able to do her earlier inspection for evidence of other people, although none of this could be put into words at this time. She would then perhaps come out of this to be a child and might begin to draw with her finger in the sand and ask me to guess what she was doing. I was not usually allowed to be right at this time but in a sense was to be put in the wrong. The kind of bird she drew gave a clue of the sorts of Sally on the surface; a robin might mean friendlier demeanour or a buzzard that something more aggressive might emerge. This interaction might vary in length of time from a few minutes to longer but then there would be this sense of grim determination to destroy the growing understanding. Sand might be tipped out and then the struggle to contain was strong versus the struggle to destroy. The sand tray was used to indicate the sign or omen of the session.

Understanding is hated, because to experience being understood implies that there is another to understand; but also it causes envy of the object that has the capacity to understand, one has to confront difference. Hate is important because it is a rage at the reality of separate existence, but it may also offer the energy to fight which eventually will be in the service of development. Several authors have usefully commented on the difficulty of working with these primitive and powerful feelings. Cantle (1983) discusses hate stirred up in the helping professions, referring to Winnicott's earlier paper (1947). He writes about the part of the client that cannot be borne by himself, particularly in relation to psychosis: 'it seeks refuge in us' (Winnicott 1947: 9) until it can be borne by the client. Winnicott is helpful in thinking about hating the child until they can become lovable again. The importance in this process is also that the therapist needs to be able to contain their stirred up hate, both so that it can be eventually introjected in a modified form but also as a model for the eventual containment of ambivalence. Wood (1997) thoughtfully explores the facing of fear and terror with adult psychotic clients. Her work is informed by Bion's imagery of 'nameless dread', as a state of meaningless fear that comes about in the context of an infant with a mother incapable of reverie (Hinshelwood 1991). The infant therefore reintrojects not a fear of dying made tolerable, but a 'nameless dread' (Bion 1962a).

My understanding of the shift in analytic technique here is that Klein's awareness of the deep conflicts precipitated by psychosis enabled her to contain and detoxify some of the destructive aspects of the patient's mind while working alongside the life supporting aspects.

(Wood 1997: 43)

Greenwood (2000) has very helpfully discussed the inability to function in the therapist when under attack from a traumatised adult client. She describes how an absence of a capacity to think reflectively leads to a shift within the therapist to do with survival rather than 'being understanding' as the terror becomes located in the therapist.

Clay-work: nests of babies

Sally's first successful three-dimensional shape that was completed and kept was a bird's nest. These began to be made as she came out of dog play. They were made empty and open, or with eggs inside, alternatively they could be enclosed, the edges folded in, again, with or without eggs (Illustration 7.3). The first nests were made very simply and were a response to a sense of containment in the session, accompanied by a feeling of calm. The nests were first, a symbol of potential containment for unintegrated parts of Sally. (It is possible that the parents' bedroom had acted previously as a concrete container for anxieties.) However, eggs then appeared at the same time as I was becoming aware of sibling rivalry, so that they seemed to represent mother's

Illustration 7.3 Sally: Bird nests.

fertility and possible rivals as well as her own wish to be that mother having those babies, all these feelings very confused and evident in relation to the therapist in the transference. As to whether the nest was closed in on the eggs or open, this also mirrored separation issues and the claustrophobic/agoraphobic spectrum which is connected to it. The 'nest of babies' fantasy, described by Tustin, is the traumatic awareness of *otherness*, as one comes out of the autistic state, which brings sibling rivalry, in the sense of having to face the fact that one cannot possess everything (Tustin 1972; Houzel 2001).

Session: nests, eggs, and birds

Sally went to get clay and sat on the floor with some on a piece of paper. She began to make a kind of container shape and I asked what it was going to be and she said a nest, a bird's nest. She began to make some eggs while I sat near her. After making quite a few, about eight, she said she wanted to make a bird. I asked if it was to sit on the nest and she said yes, but she could not do it. 'Make me a bird.' I said that I thought she could but it was hard to do. I said that if she could make a start then we could think together about how to make one. This took a lot of patient negotiation. She wanted me to do it for her or to at least start it. If I did that it would immediately have my handprint on it and this sets up a complicated dynamic of comparison and use of the therapist. There is also the difficulty she has in giving worth or valuing herself and the things she makes to consider. When children and adults are projecting themselves into other objects they have very little sense of who they are and what they can do. It feels essential that they have at some time in the therapy to confront their limits and start painfully from their actual ability; that is the only way they will start to grow. I began to wonder out loud about what made up a bird. She said 'beak' and asked me to draw her one. When I said that I thought she could draw a beak she got pencil and paper and drew a very good bird with eggs underneath. She was then able to begin the clay bird making the beak first. She was able to make a separate body and head. The head was then given another beak, pulled out from the head and eyes and then she was able to join the head and body. She then put the bird on the nest but it got smoothed in and attached to the nest with the force of her movements in joining. She took a clay tool to make feathers on the wings. It looked like a bird but the nest and bird were practically joined and the beak was very prominent.

She was able to leave this session in reasonable order and to say the time and day of the next session. The feature of a bird that most attracted her was the beak. This is both a bird's means of feeding, attack and defence (in body terms suggestive of nipple/penis). It was interesting that the eggs were both contained but almost 'inside'. This echoed the separation difficulties. Two sessions later she went to look at the bird/nest and wanted to lift the bird up to look at the eggs. When she was confronted with the two joined there was a moment of panic when she broke off the beak. At this moment in this session she was more in touch with possible movement and felt the panic of being trapped inside but when she had made the bird/nest she had been more in touch with safety and security of being 'inside'. I talked about this difference but she immediately became a dog to shut this out.

Dreams

During this chaotic period Sally and I had begun to have disturbing dreams about each other; in the same week, I woke in the night and 'saw' her face whereas dreams she had had suggested a male transference, and that I had been experienced as a daddy coming between her and mummy. To some extent the result of the dreams had borne this idea out, as when she had woken up frightened from dreaming, she had got back into mother's bed and father had gone into her bed.

Working with confused and entangled children is deeply stressful to therapists, because there are inevitably times when they seem to be able to get right inside you by virtue of their quite pathological processes and use of intrusive identification. When mother and child are so enwrapped there is inevitably going to be a testing time for the therapy as the treatment begins to bite. It is at this point that children are often withdrawn from therapy. Change is frightening, and challenges past ways of being. At a parent meeting, mother had been insightful in thinking that Sally had been angry with me for setting limits in the sessions. At this time we had a short break and then started therapy again. A good relationship with Sally's escort, who received her coming out of therapy, had a drink and biscuit with her, before taking her back to school was crucial, giving a model of therapist and escort as two adults working together.

Stopping the session

There has been occasion when I have had to stop a session with children who are in these extreme states of behaviour – this situation where possibly one might feel failure is little discussed in the literature. This has happened when any part of a therapeutic alliance has been submerged by perverse destructive feelings and to continue would cause harm to both of you. At moments like these the therapy is at risk: if a child is uncontainable, if one of you might be harmed, if the therapist feels pushed out of control by the maddening behaviour, or if the child is escalating the violence through fear which cannot be reached by words or action. In these situations having help from other members of staff is realistic and offers a model where one parent who cannot make a situation work hands over to the other so the situation can be managed together. I would reiterate the time of the next session and day very clearly, and say that I was stopping in order to keep us both safe. It is helpful if there is a safe, neutral space for a child to go to with a member of staff until the end of a session, when they can then leave as usual. In this way the remaining part of the session is a conceptual or notional one in an in-between place that is neither the therapy session as such, but is also not returning to the everyday world. At the height of this spiral of mess and chaos I stopped the session a couple of times with Sally, and in doing so was setting limits as to what was acceptable. She responded in an interesting way the third time I reached this moment, saying very clearly, 'Let's talk about it, I want to stay till the end of the session'. This echoed my own model of saying, 'Let's just think about this for a moment' in the middle of play, and also the model at school of having time to talk things over instead of going into action.

Furniture jumping

One change that I noticed was that the physical attacks on the room and therapist could become more contained into a physical activity that was not destructive as such. For example, Sally had been asking for water to drink and then both drinking it and spilling it deliberately. She wanted to drink from the session and take something in from me but feelings to spoil this were also coming to the surface. I talked of this and as it got near the end of the session her behaviour escalated. I tried to talk calmly of Sally upset, upset Mrs Case, Sally upset, upset mummy. She then began to move the furniture so that she could jump from one piece to another around the room. She held my hand while she did this, leaning heavily on me. In this way she was able to come into acceptable physical contact and gain concrete support from me that she could feel. She was also 'jumping over the gap' between this session and the next and trying to jump over the painful feelings that the coming separation aroused. It was a rather manic, speedy defence to keep ahead of those feelings. After a while I said 'Sally flying' and she said 'like a bird', grinning with pleasure. These moments of attunement built up and we could enjoy a moment together.

Children who have been lost to a sense of self with such separation problems do not feel as if they are properly in their bodies. This is in stark contrast to the dogs she had become. Sally had had a kind of stiff body armour of encasement and a clumsiness and difficulty of smaller accurate movements. Other children can be the apparent opposite and feel wobbly and pliable with no backbone (Alvarez 1992). The furniture jumping game allowed a stage of body-self exploration with the therapist: a discovery of boundaries and limits and extent to the self. Who am I and what is this body shape I inhabit? With this game there is more room for the possibility of play. She might make as if to punch the lampshade and I could say, 'I think you are teasing me'. It still has moments of more forcible aggression. I could feel giddy with Sally's jumping and moving in a fast circle or that there was an element of coercion in her leaning on me so that it had to be carefully monitored. Physical contact like this or quite often ball throwing between therapist and child can be a way of 'getting in tune together'. There is often a sense of delight to this as a new experience of togetherness. It is a precursor to 'being in tune' in one's mind with thoughts and words.

The struggle of love and hate

Children who fear separation want to keep an experience of 'no difference between us' from being challenged. They seem to find the perception of another quite overwhelming and it may be that they are more sensitive than the ordinary person to awareness of another. It seems to bring with it an explosion of feeling perhaps related to the experience of falling in love and feeling lost in it that the ordinary person might consider unusual phenomena. The awareness of the separate other is like an emotional explosion leaving the child defenceless and open to a maelstrom of love and hate with the realisation of the gap and difference between you and them and the realisation that the other is not under their control. It can be seen how wearing they are for parental figures; the mother particularly. The therapist is the recipient of these strong emotions in the transference. It seems usual for the emotions of love and hate to flip from the former to the latter in a moment. In a sense such intensity of feeling cannot last. There is a suffusion of love, a flip to hate, a maelstrom of aggressive feelings, chaos created and then it comes to an end in exhaustion. Underneath all this is intense fear to keep in mind and with the loss of good object or internal mother at the change from good to bad a strong sense of mockery and triumph. A good internal object is overcome and there is triumph but underlying this destruction is hopelessness and despair. For a child to be put in touch with the destructive part of herself brings more difficulties. It is as if they are a catastrophe that causes damage to their good objects both internally and externally and so there is intense guilt that they will try to defend against feeling. During the chaotic stage, Sally frequently drew a bone in the sand tray at the beginning of the session. This could be seen as 'being under the sign of the bone', which will be returned to in Chapter nine.

Chapter 8

Things that go bump in the night, the 'fish pictures' and the development of clay-work

As far as we know, the unconscious has no vocabulary in our sense; although words exist in it, they are neither more nor less than any other object representation; they do not possess the overriding symbolic function that they will acquire in adult language. They are mainly pictures, images and sounds which, without much ado, change their meaning or merge into one another.

(Balint 1968: 97)

COMING UP OUT OF THE SPIRAL

The third phase of the work could be characterised as coming up, out of the previous spiral of descent into severe disturbance. Children at this stage begin to have moments of being in reach. The themes and behaviour that emerge are testing on the therapist, showing confusion about relationships: sexuality, babies and separation. Sally's battle with destructive and creative urges was given a boundaried arena in clay-work which developed from imprinting to the delineation and cutting out of a shape; producing many opportunities for discussion of substance and realness. During this phase possible trauma was re-enacted by the creation of *mise-en-scène* in the therapy room suggesting both what she may have witnessed and also her fear of abandonment by mother. One day when I had arranged to have the regular session, even though there was a local holiday, Sally remembered, and reminded her parents that there was a session, even though they did not think so. Climbing slowly and painfully up out of the spiral, moments like these were beacons of light, and gave a strong sense that she had the session time and therapy firmly inside. Sally's escort said one day, how much Sally looked forward to each session. There were moments of light-hearted playfulness in the sessions and a huge effort from Sally at these times to articulate carefully rather than her more usual painfully incoherent speech. She really wanted me to understand what she was communicating. At the incoherent times, speech felt strangulated and she often stammered. Many changes were happening in Sally's presentation and she showed a developing personality with aspects of humour and playfulness so that destructiveness was modified. There was movement from the previous chaos to the discovery of some form. A series of fish pictures, play as the *Terminator* and her modelling: these different languages all showed a growth towards differentiation and symbolisation.

Self-containment

In the following session Sally stopped herself enacting a feeling physically and expressed the feeling in play.

Session

Sally had come in and begun to play without speaking. Drawing with one finger in the sand she suddenly threw a large handful of sand out on to the floor. It seemed to be an enacted but potential communication, of a feeling not contained. I wondered if she really wanted to say something to me, let me know that she was feeling upset or tipped out. She held a long look to me, then silently got a piece of paper and tried to scoop the sand up on to it and made a funnel to tip it back into the tray. She then became a dog and told me 'to the shops'. There was a long game of serious play where dog and owner are constantly lost and reunited after a search. I started to wonder out loud about the feelings she might have between the sessions. 'No Mrs Case, where is she, what is she doing, look for her, feel love, feel hate, feel lost and tipped out'.

Discussion

In this way more fluid moments where Sally could tolerate my thinking out loud about possible thoughts and feelings began to be possible. Little islands of reflection happened now and then, interspersed with dog play, chaotic times and spirals of destruction. There were moving moments too. Once, while chasing as a dog, we had both laughed, as I had talked of her love of being chased and the delight of being found; but how she mocked me, who was not to be able to catch her. She declared that the whole room was her den, i.e. a place of safety. She stopped and put her hand on her heart and said, 'I can hear it beating'. She took my hand and said, 'feel it'. I could feel her heart beating wildly but also the sense of connection to parts of her self because the rigid body armour she had had was softening. When Sally surprised me, I thought that she also surprised herself, an important element of play, as something new comes into being (Winnicott 1971). There was an emergence of a Sally who looked better looked after, because she was allowing care and was more rewarding to care for. She had amazed her mother by bringing her a cup of tea when she had not been well and had attempted to make her toast.

I began to notice her use of phrases that I may have used months ago and also that she was repeating what I said to herself, mouthing the words.

Babies

Therapy is about the constant revisiting of the same material but on a new level towards understanding. Children in these states of mind use evacuation as a defence against unthinkable thoughts and feelings so that progress is slow. There is also a perverse wish to hold to theories that deny difference, to avoid the mental pain in accepting reality, which has been exacerbated by the lack of internalised containment (Dubinsky and Dubinsky 1997). This is particularly so around sexuality and gender, leading to a struggle with 'good' thoughts versus 'perverse' thoughts (Meltzer 1973; Haag 1997).

Session

Sally talked about having two girl dogs that were going to have pups together. I wondered if two girl pups could have a baby. She replied, 'they can, they can,' as she farted and did gymnastics around the room. I said that she seemed to be blowing my question away with the fart out of her bottom. I wondered if she might be wondering if babies did come out of bottoms. She was looking at me and farting saying 'what's that noise?' in this way equating words as farts: an attack on meaning and the process of thinking and communication. She then went to the wastepaper basket and tried to put herself in it. Although she was laughing and tumbling about there was a very sad aspect to this in the clear lack of worth that she felt on a deep level.

Discussion

The phantasy that she has two girl dogs is a reference to ourselves, and curiosity about what we might make together; as well as to phantasies of herself and her mother. She does not want to entertain any thinking, however speculative, about how babies are actually made, the origins of babies. This would bring with it a challenge to infantile theories of birth and reproduction and to gender. Underneath this is her appalling lack of self worth, really she equates herself with rubbish and worries that rubbish can only produce more rubbish. At other times it would be a boy dog that has a shit and then has babies. When I tried to explore this she insisted that boys could have babies. Naumberg (1973) has an interesting discussion of a case where a boy used animal images as a 'screen', to explore his concerns and infantile theories in regard to birth and sex. Two further discussions of case material with animal images are Rubin (1978) on work by a schizophrenic child, and Karbin and West (1994) describing animal images as a safe way to explore aspects of self in prison, the work of a schizophrenic man.

Jaws and Charlie – live babies

Two sessions after we had been struggling with material around shit and babies Sally came to the session looking contented and relaxed. She opened her bag and took out a bottle of water with two live tadpoles swimming around in it. There was a lot of conversation about them which was quite clear, and understandable. She was delighted in showing them to me, commenting on their food and how they swam, and their little eyes and mouths. She was clearly pleased to see them swimming and alive. Like Dorothy in the 'Alphabet' (see pp. 22–3) we are engaged together in animal watching, which stimulates thought about herself; looking on parts of her, from a perspective. The tadpoles had different characteristics, one lively, the other quieter and more content to rest and swim occasionally. She told me about catching them and having a large container at home and then very much wanted me to keep them here. They seemed to represent two kinds of baby self as she named them Jaws and Charlie. Jaws bites and might nip me. She wanted me to have room, for the two parts of baby Sally, one that is aggressive and active and might bite, and the gentler quieter one. Worry about this one was occasionally expressed – is it alive? This adds a different dimension to some of the very active behaviour of early sessions in that one part of it may have been to keep feeling alive inside. I talked about her pleasure in the tadpoles and my interest in seeing them and thinking about them with her, but also said that they needed the right habitat to grow. They would be happier in the large container she had at home where they would have the right food. I acknowledged her wish to have these baby self–tadpoles staying with me. In response to my mentioning what they might need to grow she opened the window so that they could have fresh air. In that session we were able to explore her worries about keeping something alive. She went out to the toilet and was anxious that they were still alive on her return. She talked of having tried to bring up baby tadpoles every year for ever but they had always died. There is a sense here that in bringing them to me that I might be able to help her to do this. A similar situation with a child and a plant is described by Rustin (2001). An expression of hope that we together might be able to keep her baby self going which she has not been able to do on her own. At the end she did not want to leave the session, but she was able to verbalise this calling me 'a jobbie' and did not spiral down into chaos.

Things that go bump in the night

Sally's theories about babies suggested the difficulty in accepting mother and father's relationship as being the one from which babies might be made. More awareness of others brings with it the pain of allowing oneself to realise that other people can have relationships between them. This was at first expressed in an inchoate way, i.e. in dumping sand on other chairs (absent, but present, other people) in the room in a rage. Over the next phase, fragments of play gradually enabled a piecing together of why night-time was such a difficult part of family life. It will be remembered that all the family had slept in one room, to counteract primitive fears that they would die in the night if separated. The impact of bereavement trauma in the family and Sally's natural endowment and constitution had combined to produce the entangled picture present at assessment. The entanglement and confusional state of mind had led to a denial of difference and resulting confusion about sexuality and gender. Sexualised behaviour emerged when Sally, was not a dog, but a girl. This was after the soiling and smearing had stopped. A sexually exciting world and masturbatory behaviour can emerge as a way of not experiencing emotional attachment or intimacy of mind. It can also be a way of being joined together in phantasy, stopping actually getting to know each other. It can be as a result of sexual abuse and behaviour becoming sexualised, or result from exposure to adult sexual behaviours. Children learn what is socially acceptable, and what usually takes place in private; some sexualised behaviour in sessions may be because that has not yet been learnt. It may be that the behaviour is in the wrong place, not appropriate to this situation. With some autistic children, height-ened levels of social stimulation, from which they have been cocooned by their defences, can lead to a more general arousal and masturbation, as these defences break down. When these body excitements occur in a child's ther-apy, the countertransference is a most useful and reliable tool in thinking about what one is experiencing.

Dens

Sally began to build dens out of the furniture, often partly under the opposite table, where she had a perspective across to the therapist, and then could become sexually aroused, while inside the construction; awareness of other-ness, was countered by joining-by-masturbation. Again, as with the aggres-sive behaviours, this needed to be spoken to simply at this stage, using one word or short phrases to capture whatever feeling was present such as: lonely, frightened, want mummy, suck thumb, feel better, touch bottom. These episodes in the sessions would sometimes end with her going out to the toilet and on her return she would be in a complete change of mood. This suggested that one set of feelings had been evacuated down the toilet (in phantasy). There was sometimes a switch between a glazed, empty, hollow masturbatory state of mind to a more glittering, possessive attacking feel, an attempt to dominate (Pundick 1999). An original glimpse of awareness of a possible relationship was wiped out by a masturbatory phantasy, avoiding the pain of separateness, but coming out of that brought with it intense pos-sessiveness and destructive angers at being thwarted in attempts to be joined together. Later in the therapy, I spoke quite clearly that this was not appropriate, and that she should come out of her den and talk to me with words, not actions, and she was able to respond to this 'paternal' response (Rhode 1997); whereas at the beginning and at other times it needed to be worked through and understood, reaching the fear of being alone. Like the other disturbed behaviour of soiling and smearing it arrived in an explosive way but gradually extinguished in intensity as thoughts and feelings could be put into images and words between us.

Night-time play

At this time in the therapy, Sally Dog was woken up in the night hearing noises. There are many alarms in the night and this was causing me to wonder about whether it was actual or phantasied activity between the parental couple that caused such alertness. It bought to mind the 'combined object' of the parental couple in intercourse to the eyes of the small child (Klein 1975 [1932]). Sally would create two *mise-en-scènes* with the furniture, the blanket and herself in the semi-darkened room with the curtains drawn. The first was a tangle of blankets, arms, and legs, in a construction which gave me the experience of looking at two people in bed together. The second was made with upside-down furniture and blanket, Sally peering out between a tiny hole, staring at me, which created a child in a cot at night. Children can rapidly create a *mise-en-scène*, with just a few props. This is particularly so for those most disturbed and traumatised by what they have witnessed (Case 1994). At these moments there is no 'as if' we are in another time; there is no difference in the child's mind. We are there at something in the past and it is powerfully created in the therapist through the transference. This creation of a scene in the therapy room is representational of a traumatising event. These moments emerge out of the usual themes in play, but then one has moved on into something deeper. At these times the months of repetitive play around particular themes gets put into place, of preparation for whatever it is to emerge.

Session

I had become very aware of the vigilance Sally had for 'night-time noises', on guard for any evidence of parents together and how disturbed she was by a host of feelings engendered by separateness and wish to have mummy to herself. Sally would draw the curtains saying that it was night-time and I would pretend to go to sleep on the chair and she as a dog on a blanket on the floor. She would crawl across the floor to under the table near me and begin to make a succession of eerie noises, growls, howls, ghostly wails, farm animals, birds and wild animals. It aroused a disturbing quality in the room in the half-light of being in a ghostly jungle where anything supernatural, wild and untamed could happen like the loss of civilisation. The difficult therapeutic task is how to differentiate in this cacophony of different sound/feelings and find words for them.

In the session Sally arranged some furniture and suddenly was a baby in a cot or pram. Inside the frame the atmosphere altered and it was quite eerie. She lay like one dead, then alive, and then like one dead silently clanging at the bars. I had a powerful feeling of being alone in a cot. She began to call for 'mummy' in a small voice that felt eerie but also real. This felt particularly shivery and important after the animal voices that I had heard calling from dark woods over the preceding months. It was very painful to hear her call. I had talked about this calling for mummy and lying in the cot/pram alone and wanting mummy.

In this stage if her feelings got very strong and she began to kick at the furniture I was able to talk about the Sally that could think with me and the Sally that got filled with monstrous feelings. This Sally tried to kick away the feelings because they were so painful. She would abruptly stop and turn towards the clay. This change to clay felt safer and more contained. Bringing in a medium brought in a useful space enabling slightly less direct communication person to person, which was more bearable. The play as a dog was beginning to state a problem or question. She would then change to being a child exploring the issue in clay. Clay helped to create a benign work ambiance.

Clay-work

Sally would say 'clay' or 'get the bucket' and there was the most precarious sense in the room of something on a knife edge; as if the situation could collapse. A fragile transitional space was coming into being, which eventually became her creative space. Oremland writes that the: 'primary anxiety in creativity is the anxiety of aloneness' (Oremland 1997: 55). He links creativity with the recreation of the transitional mother – a protective aegis under which exploration (separation) with safe reunion can occur. Clay, with its strong pliable body qualities, has the power to stimulate primary sensory experience, as well as absorbing and giving shape to powerful feelings. The fact that it can transform through a cycle, from wet, to dry, to being fired, to being permanent, having many different qualities on the way makes it a versatile medium able to survive ill-treatment by the handler, yet sensitive and responsive to the lightest impression. Many art therapists have discussed its propensities. Lydiatt (1971) gives an accessible, jargon free 'feeling response' to the modelling of psychiatric patients in a studio setting with many quotes on their own thoughts about the things they made. Kramer has numerous references to clay in her work with clients; here I shall mention Dwayne, who worked through trauma in sculpture with clay, and a blind child, Eduardo where clay functioned as a transitional object (Kramer 1979).

Kramer comments: '. . . a forgiving material that can endure endless doing and undoing, absorb destructive cutting and poking and still permit the making of well-integrated handsome sculptural work' (Kramer 1999: 10). Henley (2002) gives a good wide practical overview of the uses of clay with children both individually and in groups with some interesting examples of work with children on the autistic spectrum, from the perspective of the art therapist potter. Some earlier papers are also relevant, on annihilation anxiety and the use of clay in facilitating the development of object relations (Henley 1991, 1994, 2001). Rubin (1978) writes on the parallel of clay structures and internal structures becoming firmer; Kwaitkowska (1978) with families in art therapy where there is a child with schizophrenia; Dalley (1990), on clay as a container for vulnerability with children; Robbins, as an aid to regression (1987); Serrano (1989), Anderson (1995), Nez (1991), Waldman (1999), with survivors of incest; Gerity (1999), with dissociative and borderline patients, discusses how clay both physically and psychologically is able to absorb toxins. In psychotherapy, Gampel (1993) follows Pankow (1961, 1981) in aiming to access the archaic preverbal which is held within body-centred experiences, through the making of Plasticine images *before* coming to therapy, though this approach loses all the dynamics of the making in therapy as material to be worked with.

Cutting out

Sally using the clay made a space together in which something new could form. The imprinting of animals had been a first kind of impression into the body of the clay; and was followed by delineation, as she tried to draw a line in felt tip around the animal, but, the colour got lost and absorbed into the wet clay. A new development was to want the animals pressed into the clay as before, but then cut out (Ilustration 8.1). The most enormous tension accompanied this activity between whether they would be cut out or cut up. One could feel the strong impulse to cut across the animal body; a powerful wish to annihilate. Talking about this, I would do most of the cutting out at first, gradually letting her take over as she grew in confidence. She needed a model to watch. She had little capacity to vary her pressure, or control the heaviness of her movements; she needed to see the possibility in action. This tension is indicative of the pull towards destructive impulses and the wish to make creatively. Sally struggled with the wish to stay part of the whole-mother-clay-body. Movement towards separation, brought realisation of otherness, a rage that would cut it up, was battling with an emergent new shape. Stokes (1972) associated the two modes of art, carving and modelling, with the paranoid-schizoid and the depressive positions respectively. He wrote that: 'A powerful sublimation of aggression contributes to the "attack", as it is called, in the use of the medium of an art, irrespective of what content is communicated' (Stokes 1955: 419). He thought that each work of art, combined fusion

Illustration 8.1 Sally: Cut-out imprints.

and 'object-otherness', in differing proportions (Stokes 1973). The cut-out animals, separated from the ground of background clay were part of Sally's taking on a shape apart from mother; which was experienced as a painful struggle, literally cut away. She was developing a growing sense of self.

At first, I could only encourage her to make a token attempt at cutting round the pressed shape of the animal she had chosen with great difficulty. Then she was able to do the cutting with my holding the wet clay still for her. I would withdraw my help or modify what I would do depending on what she was able to attempt. She was soon able to cut more and more and I would lift away the excess clay as she went so that she could see the shape emerging. In the next stage she began to go over the cut-out shape and modify it. One could see the sense of ownership and achievement developing, and the moderation of aggressive impulses, as care for the object grew stronger. What she was doing seemed to be in tune with the ambience of the session and to be an expression of the transference so that a quiet feeling of togetherness working around the cut-out animals might produce a mother and baby. She would put them together saying, 'Baby', smiling. Conversation around the animals would lead into an exploration of differences through thinking about the different quality of each animal.

Inner space and language

In the last week before a long break there was confusion about sessions, partly due to outings in the institution. Sally was not brought for therapy at the right time but I had been able to suggest another time in the day that would be our last session.

Session: insides

Sally arrived clutching a bag of plastic animals that she had evidently planned to bring to use in the session with the clay. I said that I thought she had been expecting to see me in the morning and she said, 'yes', and I said that I had been expecting to see her too. Her eyes widened intently listening to me. I talked about the muddle and how confusing I thought it had been for her. I commented on her bringing something in with her and she showed me the animals and added that they were hers. We talked of the work made here which is to stay in the therapy room until the end of our work together and I clarified that we were at a break not the ending. We also talked of these animals that were hers to take away when she wanted. Various animals were drawn round and cut out of clay. She then took a baby hippo out saying, 'this is a verraay difficult one!' I wondered if this was a challenge to me, to be able to cut it out. She smiled and began to make Donald Duck noises. I wondered if these were to be encouraging or to put me off cutting carefully. She laughed and made more noises. I wondered what had happened to her voice and where had it gone. I began to talk of the difficult shape of the baby hippo that had fat little legs. After making a few more noises she joined me in commenting on the hippo. She was enormously interested in the shape and if I could cut it out successfully. She is talking to me as if I am the risky part that might suddenly cut into the baby hippo's body. Here, the destructive risky part has been split off into me and she can relate to it, as I take the risk in cutting. It is my ego that has to bear the strain. It is possible to see the importance of splitting in such an interaction. The weight of impulses to harm is safely on my shoulders and she can enjoy the peaceful atmosphere of working together. I talked of how the clay gives an impression of the hippo. The idealisation of our relationship, which is a consequence of splitting off the more aggressive feelings, was then clearly shown as she fabricated a story of having two turtle-doves as pets from the pet shop, which went coo together.

She had taken the image of the doves from the wood pigeons that billed and cooed outside the room in the trees that she sometimes enjoyed watching (see Chapter three).

In this ideal atmosphere she began to ask questions about the pig, another little plastic animal. 'Was it real?' I said, 'No, it is a model animal'. She then asked what was inside. I talked of her curiosity about insides and said that I thought it did have an inside and was not empty. She then pointed to an impression of an animal in the clay and said 'Is this full?' I said, 'No, it is the hollow of a shape of the animal'. She then started making noises, torn between wanting me to talk and hating it. These are really philosophical questions on the nature of realness. She is struggling to understand the representation of a pig, which is a pig, but is not real. They also illustrate the convex/concave planes in her mind and her struggles with what is real. How do people and things have an inside and outside? One consequence of confusional entanglement is that the child's development is affected, and with this the lack of a mind that can have a space in which to think thoughts. While I was cutting out the next animal she pushed the following animal into the clay to make an impression so that we made a production line of clay animals. She began to visit me with the cow. It dabbled its feet in the clay nearby where I was cutting and she mooed realistically. There had been a discussion about udders while I had been cutting out a cow and she had asked if men cows had them. The cow went away and found the calf that now fed from the mother cow. The session ended with our washing the clay bits off the animals together and this brought forth new questions about realness as she put the animals to dry on the window sill. Was it important that they were dry; could harm come to them if they were wet?

Discussion

It can be seen from the material that the clay-work offers many opportunities for exploring realness and dimensionality. Questions about animals enable questions about aspects of our animal selves, like sexuality, feeding and nurturing behaviour. With the splitting off of more aggressive feeling she is able to enjoy feeding from the opportunities that the therapy has to offer. Added on to this was a new playfulness with the animals so that if I were helping to cut out a particularly difficult shape another animal would come to visit, sometimes expressing jealousy by impatiently digging hooves in the clay beside where I was working. She was very painfully struggling towards some separation with awareness of others, in questions. Who else came here? What did they make? Will they touch my things? Rather than being expressed in a dog guarding its territory it was in questions from a human girl. Britton (1989) has very helpfully described the collapse of the 'spatial structure of experience' in terms of failure to achieve a triangular space in which thought can occur. If a paternal element is not securely established then the child becomes confused with mother and thought does not develop (Rhode 1997). Bringing in a medium creates a triangular interaction, which fosters the third perspective of the oedipal triangle.

The clay, with its solid down-to-earth and concrete nature, promoted a burgeoning interest in words. For instance, Sally came into a session and in rapid succession was a dog that caught a fox and then similarly stalked and caught a cougar. She then stood up and was a child going to get the clay. I talked about how she had wanted me to know about these three different parts of her here today, the dog Sally, the fox Sally and the cougar Sally. We knew from previous work that they represent: a part that can interact, and work with me; a wily part; and a wild, aggressive part. The dog part of her had to stalk and catch the other two parts before work could be done. She then made three cut-around animals, struggling very hard with the cutting until a donkey, horse and bull emerged. To my surprise she asked me to write 'donkey' and then horse and then bull. This naming of things seemed to follow directly my naming of parts of the self. She then took it a stage further by asking for paints. These were in a wrecked and smashed up state from past rages but we were able to find a range of colours and arrange them in the broken lid and the animals were coloured appropriately. She talked of the different colours. The struggle to learn is a difficult one because the opposition is both wily and aggressive. This was clearer when there was a calmer space to see the struggle at work. This combination seems to contribute to perverse behaviour.

Changes

What is being made is now clearly related to our relationship and a response to what is happening in the sessions but external events in her life are also being brought into the session to be thought about. Two years into the therapy her pet dog died and was replaced by another fairly rapidly. She told me about the loss of her dog and then she started furniture jumping, holding my hand. I talked of the death of her dog and the deadening feeling inside her and the wish to jump over that feeling. She then tried for the first time to make a dog without using the plastic animals. She did a clay ball for the head and then facial features, naming these. She then made a fat ball for the body that was stuck on and then a tail, showing me. She talked of her new dog wagging his tail. It was too much for her to get a head and body joined which symbolically might be like joining thoughts and feelings – she scrunched it up. To make a shift, to the making of things entirely of her own, was going to mean the development of toleration of frustration as well as toleration of feeling. We knew from past behaviour that angry disappointment could be overwhelming. She had to struggle with her own inner destructiveness that could be opposed to anything whole or good being made, as well as the limits of her ability. To some extent they intertwine. She was moved to try to make a dog without using plastic animals as a response to loss; as a way of preserving some loved qualities in her pet. Clay is able to take a lot of bashing, cutting, smearing and other attack without losing its essential qualities. This sense of clay having a body, that can survive punishing behaviour, is useful.

Mother had reported to the family worker that Sally had made her first friend locally at this time. This could be seen as an advance in different ways. It is reaching outside the family, to what another, representing the external world, has to offer. It could be a great help to her in growing awareness of another point of view. It was also a sign of a move towards latency and normalisation.

The *Terminator*

Development in therapy commonly loops back, just as it does with ordinary development in children. Changes are happening but one suddenly realises that an emergent state has firmed up and become established. Sally had become looser in feel and less physically armoured. This brought with it the sensation of pain if she hurt herself which she had not apparently experienced before. As one might imagine, being a dog or other animal means spending a lot of the session time on all fours and she would now complain and show me rubbed knees and would also be aware of banging or knocking herself while active in the room. All this gradually crept into the session.

A robot character appeared in 'hide-and-seek'. Sally would hide under a blanket standing stock still in the room or lie in the middle of the room on the floor. In each instance a little bit would come alive at a time, a hand twitching and then an arm moving and a foot, then leg and so on. She would then suddenly jump out and 'It is Sally!' Later this was played without the blanket but with her face hidden by having her eyes shut and her head down and she would emerge in a similar way. She sometimes named herself as the *Terminator*. There was a spawning of a whole series of these action films with hero's part human/part robot, with the human part breaking through bringing vulnerability; others are wholly robot and unstoppable forces of destruction. All give some form of expression on the screen to the wish to be invincible and beyond hurt; to eradicate all trace of vulnerability, dependence and helplessness, although, all too human emotions break through.

This move felt a significant one for Sally. Previously she had been held in by physical body armour, with emotions apparently eradicated. Now she could have tears in her eyes if she hurt herself and was also vulnerable to the ebb and flow of school group relationships as well as family sibling rivalry. The body armour could now be symbolised as she played out being the *Terminator*, enacting the emergence of Sally.

Humour

Another emergent part of Sally was her humour. I would talk about the teasing Sally and the humorous Sally. Physical humour, of the slapstick variety, had come first; over being a dog and wanting to be chased. The teasing naturally developed out of a growing ability to control aggressive impulses and just making as if to do something destructive, in order to try and get a reaction from me. There is an enjoyable sense of power for a child in this. 'I could do this to upset you and hurt you if I wanted to, but I won't'. The impulse is moderated by love to the object and perhaps awareness of the consequences. The carrying through of the destructive impulse destroys the positive feelings present. Some of the aggression is moderated and converted into teasing and becomes more socially acceptable. Verbal mocking humour then developed.

This was a great relief because it brought attacks on the therapy out into the open, but in a more workable form. The humour brought a lighter quality; even though it was attacking, it was not physically attacking. I was not having to be aware of our safety; and could think more clearly in the spaces that were available from time to time. An example of the new mocking element might be that she would ask me to train her and I would talk with her about what this might mean in the context of that particular session. She then said that I had to ask for 'paw' which I did, wondering where this was leading. After doing it 'correctly' she followed this by presenting her back leg having turned round, as if the dog had got it wrong. Her smile and general demeanour showed how aware she was of what she was doing. It was funny, but also mocking, and vividly demonstrated how she presented me with her bottom or rear end instead of responding with her head and thoughts. She seduced me into play and then turned the tables on me. TTP (Taking The Piss), the adaptive mechanism of humour on a social and mental level, has been discussed in work with adult psychotic patients (Greenwood and Layton 1991). It can allow very powerful feelings to be stated in a bearable manner. In a similar way with many of her emerging questions about life and three-dimensionality she embarked on something meaningful and then the desire to pervert it and give me her rear end was strong. The Donald Duck language which she would revert to when not able to maintain meaningful thought was a kind of talking with your bottom.

Playfulness

The emergence of playfulness brings with it the possibility of more flexible role-taking in play. Such reversal is very useful in the therapy as it enables the beginning of seeing another point of view. For instance she is playing at night-time and I am to be asleep and so is she, as my dog. Each time I am to be woken by bangs, thumps, tail thumping, and sound in the night. This was repeated many times and I was to settle her each time. I then changed from talking about the puppy that hears noises in the night and cannot bear to be apart from its owner to trying to think how this was like children who feel left out of their parents' bedroom at night. They are unable to sleep because they want mummy or daddy and do not like to feel left out of whatever they are doing. Sally began to shout 'Go to sleep' at me, trying to stop me talking. This suddenly changed to 'Go to sleep, baby'. With this shift we had both become human and she was now a tired harassed mother, who I, as the baby, had been keeping from sleeping. Sally, in this unaccustomed role, was suddenly speaking very clearly. She became more insistent and threatening, 'You'll get a tanning on your backside!' She continued, 'Go to sleep!' very firmly. I was then able to verbalise how left out I felt and wanted to know what mummy and daddy were doing in my role as wakeful, curious and disturbed baby. Later, I was able to talk about how very painful it was to be apart from mummy and for mummy and daddy to be together. Talking about feelings was likely to send her into manic activity and diversionary tactics. If it was possible to put them into words in role as the baby then she could both hear the feelings but also feel relief that I have them, not her. This is in a similar way to taking the brunt of the anxieties around cutting out and cutting up until she is able to let these things be felt for herself.

I realised that each move forward would happen first of all on an animal level before the human equivalent. Therefore, the beginning of thinking with me about thoughts and ideas and feelings took place while she was in a collie form of a female dog. The dog would look as if she were struggling to understand when I spoke, but it is in another language; which it must have felt like at times. I wondered if Sally located herself in animal form because of the seemingly incomprehensible nature of human activity.

The external world was beginning to attract Sally and parallel with this was her use of different tenses while talking: she has a future and a yesterday as well as the present. One day she surprised me by beginning to talk about today, that is, ordinary events in school, and the fact that she was going swimming tomorrow which she likes. It was not straightforward to understand each other as I thought at first she was having a bath tomorrow, but she was able to clarify this mistaken understanding by making vigorous swimming motions. It can be seen that the external world is exerting more pull on her and that there is a growing part of her that can respond. It has always been there, but something inside and her external circumstances have combined to make her not take up what it has to offer. Her hands were beginning to heal and there were long gaps before something happened that resulted in her attacking them again.

Language: consonants and vowels

One possible explanation for Sally's language distortion became apparent. Two extracts, one from the start of therapy and one in the second year will help in the elucidation.

Session: start of therapy

She was staring at me and moving her hands about in the sand so I asked if I looked the same since the last time she saw me or had I changed perhaps? She said 'Your hair'. I said 'Does it look different, longer? She said 'My mum, it's the same as my mum'. I said, 'Your mum and I have the same hair, I remind you of mum'. She looked down and moved the sand and then said with great difficulty, 'C- a- r- o- l- i- n- e'. I said, 'Yes'. She said, 'Your name is Caroline'. I said, 'Yes, Caroline Case'. She enunciated each individual letter sound so that it sounded both grotesque and beautiful. I thought, repelled by sounds and touched by feeling. She then said 'paint' flatly, moving to the sink.

Discussion

There was a great contrast between her sentence and this flat one word monotone which seemed to take us back into the realm of the dead. She is clearly in a powerful transference to do with her mum and this elicits both the grotesque and the beautiful; that is, perhaps, the dilemma of the entangled child. It is both to be entangled with the desired object but also to be in a grotesque confusion as to what feeling and experience belongs to whom. Each sound seemed to have a separate feeling, separated from meaning. At this point in the first weeks of therapy I had heard the grotesque and beautiful mixture but I had not registered that it might relate to consonants and vowels.

Session: second year

As she began to leave limbs sticking out from under the blanket in a way that suggested two people, I was being given the experience of seeing two people in bed and being the third. I talked of this and she responded with Donald Duck noises and abruptly left the blanket and came to the table to make something with clay. I talked of the exciting and painful feelings when she felt left out of mummy and daddy being together. I thought that she had turned to clay today as a way of getting away from these feelings. She then said, and wrote, 'f-u-k you' and wanted me to say it. I was interested in her speech because the way she says this separates the vowels and consonants as distinct entities. Later, she wanted me to say 'f-u-c-t' which is a combined fuck and cunt. Wrestling with painful awareness she began to draw on a picture on the wall in my room, a picture of *Jane Seymour* by Holbein, which is a sketch, combining clear lines and suggestions of lines (Case 1995, 1996, 2000a). She was interested in tracing the outline of the figure, keeping on the line.

Discussion

Awareness of sexual difference and of the coupleness of parents can be painful. Her struggle has been to find the outline of herself in relation to her separate parents, particularly mother. One of the reasons that she may have found speech so difficult is that consonants are hard and closed in the mouth and vowels soft and opening. They correspond in this way with the first combination in the mouth of hard nipple and soft lips and the later sexual coupling of genitals in intercourse. If you are struggling to keep any awareness of relationship from your mind, then the discovery of sounds and words and that put together they have meaning will be hard to develop. It took me back to the first saying of my name by Sally when each letter was given an individual sound. Meaning is destroyed, if no connections are allowed to be made. Sally's voice from the grave at the beginning of therapy could be thought about as a voice from which all emotional link had been eradicated. In this session, although she is fighting my making of meaning from what she is showing me, her drawing self traces an outline, which suggested that this painful struggle was giving her a sense of where she began and ended.

Just before a break, shortly after the above session, she was feeling like rubbish that I was throwing away. She showed this by standing silently and robotically in the wastepaper basket. I asked her if she could find some words for how she felt about the break. She at first created a messy room of spilled out sand and water and I talked of how this might feel, but could she put it into words, not action. She responded by writing, 'fuck y crlne'. In this, most of the soft vowels are left out and the hard consonants remain. I talked about the loss of loving feelings at this time and how mainly hating feelings were left as she felt I was leaving her and would not have thoughts of her in my mind over the holiday. Amongst the mess she had made she took out a piece of paper with wet sand on it and named it sand paper. As she separated this, from the mess on the floor, it suddenly felt more contained. She had a mixture of abrasive and soft and this seemed to be a way of combining some essence of loving and hating feelings. She had found a way to name this, perhaps a concrete pun, because it needed the actual object to be present. Tustin (1972) describes 'intolerable frustration' experienced by autistic children in their early development:

> It has been my experience that at these levels, the painful tension of pent-up frustration is experienced in a bodily way as grit, gravel, prickles, tiny broken-up bits of crunchy stuff, bits of broken glass, or some such discomforting irritant.
>
> (Tustin 1972: 82)

In sessions, we struggled to develop a shared communication; images or words that we could both comprehend. Space does not allow for a further discussion of speech with children in these states of mind which will be put into a future paper, but Sally's use of language does suggest that we use language with an element of idiosyncrasy, in our gesture and inflection, which has a three-dimensionality, a unique voice; as well as language shaping our relationship to the world, in the sense of social discourse, both take place. Meltzer's work has been helpful: '. . . inner speech, must find an object in the outside world which has sufficient psychic reality and adequate differentiation from the self, to require the vocalisation of this inner process in order for communication to take place' (Meltzer 1975: 193).

In Lacanian therapy the formative role of the desires and demands of 'the Other' in shaping the desire, identity and symptoms of the child, is given a large weight. Lacan sees language as the structuring medium of human intersubjectivity; even 'preverbal interactions' of mother and child are 'linguistically mediated interactions'. Mannoni thought, in a Lacanian mode, that the mother's fantasy and history are 'inscribed in the emotionally troubled child's symptoms, body image, and capacities for verbal and artistic expression' (cited in Brenkman 1999: xxiii). The child's own desires and fears have to be separated from those of the parents.

The fish pictures

The first picture to emerge out of the chaotic and aggressive stage had been a fish picture. At this time a new dog game had developed: the owner went to the park and the puppy did not want to come but then escaped from the house where it had been left and surprised the owner at the park. She had found this very funny, especially the surprise bit and that the puppy had been out alone. She had been playing out a wish that she could follow me and appear in my life out of the session, but also with the idea of independent moving and thinking. One morning I had sat down after a short time and had said that when one was chasing a pup it was better to sit down because then they were curious about what you were doing and came to you. She had said 'No, they did not', but had sat down as I had on a chair, and had asked if I had glue.

Mummy fish and baby fish

There had been glue, because I had gradually been replacing materials lost during the chaotic period. She had got one blue sheet of paper and two white sheets and had taken them all to the table. She had folded the white paper in half and had drawn half a fish, then had cut it out. She had called the fish, a little fish, and had made a black eye and rough marks in black felt-tip. She had commented on the fish shape remaining from cutting out the fish, and had said to 'keep that'. I had said that it was the shape of a fish and a whole fish and she had said 'I was talking crap'. She had been annoyed that I was making a differentiation between the two shapes, the figure and ground. I think there had been a difficulty here in having a negative shape, leftovers, or pieces that one might normally throw away, because of the difficulty of separation. This is very noticeable in children who are struggling with separation or denying it, that they must also keep the background – although it has been cut out it is still psychically part of the whole (Case 2002).

She had decided to cut out a big fish. She had kept repeating, 'This is a big fish, isn't it? It's a mummy'. The little fish was stuck to the third piece of paper and cut out, so that she had a little fish with two sides. She had then stuck this on to the big mummy fish (Illustration 8.2). She had got her felts, and had begun to colour the big fish's fin. There had been accompanying talk about it being a colourful fish, that these were nice colours. She had been colouring really carefully and then had hit a patch of glue that affected the felt, but had managed to weather this setback, which had been quite an achievement. She had then done scribbly colouring in the main body of the fish. As she had coloured on she had become self-conscious of doing something 'nice' and shouted 'What!' at me.

This is a difficult transition, when children have been continually overcome by a destructive part and begin to come out of it. It is quite fragile, a new-found enjoyment and investment in producing something whole. At that moment when she shouted 'What!' she projected on to me a question from

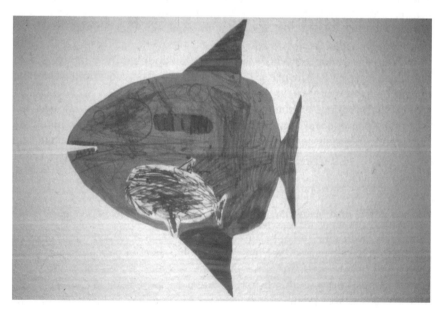

Illustration 8.2 Sally: Mummy fish and baby fish.

within herself as to what she was doing, which was aroused by my attention to her. She knew that I was a separate person having thoughts of my own. It was as if part of her could not believe what she was doing (so carefully). As she coloured on she had continually asked 'Is it nice?' I had wondered whether this was a wish for reassurance, or a difficulty in knowing what was nice or nasty, or if she was scribble-colouring an attack on the mummy and wondered if I knew, or if she had been drawing some of the confused feelings about her internalised mother. I had talked about the difference between the black baby fish, the brightly coloured fin of the mummy fish, and the scribbly body. She had said that the baby was black but would grow into a big colourful fish like the mummy. When she had finished it had been folded up and put in her folder. The baby fish that was stuck to the outside was a good representation of the difficulties of mothers and children struggling with separation. If you are stuck like glue then all goes swimmingly well. This first fish picture became part of a series, where feelings could be symbolised. The pictures enabled talk around painful areas of her experience. They had a different quality to the earlier 'pets-that-were-also-her' pictures.

Killer whale/Free Willy

As before she suddenly asked for paper, felts, glue, and scissors and drew a large fish. She mentioned several times that it was big. She began to ask me about what I did with other children who came to me for sessions, some of whom she knew. I answered straightforwardly, and repeated what she knew, that I did not discuss other children's work. She then scribble-coloured the fish and called it a Killer Whale/*Free Willy*, as she did the teeth. It is both an image of aggressive feelings now more under her control, and an image of the struggle towards separation – the killer whale that needs help to come out of confinement in the film of that name. She then drew a dog she had been playing, who had pups. She wanted me to write the words for *Free Willy* and I wrote them on a piece of paper thinking that she would copy them but she cut them out and stuck them on the picture. The dog with pups is a separate image of mother/therapist with her other children/patients. She then drew her bird, Sparky, and this brought forth some talk about him, how he lived in her room and kept her awake with his 'chattering'. She had frequently told me to stop my 'chattering', so that I understood this as an image of the therapist who keeps her awake with the thoughts she has and communicates to Sally.

Mummy, baby shark, and very big fish

In this session, with the Christmas break approaching, Sally was in a hard aggressive mood that felt as if it would deteriorate into something destructive. The initial dog play replayed themes back to the lead, the shop, and the park.

She then picked out a small piece of black paper and drew a shark that is a baby. She then drew a mummy shark on white paper that has teeth. They were cut around with the negative shapes kept as usual and the mummy shark was scribbled in brown (Illustration 8.3). The baby shark was stuck to the mummy shark, Sally saying that they were side by side. I talked about the baby shark stuck to the mummy shark and how safe this felt but how dangerous when they were apart, with reference to the break. She replied with a string of swear words.

She then drew 'a very big fish'. This had rough camouflage lines and contained a rough fin-shape, rather penis-like and the black felt-tip went through causing a hole. This was the mummy fish me, containing daddy's penis and all the feelings she was struggling with, of me with my partner before the break. She was commenting on the big teeth that the fish had and how it could really bite me. She showed an orally based anger about the break and talked of her dog just having a bone, so that it felt as if the breast was somehow denuded, stripped bare by her anger and realisation of loss with the break. At times like this, words feel very attacking to her, as if I have the bigger teeth.

Dolphin

Through the animal world she is able to explore ideas and play with them, finding some containment and expression in the images. After the Christmas break, she made a fish shape, on white paper, calling it a dolphin. She did

Illustration 8.3 Sally: Mummy shark and baby shark.

some teeth and then asked if dolphins had teeth. We talked about this and she said that they are friendly to man. I was then to keep hold of the dolphin and the surround. A much larger shark, on black paper, followed, with much larger teeth and she said that the shark is larger but the dolphin can fight it better and win (Illustration 8.4). There was some play with the two of them, their mouths against each other. I talked of the dolphin that is friendly to man and the shark that we think of as being able to bite or attack man. She needs to continually play out and play with this problem for her which is about the two conflicting feelings she can have towards the same person. There was a move forward from the two tadpoles some time previously, as the dolphin, friendly to man, although smaller, is stronger in the fight between the two sides. Previously the larger more active tadpole, Jaws, 'could bite me'.

There is now a balance between the creative and the destructive and between the speaking and the devouring in the work with Sally. Cirlot writes: 'The mouth is the point of convergence between the external and the inner worlds' (Cirlot 1962: 222). You cannot bite and speak at the same time. The making of the fish pictures enabled talk around these painful areas. Sally had moved from an adhesive identification, to intrusive identification, to projective identification that could be used for communication rather than just evacuation of unprocessable feelings. A potential space had developed where the making of images fostered a symbolising capacity. The use of

Illustration 8.4 Sally: Shark and dolphin.

clay allowed her an experimental field, fostering these developments as well as providing feedback in a physical mirroring of psychic developments, alongside the relationship with the therapist. The original selective mutism had been like an internal loop but now she was moving towards a distinction between internal and external experience.

Chapter 9

The heart and the bone

Often the hands know how to solve a riddle with which the intellect has struggled in vain.

(Jung 1960: 86)

NURTURE AND NARRATIVE

In this fourth phase of the therapy, several developing themes emerged in the clay-work. The first of these was the 'encasing of animals', demonstrating the wish to be out in the world (heads showing) and the other impulse, to remain in her defences. The second was the making of 'animals in an environment with nurturing elements', which facilitated the developing internalisation of the elements necessary for maturation to take place and brought discussion of specific feelings on to the agenda. The third was the move towards three-dimensionality in her clay modelling. This was instrumental in her psychic development. In this phase it became more possible to understand the signs in the sand tray: the heart and the bone, as a metaphor for her internal struggle with three-dimensionality and flatness. Sally went through a 'lion phase' which was linked to her courageous psychic struggle to 'make something that looked real'. Interwoven with her clay-work were developing scenarios and narratives based on dog and rabbit characters which gave expression to, and experimentation with, her preoccupations to do with relationships.

Clay-work

Sally had developed a ritual at the beginning of clay-work; throwing me a lump of clay and asking me to roll it into a ball for her. This had been a moderation of an impulse to throw it at me/to me, which at first had fought inside her. As she got the clay out she would frequently throw the bucket, that the clay had been in, over her head, across the room. There was a ritual quality to both these actions. She seemed to want me to touch the clay, as if it would be imbued with some of my qualities, in a magical way, before she used it, suggesting participation mystique. At first, when this space for making had been so precarious, I had not commented, but now we were able to talk about it. The throwing of the bucket, which was deliberate, had a sense of 'we have no need of containers', and I approached this at first in a practical way, rather than the psychological; clay needs to be kept in a container or it will dry out, and be unworkable, everything needs particular care in order to work at its best. Later, it could be approached more directly in relation to *her* need to be looked after, to be contained.

A fear, that the things she made might be touched, spoiled or interfered with was present at this period. Various hypotheses jostled for attention. First, she was very worried about other children touching her things, the old issue of sibling rivalry. Second, Klein (1928, 1929) has written about the fear for one's own babies/productions being damaged by attacks by mother, in the sense of retaliation for one's own attacks on mother internally, in phantasy. Third, touch seems to bring life to her clay-work after the clay is handled by the therapist; could it also bring death, by a bad handling? Fourth, 'bad touching', also brings to mind physical abuse and/or sexual abuse, but there was no evidence that this was present. Alternative ideas have to be held in mind, until the material is clear, as will be seen later in the chapter (pp. 193–4). There was a struggle stage by stage, to gain skills and independence. In children with such intense separation difficulties, the more ordinary sense of achievement in a new skill is rarely as strong as the wish to be the looked-after baby. This pleasure in new skills does get established, but it is often a slow and tortuous route.

Fear for objects made/encasing of animals

Session

Sally got the clay and ordered me to 'Get the animals'. I questioned this, saying to her, that she had legs and would be able to find them in her box. She suddenly began to play at not having legs, smiling and saying, 'no legs' making her way on bottom and knees, squirming to the box and back. I talked of a baby part of her that did want Mrs Case to get them, and a more independent part, who could enjoy going to get them and be pleased at being able to do this. There was a warm atmosphere in the room and she chose a lion animal to try and press into the clay. She had some struggle with this and was making it difficult by pressing so hard at the clay. She shouted 'What!' at me, which she often did when there was a feeling of warmth and intimacy: the 'What!' distances. When the lion had been cut out she thought about making something else, but then smeared clay on the wall. I talked of her enjoying the feeling of being here but how another part of her wanted to destroy that warm feeling and the calm and safety. When she continued, I stood up, and caught her hands and said that I thought she was misusing the clay and that she did know very well how to use it and other materials, pencils, paints, etc. She several times said 'nah!' Then, she did sit down and settled to making a nest shape.

The lion she had cut out was going to be 'Simba' the son of the Lion King from the film of that name. She now said that she was going to make a den for Simba, from the beginnings of the nest. She said that I was not to touch it, expressing fear for her creations. She vacillated about the den. She both seemed to want space for the lion and yet also to protect him, so that she made the opening larger and then smaller in turn. She then covered the lion in a blanket of clay so that the nest/den was open but the lion was covered. She added a name-plate in clay, saying Simba.

Discussion

The Disney story of Simba is one in which a lion cub loses his father but then has to find his way to take his place as king of the pride of lions. The play and work showed the helpfulness of this identification with father, in aiding her independent action. The encasing of animals went on in the following sessions (Illustration 9.1). I talked about this in several ways. An image of herself and how she was pulled between wanting to emerge (most of the encased animals had their heads sticking out) and wanting to be safe and

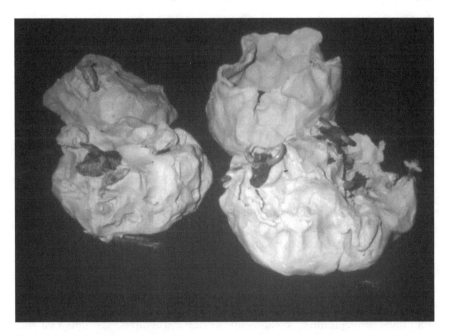

Illustration 9.1 Sally: Encased animals.

protected inside, hidden from the world. I talked of the wish to be in and the wish to be out, of how she could feel safe inside but also trapped. Of how she could feel enjoyment of being out but also scared. Meltzer's claustrum theory (1992) is helpful in thinking about the powerful phantasy of being inside mother's body. This had been evident from the beginning of work with Sally in the making of dens, and hiding under my chair, peering up secretly watching me. The encased animals with their heads sticking out suggested that she had reached an important stage of transition, poised on the doorstep of the inner/outside world.

The beginning of a sense of containment for chaotic feelings (the first nests), had been swiftly followed by primitive sibling rivalry (the nests of eggs). Oedipal rivalries are a consequence of emerging. The pain of having to share the therapist with therapy siblings, sharing mother and father with siblings at home, as well as wanting mother or father to herself, were reasons not to come out. If she stays mentally encased in the psychological equivalent of clay casing then she does not have to feel or experience. During this period she also encased animals and asked fiercely if other children would touch them. She checked again and again that I would keep them safe. At this stage her relation to her objects made was neither truly concrete nor truly symbolic: they were experienced as part of her and also as part separate.

Development of three-dimensionality

As a medium, clay offers enormous potential for the exploration of realness, and its use offers insights into two- and three-dimensionality. Several writers have discussed the importance of clay as a medium in work with psychosis in adult patients. Killick (1987, 1991, 1993, 1995, 1997, 2000), in her work at Hill End, has been influential. Goldsmith (1992) who followed her in work at Hill End has described the use of the room environment and the materials as a container, as a precursor to engagement with another person:

> Through the recognition of the value of working with the 'concrete' level of functioning we aim to utilise the actual spatial locations and their experimental components as part of the basic 'work' and not only as the frame or context of the work. In this way the department itself partici-pates in our techniques by enabling us to reduce the otherwise implicit demand, that 'clear cut' therapeutic spaces make, for high level function-ing of a more integrated 'self' than can be immediately achieved by these patients.
>
> (Goldsmith 1992: 46)

Patients were able to have a table for their sole use in this studio setting and build a beginning relationship with the therapist through concrete interactions around the materials and objects made, as well as negotiations around practical issues. Killick movingly describes the making of clay images by her adult patients and the change from 'meaningless' defensive use of imagery to evolving 'meaning and mindfulness within the therapeutic relationship':

> ... the value of the realm of experience offered by the concreteness of art-making processes available within the art-therapy setting, which can form a transitional, or intermediary, area of thinking for the patient in relation to the living presence of the therapist. The pre-verbal thinking functions involved in the creative use of visual image-making can contain and transform the raw material of experience within the therapeutic relationship, paving the way for symbolisation, and the experience of relatedness to the therapist can foster the possibility of a symbolic relation to the images.
>
> (Killick 1993: 30)

Greenwood (1994), working with adult psychotic patients, discusses the collection of a person's work giving them feedback of identity; Hershkowitz (1998), with a similar client group, comments on clay's fusional qualities. The use of clay with adult psychotic patients, and the way that clay and Plasticine work as experimental bodies has been explored by Foster (1997) who was influenced by Killick, and Pankow's (1961, 1981) work around dynamic structurisation, an analytic approach using the concept of the body image. She explores how working with three-dimensional materials evokes similar psychotic anxieties to those evoked by patient to therapist emotional and interpersonal contact. She comments on how they tend to flatten the material which may be both a method of control over it and because of a fear of it becoming a container for persecutory forces. Foster comments on how clay fosters tactile sensations: 'They can provide a feeling that one's finger is in something, that one has entered into the inside of a body-like form and/or that the substance engulf's one's finger' (Foster 1997: 54). Foster explores a line of development in her patients from two-dimensional work, to three-dimensional work, to direct interpersonal forms of relating with another human being.

The emotional charge of the break

It was possible to see the progress Sally was making in her ability to manage some of the feelings aroused by the natural breaks in therapy.

Session

In the last session before a break Sally at first felt hard to contact. She played through a whole repertoire of animal and dog scenarios but it did not feel very real: she was going through the motions of playing. I commented on the difficulty of finding an expression for how she felt, as if she had been trying out all she knew, but none was right. She then abandoned this play and got the clay out. She wanted all the plastic animals out and for a production line of cut-out animals to proceed. Again, she is turning to a previously known expression. She showed a lot of patience in this session because the clay was rather crumbly and it was difficult sometimes to keep a shape. She also had very clear speech. She was cutting out for herself but with a wide margin and wanted me to help her cut a better, more defined shape. I said that I knew she could do this and also make her own things of clay. She began to make a large, thick-walled nest of eggs and then formed a whole dog, made with all its facial features, guarding the nest (Ilustration 9.2). She lay the dog across the top of the nest, finally able to make a whole shape herself without smashing it up. I was able to talk of how much she wanted this space to be guarded while she was away. The nest space represented mother's womb/mother's lap and she fears who will get into it while we are separated. At the end of the session she began to tip furniture about and I was able to talk about her tipped out feelings, being tipped out of the therapy.

Return after the break

On returning after the break Sally played various games of hide-and-seek. While doing so, she became a variety of different animals, all red in tooth and claw. I talked about the feelings aroused by the holiday. How it felt that I had

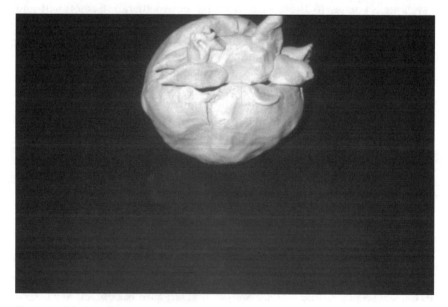

Illustration 9.2 Sally: Dog guarding nest.

been hidden, and her from me, by my absence and how pleased she was to see me and be back in therapy but also how angry and scratchy she felt to me. She then turned to the sand and invented a new game of hide-and-seek in the sand. She made a hand print in the sand and then covered it with more sand and then I had to find it: an impossible task. It suggested how difficult she felt it was to find each other after a break; almost as if she does dissolve into tiny particles and no clear person is remaining. There is disbelief that we can find traces of each other after the break. She was cross with me when I talked about how impossible it felt, clearly not the right interpretation, and turned to the clay. She made a nest of eggs with a small lump over the top that she said was 'holding on'. Both the image of the dog guarding the nest or therapy lap from before the break, and this lump that holds on, suggest that she is able to guard and hold on to something positive in thought about the therapy during a break but also the terrific strain it is for her.

Pancake dogs

Sally had been able to make a three-dimensional dog while under a strong emotion at the break but was unable to repeat it. It was as if she had done it once but then had to slowly learn the stages, as it got established inside.

Sally wanted to make a dog that 'looks real' but felt it was not possible. This creative impulse clearly came from a part of her that wants to grow. I encouraged her to try, and then she did make a dog. It had a large head and a flat body, like a pancake dog. It took several attempts to get the pose she wanted; which was of a dog lying down but looking back into its body in a way that dogs do lie. The head of this dog is three-dimensional but the body is flat with the accompanying right number of legs and a tail. It was at a mixed developmental stage, containing something expressive in the pose, a certain solidity. She put in, like a younger child, what she knew to be there. She was very pleased with the dog and was grinning with pleasure and it was delightful to share her pleasure in something she had made by herself (Illustration 9.3).

She now made a nest of eggs and added a white paper mother bird (Illustration 9.4). She then made a tree of black paper and stuck the clay nest to it. She added a piece of white paper, for water, because the tree needed water. She just managed to get this all stuck together, with glue before the end of the session. She washed her hands and left the session quite relaxed.

Discussion

This was a huge step forward all at once. The dog was lying free and separated and there was an awareness of the eggs in the nest in the tree and the tree's need for water. This resonated in me with the-child-in-the-family-in-the-community (Harris and Meltzer 1977). In this phrase is the idea that mother can care for baby within the loving circle of father's arms. Father mediates

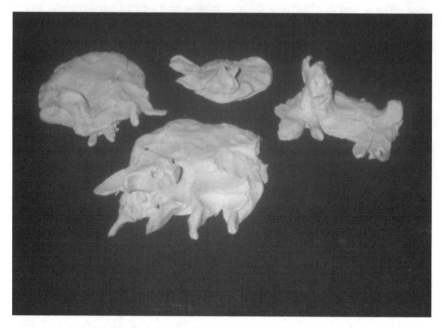

Illustration 9.3 Sally: Pancake dogs.

between mother and the community but they are also supported by the community. The nest in the tree, and the tree's need for water, symbolised this move out into an awareness of nurturing needed in a wider circle, the community. We can look after others if we are looked after ourselves. This new awareness on Sally's part reflected the goodness of the institution and workers who had struggled to help the family get established as a viable unit and had taken them out of their isolation, giving them access to a community.

Sally made a series of nests with eggs, and a mother bird made out of paper, that sits on top, partially folded into the clay at the top of the nest (Illustration 9.5). It was the beginning of recognition and acceptance of mother's role in nurturing and protection and therefore of the need for a dependent relationship with another. The mother bird was one-dimensional though, as if there was only one perspective. This could relate to a difficulty with being able to imagine, or to let the mother have, an existence of her own (especially with father), or to experiencing mother as vulnerable 'paper thin'.

Dogs with feelings

Session

At the beginning of the next session Sally was touching both the most recent clay creations but also older ones of animals encased in clay. They were dry

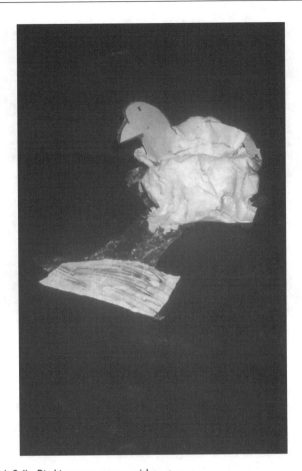

Illustration 9.4 Sally: Bird in nest on tree with water.

with the animals inside, heads showing. She asked if the animals would come out and I said that they could only come out if the clay was broken. She said, no, 'never, to stay in'. I talked about this, how they were protected and safe but not able to move freely. She then went over to the sand and drew a heart with one finger. She had a different presence today. She felt calmer, more present and in good eye contact. We went through the usual ritual of the clay being thrown to me and back to her. This time there was more of a light-hearted game feel to this rather than a ritual. She then said that her dog from last week was not a dog. She wanted to make a dog lying down but could not. She is aware of the flatness of the body and wants it more lifelike, more three-dimensional. I said that I thought she could do that if she could get a picture of a dog she knew in her mind. She had done it before. She then began to make a dog lying curling round. It had its head over its tail, front legs

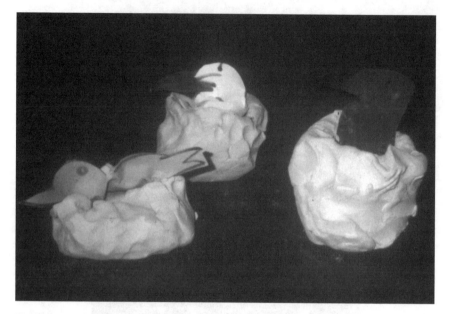

Illustration 9.5 Sally: Birds on nests.

forward. She built it up slowly. She talked about each piece. There was a flash feeling of warmth as she talked of her dog and how it sometimes lies with a foot over its tail. Then, when it was finished I put it on the window sill to dry.

She now wanted to do a dog lying flat, mouth open. There was a lot of worry about this, that she would not be able to do it. This was built up in the same way, a piece added at a time. Again, the clay was thrown to me, for me to handle, she had to start as if it was the beginning of the session. She made a dog's head at first with the mouth open. She made teeth and then realised she had forgotten that she wanted the dog's tongue hanging out over the teeth so she took the teeth out and started again. She was quite impressive with how she was able to persevere with this setback. I said that the dog was panting and she asked me what that meant. I showed her and explained why dogs did this and she copied the action and smiled. I talked of her interest in new words and what they meant. When this was finished and also put to dry, she now wanted to make a 'sad dog'. She again threw the clay to me.

She wanted to make 'a sad dog in a dark background with snow'. This was an immense description of a feeling mood from her and was a development related to the eggs in the nest, with mother bird, and the tree with water, of the previous session. It is a development of figure and ground, of subject and object. She started the dog lying head on the ground, face forward, front paws forward. I asked why it was sad and she said it was sad because people had got at it, not leaving it alone. As she was making I wondered what made her feel sad. She asked me what time it was (avoidance of question) and was it near dinner time, as she was making a bone for the dog. I said that she was hungry and thirsty and needed some food and drink, to take in something good, but it was difficult to think about the question. She decided to make a bone for the dog and then a bowl for the bone. As she did so, the bowl that had been made from a ring of clay with strips across the bottom got bigger, and she decided to make a basket for the dog. She scrunched up the first one and made a 'very big basket'. She tried out the dog in the basket, widening it. I talked of wondering if she felt sad and if she could perhaps feel these feelings as a dog but it was difficult as a girl. She said 'I am a dog'. I said that she could express things as a dog or in dog language and perhaps it felt safer to feel as a dog, not the pain of a child.

She made a large basket. A hole became the place where the dog came in and out. She pressed the dog into the basket and said that it was showing its teeth. She talked of how her dog does that when it wants to be left alone, lying with its ears flat down. The clay dog was made to look like this in the basket and then she made a cover for it out of paper. She wanted me to cut it out in white paper and then did red stripes on it. All was then glued on to a black background and she painted white snow. She now wanted to add a house (of paper) to the model although it was getting near the end of the session. The dog is outside the house in its cold, snowy landscape. She then quickly made a figure out of paper too, who is coming to annoy the dog. The figure is looking in an enquiring way and smiling. The dog is showing teeth. I said that the dog felt it had to growl when it felt sad, and show teeth to keep people away who annoyed it. I said that I thought that she might sometimes feel the same way when I annoyed her by the things I said. At the end she dropped water drops on the heart in the sand tray, in a slightly mocking way. It is very difficult to keep in touch with warm feelings, when you feel you are being chucked out at the end of the session.

The heart and the bone

In her clay-work Sally made good use of the developing transitional space. She had some autonomy, but could also ask for help and when I challenged the need for help, she sometimes found that she could in fact do more. She was developing a capacity to be alone in the presence of another (Winnicott 1958). Two different parts to the session delineated two different aspects of therapy. In the dog play, the transference relationship was played out. The previous over-close love and hate had allowed no true closeness, as there was no space to move over to become close and then move away, in a natural rhythm of relationship. The questions that emerged as she came out of her entangled state could be played over as a dog. In the clay-work, Sally struggled with this emergent state, and a burgeoning sense of self, of identity. When Sally moved to make with the clay there was a struggle with three-dimensionality and she was able at times to accept a dependent relationship in a good way, at the same time being more independent, which sounds paradoxical.

While she made things in clay there were many attempts to put the clay into my hands trying to make me do it. I had to keep resisting this which was difficult, and found myself saying, 'I believe that you can do it'. Models were sometimes made in the space between my hands, as I insisted that she try, but kept my hands there in an encouraging way. During this combined lion period and three-dimensional dog period she frequently drew a heart, or two hearts overlapping, in the sand at the beginning of the session. This is a good example of an apparently casual but important use of an impermanent medium. It is just there as a sign in the sand tray, but the rest of the session might be taking place under this sign.

I had to struggle with belief, which means holding out hope for change, and she had to struggle with the courage to try, and the brave struggle with three-dimensionality; the move she was making away from adhesive identification and the attractions of the claustrum towards being a separate person in relation to another. Belief and courage are two aspects of the symbol of the heart (Hillman 1981; Case 1990b). One session, she finally managed to make a lion, on her own, not an impression, with four legs standing on a boulder or piece of rock, holding on with his claws 'like this', showing me curled fingers (Illustration 9.6). The emergence of ground and rock beneath the feet is interesting, as she has moved from nests, to animals impressed into their background, to animals defined against a background by being cut out, to encasing of animals looking out, to a safe place in an environment. This then broadens out into an environment/piece of ground beneath the feet. The lion has to claw a hold, suggesting that it has had to be fought for, and is precarious, but also the tenacity of her grip. She left a piece of clay in the container for 'next week'. This was the first time that she had been able to leave any clay; usually she had to use it all. So there is a new sense that she can trust in a 'next week' and that there will be more, or what she leaves, will still be there, rather than used by imagined rivals.

In the past, in the chaotic stage of therapy the sessions had been under the sign of the bone: frequently drawn in the sand tray. These could be considered as opposites, in that the heart can symbolise love, courage, and belief – what one puts one's heart into, in the sense of commitment. Whereas the bone symbolises the stripping and denuding of flesh and fullness, the bare bones, it is what is left to worry at and gnaw. Bones are hard and splintery, offering no nourishment: 'skeletons' are associated with death. Our sense of engagement with life comes from the soft and vulnerable palpitating heart. Two hearts suggest the engagement in relationship. The emotional poverty of the bone is shown in the skull and crossbones as a symbol of the pirate, who takes what

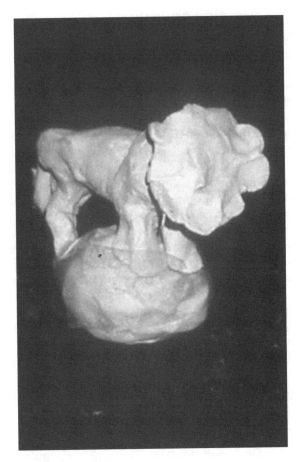

Illustration 9.6 Sally: Lion on boulder.

he wants without mercy. These opposite signs characterise the dilemma of the child emerging from a previous autistic state to a disturbed/psychotic phase in therapy. The trauma they have experienced leaves a vulnerable part that wishes to engage at the mercy of destructive forces which protect in their own way, but leave the child out of touch, with the phantasy that there is no need of parental figures. Rosenfeld (1971) has described this as 'destructive narcissism'. The lion came on to the agenda in therapy at this time. At first, a male lion that is synonymous with courage and bravery and masculinity – the king of the animals, offering a paternal identification, which can aid development, later, the female who has the capacity to work with others.

Collapse into two-dimensionality

At this time Sally had had several productive weeks in school and was making moves forward in therapy and then it suddenly collapsed. It was difficult to know what had happened. There was illness at home, stomach upsets and diarrhoea and family work also came to a halt. This kind of setback is not at all unusual when things seem to have been going well. The whole family is adjusting and making changes in how they live with each other and in understanding, and this is an enormous strain on inner resources.

When Sally came in the next session, the collapse back into something flat and two-dimensional was plainly observable. Her hands were picked at, and she spoke in a flat hard voice, accompanied by a hard stare that felt as if it would go through me. The warmth and sense of transitional space that might be creative between us was gone. Something had emerged internally or externally, that was too hard to bear and she felt lost to me in this mood. She was using words as monosyllabic wedges into the room, flatly demanding, but not open to contact. She said, 'clay', after looking at last week's lion and then, 'knife' and cut off a small piece and began to make something. I wondered what she was going to make and she said, 'watch and you'll see'. I could see that it was a circle mane shape and she began to add pieces to it to make a lion but the body was very long and thin like a tube. She added four legs and a tail and it drooped and collapsed. She did not ever give it a face and finally attached a small piece of clay under it for a rock or boulder but it looked collapsed on to it. This sense of the body as tube resonates with the psychotic feeling that the body is a mechanical apparatus that things go in and out of, and with the robotic image that had been present in different sessions. The new lion was now put to fight last week's which was knocked off the boulder, the join broken.

Sally tried to build herself up again. She went back to the first sense of security in making a nest. She made it with very strong walls and used the clay from the outside of the nest to make the little eggs, six in all. She then made the sides very high to protect the eggs. The rim was bent down and scored heavily all round with a knife 'to make it stronger'. These cuts were quite deep and showed the ambivalence to the eggs/babies, that is present, to protect/attack. She felt out of reach. The hardness present was confirmed when she drew a wolf, with her back to me, and then turned to show me. She then got Sellotape and tried to mend last week's lion. The Sellotape fell off the dusty clay. I explained how the Sellotape picked up the dust and would not stick and how disappointing this was. In the mood she is in I did not think she would be able to listen to me and she tried to force it all together by wrapping the Sellotape round and round. It did not work as she was not able to take into account the qualities of the materials. She suddenly (it seemed to me) was wiping the table, signifying the end of this phase and was getting the dog's lead out.

She was on all fours wanting to be on the lead and to go to the shops. I noticed the glint of something by her arm and realised she had the scissors stuffed up her sleeve. I said that it was not safe for either of us to have them in the play, and she handed them to me. I did not refer again to them directly, but talked about the howling wolf/growling dog that had mixed feelings about its mistress. There was no communication except for intermittent growls so I reverted to an earlier technique of speaking, which was to ask in a stage whisper what the dog's name was and what she wanted me to do next. She had as usual with the dog play, a name, and therefore I think a character in mind and did reply very shortly; it helped to form a bridge of alliance.

We went through some rapidly different play, touching on various old themes, shops, slipping the lead and hiding, a puppy on a blanket under the table. During this she drew a heart and a bone in the sand and then quickly rubbed them out. Possibly, revisiting the therapy history put her in touch momentarily with a different Mrs Case. This was in sharp contrast to the overlapping hearts of the session before. She then became very fierce and growling, eventually saying that, a man was making faces at her. She felt quite mocked or persecuted inside. I now had to go to the shops alone and come home to find that the house had been destroyed. She was lying under a table kicking the underneath with her feet so that it jumped about as if in an earthquake. Her clay things that she had made previously and her box of toys were on this table. I talked of the battle going on inside with something that does want to destroy things and a part that wishes to grow and develop. I then had to go to the shops again and she had got her doll's house furniture and tipped it all over the floor. She said that everything in the house has been overturned and it is 'night-time'. We were at the end of the session here.

It is possible to see the difference between being under the sign of the two hearts, being under the sign of the heart and bone, or just the bone, earlier in therapy. The bone suggests that the house is destroyed when the parents come together, the feet pounding under the table. It is an account of primal scene destruction rather than primal scene regeneration. When she is collapsed into something two-dimensional rather than being able to maintain three-dimensionality, the internal object she is in touch with is denuded: the bone.

Keeping babies alive

In the animal play, an emerging theme, played over in many different ways, was of babies under attack. A mother would have babies that would be under attack from other, wilder animals. Sometimes there was a daddy, but one of the parents would be killed off. In order to protect the babies, they seemed to have to be as if dead, buried or not moving, but they would still be killed. This was accompanied by a difficulty in having two parents in the play who could work together to protect them. Sibling rivalry and an urge to attack the babies was also present in the form of children who came and looked at the animals and wanted to hurt them, Sally put this very insightfully and earnestly to me one day: 'The children think they [the animals] are better than them'. When I explored this with her, wondering why the children thought that the animals thought they were better than them, she answered that the animals were feeding from the mummy. I wondered if the children would like to be feeding from the mummy, and she nodded, saying, 'Yes'. Could this parallel, the fear that things she made in clay might be harmed (her babies)? In internal life these fears possibly related to fear of retaliation for all her attacks in phantasy, in the past, on her mother's child-bearing capacity, with her father, and her hate of rivals arriving. In external life, it could relate to an actual experience.

It became clear in a session when Sally played out being two rabbits, which mate and have babies. Two children then come and touch the baby rabbits and they die. I was struck by the way she told the story and was the rabbits in the play at the same time. The rabbits thump an alarm and are scared of the children. I talked of the rabbits' fear and of the harmful children and wondered what made them harmful. Sally then told me that this had happened in the past, when one of her siblings had touched baby rabbits and they had been eaten. Given Sally's location of herself in family pets, the trauma of this happening is clear, and also the way she tells the story; she is the children and she is the pet. In this way, external events and the power of 'bad touching' had interwoven with phantasy life and sibling rivalry to create this great difficulty in keeping something new alive. This was really the crux of the matter, as it was a great challenge to making progress. I talked with her about the strong feelings that are aroused in other members of the family when a baby is born. These may be feelings of love and welcoming the new little person but also of jealousy and a wish to be that little baby. These feelings can cause angry or harmful thoughts and actions to the new babies. I then talked about her feelings when her siblings were born and the jealousy of the children towards the parents' relationship, from which they are left out at night.

One of the consequences of being in a confusional and entangled state with another is the heightened erotic wish for that parent to be the child's partner. The mother–infant and mother–father coupling is confused. The normal oedipal situation is intensified because of the lack of aid to maturation and acceptance of being a child to one's parents, and the parents' difficulty in fostering individuation. We have seen in the last chapters that Sally struggled with desire and sexual feelings, as well as with confusion about sexuality and gender. In this last stage of therapy we worked on this area particularly, interwoven with the difficulty in keeping babies alive. Underlying this, there were feelings of abandonment and a fear of dying. When the autistic armour goes, children are left very vulnerable. Mannoni comments on how they: '. . . remain fascinated by death and run the risk of suicidal acting out' (Mannoni, quoted in Brenkman 1999: xxxiii).

The potential richness of the dog stories

Originally, it had not been possible to talk about feelings when Sally was locked away from contact in hard body armour. Then she played it out as a dog; playful, suspicious, aggressive, nonverbal; followed by play as a dog where she can describe the feelings to me. Then there had been a stage when human and animal material had been quite separated in her mind, and must not make contact. Then, it was possible to talk about animals, bringing in humans. The therapist's feeling more definite and confident that what was being shown was human material in animal form paralleled the possibility of her bearing talk about her feelings as a child. Finally, it comes close to being a human thought/feeling that has to do with her; before it finally disappears out of the game stories as a regular feature or comes back occasionally as a game we used to play. 'Do you remember when we played this . . .' part of the shared therapy history that we can recall. This shared history together forms a strong bond that is then capable of bearing or weathering breaks, painful realisations, etc. In the last stage, she has things she wants to communicate about humans but acts as if this is a story about animals, because she has become more self-aware and self-conscious.

The capacity for narrativity, as far as we know, is particularly human. Bruner describes paradigmatic and narrative thought modes. The former is that of maths, logic and computing. The latter he describes as having two landscapes:

> One is the landscape of action, where the constituents are the arguments of action: agent, intention or goal, situation, instrument, something corresponding to a 'story grammar'. The other landscape is the landscape of consciousness: what those involved in the action know, think, or feel, or do not know, think or feel.
>
> (Bruner 1986: 14)

Carrithers suggests that narrativity allows 'humans to grasp a longer past and a more intricately conceived future, as well as a more variegated social environment' (Carrithers 1991: 306). To be able to invent characters and plots supports the growth of the understanding of 'deeds and attitudes' which take place within a 'temporal envelope'. Understanding stories and making them up, helps to develop an understanding of social complexity. Hillman writes that; 'therapy re-stories life' (Hillman 1983: 47). The animal stories had begun very simply, a dog moving about the room; which was both her, and a dog character with a prototype story, as at this stage she had been equated with the animal. The stories developed characters, for instance, three different dogs, with different attitudes to the therapist. The stories became more elaborate in terms of action and plot and understanding feelings; which became a way that she could play over preoccupations, and responses to the therapist in the transference. Jones (1984), comments on the importance of story-making for its access, awareness of and management of unconscious life.

The homeless dog and the pet shop game

After the long summer break two games started in conjunction: 'the homeless dog', and 'the pet shop game'. In the homeless dog game she is a stray. She comes to knock at my door, but when I put down food for her, she cannot let herself eat or drink, in case it is poisoned. She flinches about the room, sidling up and away and then under the table saying she had nothing. There is great difficulty in trusting what is on offer – the therapy food – that is the thoughts and feelings of our work. This is a dog that has to look after itself (as she felt she had to over the summer). The fact that it has come into play means that it can be symbolised and is therefore nearer consciousness as an issue that has to do with her.

In the pet shop game I have to go into a pet shop and choose a pet. She describes to me how there are cats down one side and dogs down the other. She is on the table as if on a shelf in a cage and rapidly becomes different dogs that I might choose. There is enormous tension about my going around the pet shop to choose. In contrast, in these two games that intertwine is 'homelessness' and 'being chosen and taken home'. Also, not being able to trust in what is on offer and therefore feeling that you have nothing and, wanting to be chosen. Each chosen dog has a brief existence when it is very farty and blowing raspberries as if, to contradict that she wanted to be chosen. It then quickly dies, so that we can play it over again. The farty and raspberry noises seem like a talking out of your bottom but in a much lighter way, playfully, rather than the thinking with your bottom that seems to inform perverse thinking. It is as if, despite the mocking part of her, another part has to continue to produce a new variation on the story, trying to communicate a thought or feeling that she hopes will be understood. I talked to her about the wish to be chosen from amongst the other pets in the shop (from amongst the other children I see for therapy) and to be taken home. The wish is expressed for a special relationship with the therapist, and how painful it is that it is kept as a therapy relationship. Sometimes, in the pet shop game, I have to wait for a pet and am continually frustrated. This reverses the dynamic over the holidays when she has to wait for me.

Sally had a strong resistance to my including talk about human feelings into the talk about what Sally Dog was feeling. As the pet shop play continued with its central theme of 'being chosen' and taken home, I tried to move from thinking about the dog's wish for a home to thinking about Sally's wish for a home. This had to be done very carefully in stages. At first the play alone and then waiting until it felt that she could tolerate my speaking. Then I would talk of the dog's wish for a home, generally all the pets in that pet shop want to be chosen. This particular dog that Sally is wants a safe home.

Dogs have a wish to be safe and so do children. Children have feelings about wanting to be looked after. Gradually we could move to the idea that Sally would like to be picked as my special therapy child from the other children that I see. At home she would like to be the favourite child. She is able to bear a little coming alongside these feelings, sometimes curling up and sucking her thumb and listening. There was an edge that would soon develop as she could not bear very much being in touch with softer feelings and would want to attack those feelings and get rid of them. The difficulty is that she has projected so intensely all her self into dog form that when I try to talk of these as being human feelings that she has, she experiences the violent return of the projection. She does not want to hear what I am saying. She has already successfully got rid of that feeling, why should she want it back? So the relationship is tested each time I move that thought alongside her. The therapist first of all has the role and task of thinking about these things to themselves and doing the work of this and then to judge what the child is ready to bear in small doses.

Material from current anxieties

Sally began to draw on stories from film and video, with animal characters, adapting them, or choosing elements that had a resonance in her present everyday life. Something in the story struck a resonance within her in relation to a present concern or worry, the difference being that she is able to select a character to help her communicate what is troubling her, rather than being the family pet. The difference from the previous use of, for example, *The Lion King*, is that it could be related to her *current life* as a child.

Session

She painstakingly told me the story of the film, *Beethoven*, saying that 'She was that dog'. She emphasised how a bad man had lied about Beethoven, saying that he had attacked him when it was not true. He had pretended to be bleeding from bites. This was duly played out with my playing first, the bad man and second, the good dad who finally believes. As she sat down at the end of this I asked if this had ever happened to her, to be wrongly accused, as it had been a very intense game. She immediately began to talk of a situation at school in her classroom where she had been unjustly accused of a misdemeanour by another child. I talked about how awful it felt to have someone say wrong things about you, and asked how it had ended. She said, 'Everybody's watching to see', turning over on her back and flipping a sneaker off so that it tossed across the room and nearly hit me on the head. The feelings she must have had in the classroom, with other children all watching and awaiting the outcome, had suddenly been felt and overwhelmed her too much to contain. As she continued to flip her shoes I had a very vivid image of how words, feelings, new ideas, came to her like hits on the head, and talked about this. She then went into a superman routine which, is to be invulnerable. I talked about her wish to be in states of mind where nothing could upset her, like people telling lies about her. I talked about ideas hitting her on the head like these sneakers flying through the air. She laughed at this but was still quite wild with her flying objects.

One shoe smashed into a picture and I talked of looking after both ourselves and the room. She said, 'The room can't cry!' I agreed but said that it could be damaged and she calmed down. She wanted to leave the session early for a moment, and I said how hard it was to stay with the difficult feelings that we had been discussing.

She then took a picture by Monet of a bridge over water, *Bridge over Giverny*, off the wall, and said that, 'This was a nice day'. It was a move forward to recognise an emotion and feeling that had been put into the picture by the artist. She wanted to make a print of the picture in the sand. She made an imprint of the frame and then put the picture down and drew the picture in the sand with her finger. As she did the river she said how much she liked it. The imprint is like the wish to capture that moment that you like – the reason one would buy a picture. What she did, in the past was to imprint herself on to things, when she got a response that she liked; as she had with her dog. Locating herself in him through the mechanism of adhesive identification/equation: I am the thing that I like. In the use of the picture on the wall there was an element that played with destruction: the picture could be smashed. But there is a much stronger feeling of attachment and warmth, so that this is played with and I am teased with it, but in fact she puts the picture back carefully before she leaves and says goodbye, and waves to me several times.

Changes

Sally could now talk to me straightaway, and keep up a whole session of conversation, not reverting to a dog persona at all. The talk had the combination of being quite compelling, in her great intent to communicate with me, speaking clearly, but also stammering quite badly at times, so that she felt both, fluent, impeded and handicapped. The growth of the part of her that wants to interact, together with the terrible internal struggle with other parts of her, can be felt keenly. She is struggling with the learning difficulties and other disadvantages that she has, which can be thought of as inherited/environmental. Her teacher and I were aware that she could hide her abilities and kid on that she could not do things that she could do. Secondary handicapping, when a handicapped child identifies with the reflection of themselves that they see from another, has been very usefully described by Sinason (1986, 1992). Most difficult for her, was that a more able part could get hijacked by a destructive, perverse defence which could feel triumph that the other person had been fooled. However, there were encouraging moments of attunement. For instance, Sally made a lioness, and wanted to put it on a hill, as she had with male lions before. I talked about her feeling lioness-like today. She smiled and said that she wanted to make a whole pride of lions. I held the ball for her as she joined the lioness and said that it felt as if the lioness was 'king of the castle'. She looked up at me and grinned and we both said together, laughing, 'I'm king of the castle and you're the dirty rascal'. The new flexibility that is present in our relationship is demonstrated by the moment of attunement over the rhyme, knowing what we were each going to say and enjoying the fun of the mutual statement of position, 'You're the dirty rascal!'

Meeting with Sally's mother for a review, she talked of the real improvements in Sally at home. Sally was able to express feelings and understand what was said to her. At the doctor's where normally there would be a huge difficulty in examining her, she had been able to say clearly, 'I'm not scared, I just want to know what you are doing and what it is for'. Sally's mother also gave me the first coherent story of the traumatic background of her own bereavements when Sally was a baby. This demonstrated how parental work and individual therapy had combined to produce a certain narrative of containment for mother and child.

Chapter 10

Working towards the end of therapy and conclusions

> [O]ur genre therapeutic fictions all start at the same point the main character enters therapy . . . the story leads out of therapy into cure and the world.
>
> (Hillman 1983: 13–14)

CLAY-WORK AND ENDING

It had become apparent that Sally would be leaving her present situation and be starting at a new school. Part of these changes involved her re-assessment from being autistic to having moderate learning difficulties and the moving on to a more appropriate school placement. She had also reached the age limit of this particular placement. We were beginning to talk about this new situation and that it would mean the coming to an end of therapy too, in seven months' time.

As the 'pet shop' games continued in these last months of therapy, there were often Donald Duck noises, from Sally at the beginning. But, as the session progressed, Sally would lie and listen when I talked, sometimes sucking her thumb. The pets were bought, mated and had offspring, and all the familiar themes were played over. Every now and then, facts around differences that we had struggled with over the past three years were stated in an earnest way. When these facts were established; that is, the difference between the sexes and the difference between children and adults, the pain of change and separation, stimulated by our known end in some months' time, came more openly into the play. The ending was brought into dog play quite naturally, as the next stage, when the pups or other young animals grow up and move to a new home. In the play, the mother dog would try to hide the pups when it was time for them to go to a new home: Sally said that she died when the pups left. The old fear that separation means death was uppermost in her anxieties. Endings, in terms of the retrospective review of pictures, have been usefully discussed by Schaverien (1993); the art therapist's feelings about ending, particularly in relation to images, by Edwards (1997); and the psychodynamics in the process of ending child psychotherapy by Wittenberg (1999), Lanyado (1999), and Ryz and Wilson (1999).

Clay-work

In this last section on clay-work, the move forward from flat pancake dogs, that had more three-dimensional heads and who were lying (stuck) on a background, to fully three-dimensional dogs, standing, or separate from a background, will be traced. The clay was an agency for change. The particular characterising factor of art therapy, the triangular relationship between image, maker and therapist fosters and gives expression to the developing oedipal triangle, helping to create a third point of view, as we looked on and discussed her creations together. The cutting away of the pancake, flat part of the dog, first happened through a 'creative accident', after a session where the time of the session had had to be changed. It was stimulated psychologically, because she had had to adjust to my absence (at the correct time), and my presence (at a different time). She had been surprised and delighted to find she had two three-dimensional dogs, which she named King and friend. It was as if some of the ground had been removed from the main picture, pared away and not needed. It will be remembered that in the earlier fish pictures all the backgrounds had to be kept.

The following session, before the Christmas break, these dogs were painted. She then wanted to make a quick last dog although there was little time left. This dog had a slightly different position in that its head was lying on its legs rather than curled round more to its tail. It had a 'lying in waiting' feel about it – lying in waiting through the holiday. She wanted to know that the things she had made would be ready to paint and be dry by January when we would be resuming sessions. So there is a strong link here to her knowing that work will continue after the break. A separation, although difficult, is surmountable.

Sally's next stage in clay-work was to make a dog standing up. She had several sudden questions to me that day which started by wanting to know where I got the clay from. This led to discussion of where she lived, where her school was and where we met for the therapy session. It was clear that she had had little awareness of the outside world in the sense of where these places were in relation to each other. But now she really wanted to know. She made a dog that is standing up and it has a separate basket that it can walk in and out of. I talked of how it can walk in and out just as she can come and go, between home, school and therapy.

The next step was to make a dog in clay but, 'it is not just a dog, it is a special dog'. This was a mother dog she had been playing. She made a very moving image of a dog lying and feeding its puppy (Illustration 10.1). This image reflected the feeding relationship in therapy that we were now able to enjoy. Sally expressed the importance of the connected, feeding experience in

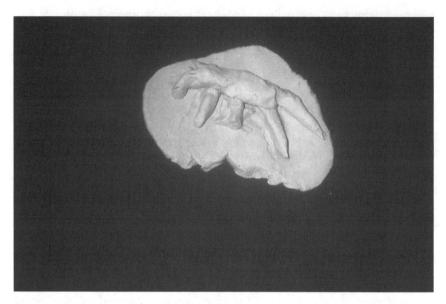

Illustration 10.1 Sally: Mother dog feeding puppy.

her own way. It had been apparent that it was happening by her change of demeanour and her watching me while thumb-sucking. But in making the image she gave expression to the thought she had had previously that, 'it is a nice sight to see a baby feeding'. There is tenderness in the image, to do with the openness of the mother dog and the acceptance of a dependent relationship by Sally, the maker.

The importance of the clay was that it was on the ground and firm, solid. Sally could see the relationship. Clay can enable both a metaphoric but also a concrete experience. The term 'concretising' often seems to be used in a negative way, not positively, as something that we should grow out of, or something that ill people do. It is seen as limiting, as the play of symbol and metaphor is not available to those who can only think concretely. However, the strength of concrete thinking which underlies abstract thinking, is perhaps also in its limits. We sometimes need to see before we can know. It was a struggle for her to make it and I reminded her of the dogs that she had made at Christmas. She then reminded me that this was more difficult! But she was able to make it. We were then able to talk of wishing to be the feeding baby, and how difficult it sometimes was to think positively of the pleasures of the next stage, growing up and being independent. I also talked of the changes that were happening to her, the change of school and the finishing here of the therapy.

Chart

A large chart of the remaining therapy months and weeks helped her with preparation for the ending. The session that this was introduced, she played being a puppy brought back from the pet shop and incorporated the chart, as a book, which is on 'how to train your puppy'. She said earnestly that 'there were no chocolate drops' – I have to train her to the book. There is no way to sweeten the end of therapy, and the loss that is involved; apart from the growing sense of what has been taken in, changes, and the move on that is now possible. It is the purpose of therapy to reintegrate children back into ordinary life and to let the usual home/school environment back into their formative role. I was able to talk to her about the chart and the ending. Wanting me to train her by the book, was asking for a particular kind of containment. We did need a structure but also to take into account the feelings involved. We needed to work to the chart which gave us a framework but also within that to explore as many feelings as possible.

This session she got the clay out near the end and had various attempts to make different dogs but none seemed quite to express what she wanted. So she screwed them up and then decisively made a very solid three-dimensional dog that is lying on its stomach and beside it an older pup that is not feeding. While she was making this we were talking of the end of term, the end of therapy, the new school and a visit to the new school and were able to use the chart as a chart to look at the time left. She was very pleased with her dogs and announced that she was going to take her different dogs in clay with her but not take the other things from the past. There was a sense here, of a wish to leave the past chaos of feelings with me.

The new sense of Sally that was apparent in the making of the three-dimensional dogs was of someone with a space all around her. My experience of being with her was that it was now possible to have a flow of thoughts both about the session but also conversation while she was making; something that took us outside as well, so that more of her everyday life could come into exploration. She had care over what she was making. She felt different to be with in the session and was not entangled. She had come into dimensionality. Previously there had been no sense of a beginning and an end to either of us in the session, and it had been terrifying, but now that she had space about her, we could come into relationship.

The next session she got the clay out and decided to make a puppy without a mother. Then to me, 'Can you do that; make a puppy without a mother?' We talked about this and she decided that she could and tossed the clay bucket over her shoulder. I said that there was to be no mother today and no bucket for the clay and she grinned. I spoke of how the clay could be out of the bucket but needed to be back in it afterwards to keep damp, and how children could go out without mothers but needed mothers to come home to. She tossed the clay to me in the way that she used to and began with soft clay to make the puppy. It was well made and she was pleased, commenting throughout that she was making it good. It lay with its eyes shut, asleep, head on paws, alone on a base. Here in the clay she was exploring a feeling that she could be alone and quite safe. The puppy has a soft base, a base of his own which is secure.

She then thought that she would make something else, a friend of the puppy. This friend is looking out and has pointed ears, straight up. I said that this friend was listening carefully. It is an alsatian who is an older female. They are best friends. When the male pup is older they will have pups together. Now the puppy is sleeping and the alsatian is watching out. The two dogs reflected our relationship, and the present variation on the oedipal dynamic. The two dogs are also the two parts of her and reflect her growing ability to look after herself. There is a little one inside her and an older one that can protect and keep her secure to some extent. A question that might be in the reader's mind is to whether she ever made human forms, and the answer is that she did, but she was not able to let herself keep them. They were made under the table, out of sight, briefly flashed/shown to me and then destroyed. This part of her, that could not be brought fully, in a sustained way, into the light of day, represented the work still remaining to be done, or, what we had not been able to do.

Ending

The ending was painful. There was inevitably a wish to be able to do more, to continue, but as frequently happens in child work, the whole picture of home, school, and therapy had to be considered. The new school was at a distance, making continuation very difficult and I had decided that it was better to end with the full support of the present situation than risk continuing and it breaking down. I also thought it made more sense to Sally, who was proud of 'moving on' and that it would have been confusing for her to return for therapy. There were some chaotic sessions as she struggled with angry feelings of abandonment, but the destructive parts did not take over and could be thought about together. Meltzer (1967) describing ending in terms of 'weaning' is a helpful model: the new school could offer a 'solid food' experience after the nurturing of the present placement.

In the last session she came with a bag, prepared to take some favourite things away at the end; we had spent many sessions in reviewing and discussing the history of the therapy together. She really wanted to do everything in the session and divided it into time to play, time to make something, and time to paint an older model she wanted to take with her. We began to talk of the possible different feelings about leaving which I named and she nodded and said 'yes' when one matched her own feeling, also very pleased when I talked of our sad feelings about ending. All change involves mixed feelings. She has visited her new school and is looking forward to particular aspects of it, proud to be moving on. She will also miss many things about this present placement, including the therapy. She now glued and stuck and painted some older pieces of work she wanted to take, and then, almost got caught up in a wish to a make a mess, to externalise the upset she was containing around the ending. Tears came to her eyes and we were able to put this into words. In this very moving way our work came to an end.

CONCLUSIONS

Being in relationship with Sally in therapy stimulated my thoughts and emotional understanding, extending my capacity as a therapist; we both learnt from each other. In the case study it has been the intention to explore the complexity of issues in work with entangled and confusional children from a perspective that straddles art therapy and child psychotherapy. I have wanted to explore the place of the image in the therapy of children who were hard to reach. Sally had at first presented with encapsulated and entangled features. Contributing to the picture had been Sally's genetic constitution and learning difficulties. Her early environment had been shot through with traumatic bereavements which had affected mother and child particularly. In these situations, one child, particularly if they are different, can collect the unwanted feelings in a family group, and then struggle to sense who they actually are. The fear of further losses and the need to fill an intense sense of loss contributed to the entanglement between mother and child. The entanglement then worked back on the learning difficulties, probably enhancing them, as a life not fully lived, loses further opportunities for learning. Fear of further losses led to a terror of separation which in turn led to all the family sleeping in one room. This nest of closeness allowed no true coming together and coming apart, and development was impeded. Adhesive identification with mother, as well as sleeping in the same room, contributed to a confusion of mother–infant/mother–father relationships. This impacted on her understanding of sexual difference and identity.

Sally took on animal personas, particularly of her pets. It is possible that this began through the sensual attractiveness and responsiveness of her pets at a time when human to human relationships felt dead through loss and depression. Taking on an animal persona may have helped to foster a sense of 'continuity of being' at a time when death and depression threatened. This creative leap into an animal skin had positive aspects for her but also negative, as she could have become trapped in it. The next stage was to find a way of being an alive and animated child. One of the great challenges of this kind of work is to distinguish internal and external traumas and how they impact on each other. For instance, the effect of a pet dying with which she was adhesively identified, plays into an internal landscape already littered with bereavements and maternal depression. It is not possible to say that the work is complete or finished or that one fully understands all that has happened, but one aims for a partial reintegration of intolerable feelings, and to set the child on a pathway towards a more normal life.

The work with Sally had needed an interactive and playful relationship to build up the necessary background for symbolic activity to develop.

> An area of play is necessary between the subject and the other so that the imagination can be accepted and the subject can take up speech. Speech is taken up in relation to someone . . . we never ask who this someone is. But a subject can have a perfect command of language without feeling entitled to use it.
>
> (Mannoni 1999: 102)

In early work with Sally, the therapist was able to begin a commentary on her activities which led to the taking on of an animal persona and the creation of the 'dog stories'. The dog persona could be thought about as a halfway house from the claustrum, with its phantasy of being inside mother, to being an outside person. This taking on of an animal skin has elements of adhesive equation and also of 'second skin' phenomena described by Bick (1968). Borrowing an animal skin is both a defence, but also a creative leap of imagination as it allows a pathway out of autistic defences towards expression and communication to others, albeit a shape-shifting, camouflaged one. The therapist needed to respond in play as well as keeping up a commentary on Sally Dog. In this way, Sally Child was able to emerge.

The dog stories became a rich source of narrative for the communication of relationships in the transference, but also for the communication of inner states, preoccupations and anxieties: 'Stories in all their myriad forms-myths, legends, allegories, fables, parables, anecdotes, etc. whether they be told visually, verbally or in the form of a written text, help us make sense of the world and construct our sense of identity' (Edwards 1999: 7).

Hillman (1983) suggests that although the stories we create may be incomplete, confusing, difficult to tell or to depict that it is through stories that we create and share meaning, a process that may in itself be healing.

Sally's language, when she emerged from selective mutism, had two modes originally. These were first, a stream of consciousness, undifferentiated chatter to her mother, and second, a two-dimensional, monosyllabic, flat use of one word, to the rest of the world, from which all emotion had been eradicated. At first, she was able to become animated in attempts at conversation around animals. She then took on an animal persona which allowed expression; mainly in dog language. It proved possible to make a link with the human child who could tell me about the dog persona that she had taken on. Over the three years it was gradually possible to talk about the dog's feelings, and for them to be linked to human feelings and then, directly to Sally. Sally's development in therapy showed how her struggle with language, in both its delay and its disorder, had been partly emotionally based in her struggle with loving and hating impulses around her entanglement with her mother. When verbal language of social interaction and communication, which is also a language between parts of the self, becomes so enmeshed in symptomatology, analytic work with art materials and play may offer a combined pathway to the outside world, for the child trapped inside.

Sally's drawing and painting had at first had a lyrical quality, with her name usually woven into the animal she had depicted. With confusional children, one may see images that look as if they are representational, but in fact, they show 'equative feelings'; of children in states of mind where there is to be 'no differentiation'. Sally used pictures to express her self/animal/pets, equative pictures, which after the period of chaos in therapy moved towards becoming part of her and not part of her, and then to being metaphorical and symbolising her relationship with her mother and the therapist in the transference. Once this adhesive relationship could be represented by a literally gluey picture, it became possible to begin putting these feelings into words. These first images to be made after the chaotic period, allowed what was being protected by the aggressive behaviour to emerge, and to be articulated.

Sally's clay-work went through the following stages. First, an attempt to control the therapist as an extension of herself, and make the therapist's hands do the clay modelling, expressing the refusal of the confusional/entangled child to live their own life and their insistence, fiercely held on to, that the adult is an extension of them. The second stage of 'imprinting' had two aspects. Forceful adult emotion had imprinted itself on to her and she in turn equated herself with the things that she liked and wished to incorporate. Its first happening in the session may have been to do with the impact of the therapist's otherness upon her. Third, clay nests acted as a first container for unthinkable thoughts and fears. Fourth, clay was the medium through which she could struggle towards separation in her creative experiments towards a separate body for self and other. Underlying this, in relation to three-dimensional material, is the presence of clay as a separate body. This use of a three-dimensional medium, is particularly helpful with confusional/entangled children. It can facilitate the emergence from the duality-unity of the claustrum phantasies. Art therapy is especially able to foster the third perspective of the oedipal triangle, in that bringing in a medium creates a triangular interaction. Art allows an inner dialogue, as well as being a form of relating to others. It has the capacity to act as an agent for experience as well as being an organiser for that experience (Oremland 1997). At this stage, she was bringing material from her everyday life as well as from internal life, the two interweaving.

With entangled children, there has been an awareness of separateness-terror and then an insistence on 'being the same'. This illusion will be fiercely defended and hung on to. The outbursts of disturbance need different interventions to those used with encapsulated children. Like encapsulated children there will be times when the child with a communication deficit or communication sensitivity will be to the fore and this will need to be attuned to and anxieties contained. However, the outbursts of disturbance need at times, robustness, and a change from a maternal mode to a paternal firmness, to hold the boundaries and contain the interplay of loving and hating feelings. Winnicott (1971) writes that it is only when the child moves from the illusion of being one with mother to disillusion of separateness that, using whatever aggressivity the environment allows him, he begins to find the imaginary resources he will later need for creativity and sublimation.

Therefore, different phases of the therapy need different approaches. In the first phase for example, the therapist talked to Sally about her activities, giving her a sense mainly through sound, of being understood. In the second phase a more robust stance was needed to resist the pressure to be an extension of Sally, a paternal mode. At this stage one needs to maintain support, and to be encouraging, talking about the difficulties of making and her frustration, but not actually doing it. When this phase has been weathered, a different approach is needed again, and was taken during Sally's struggle with cutting out, a delineation and definition of self. Here, I felt that she needed to see a model of how something was done and I had in mind a sports model of learning. We learn how to play a game by watching others play, as well as by playing; an amodal pattern. At this stage I could take on the struggle, gradually lessening what I would do, until Sally was in full control of cutting. The subsequent modelling in clay formed a building block towards the development of three-dimensionality. Making things in the space between my hands allowed a boundary to the anxieties aroused by creativity, aloneness, fear of failure, and frustration. Sally needed to be held within the space made by my hands as well as by my voice, eyes and thoughts, at the same time taking on the challenge of making her own forms.

WXYZ – FROM THE CASE STUDY TO THE CASE FOR ANIMALS

Animals, and images of them, can offer us a mirror of the human condition. Participation mystique and the concept of duality-unity allow a different perspective on three-dimensional animal images particularly, that are out-there-but-also-part-of-me. Their appearance on stage in therapy frequently assists communication and engages therapist and child in the work. We may want to deny our interdependency with animals, and nature, but it is only through seeing ourselves as part of a community in nature that we will survive, just as it is only when Sally accepts her dependency that she can let go of her crippling defences.

Sally's case material gives insight into cruelty and its sexual and aggressive aspects. In particular, Sally's play at dogs having puppies, and the two children who want to touch them illustrates the wish to be the feeding pups. 'They want to drink the milk for themselves.' Sally had been insightful, saying to me earnestly, that, 'they cannot drink the milk themselves because they are not pups'. She also said that they want to be cruel to the pups because they think that the pups are better than them. The motivation of some domestic violence seems to be set off by jealousy of the breast-feeding mother–baby couple and one can see here, the link with cruelty to animals. The deepness of our splitting in relation to animals is appalling and intriguing. We turn a blind eye to the suffering that we cause to animals. We are served by self-interest, taking what we want, like pirates, from the animal kingdom/mother nature, not caring what destruction we leave behind, and on the other hand, we can sentimentalise and idealise; both attitudes blur and prevent a healthy relationship to other animals which might vision us as having one intelligence and point of view, among others. Psychoanalytic insights could be brought to environmental and animal questions, adding weight to the writings of animal philosophers. This tailpiece, out into the world, offers three images of calves:

The absent calf

Near to my house is a large field of Guernsey cows. It is a commonplace to comment in the village on their beauty. They *are* beautiful but this is tempered by the bulging udders of the cows. The ghostly image of the calves that have been taken away, have a negative presence in their absence. We are somehow able to turn a blind eye to this distress, to mother and child. We do not see what is there, only what we want to see. Our ill-treatment of animals is based on self-interest, we want the milk for ourselves, and envy of the animal's capacity to be itself, which we have forfeited, with the gain of a language that can both enable expression and communication but also allow us to be divorced from our instinctual life.

The veal calf

Calves taken from their mothers at birth are immobilised either by tethering or by being put into crates or even occasionally with their heads in 'stocks' so that they cannot lick any part of the pen or flooring and thereby pick up any vestige of iron. The aim is to keep them anaemic and so produce the whitest possible meat. They cannot groom or lick themselves . . . For cleaning purposes they are kept on slatted floors, which is anathema to cloven hoofed animals (hence the success of cattle grids) and results in deformed feet and swollen joints. These animals are fed with a calf gruel or milk substitute but are given no water. The gruel makes them thirsty and there is nothing to slake their thirst but another dose of gruel; consequently they grow and put on weight. These calves are given a maximum of fifteen weeks to live. After that the extreme anaemia induced by their mode of living and diet would cause death in any case, if they were not slaughtered first. Antibiotics as an aid to growth and a deterrent to a too-early death are freely employed.

(Hutchings and Caver 1970: 97–8)

The white meat presumably holds an illusion that no blood has been spilt.

The white calf, Phoenix

A very different symbolism of the white calf came to media attention in the foot and mouth epidemic of 2001. Phoenix, a twelve-day-old, white calf, was named and reprieved, after being found lying alive under its dead mother. It had survived while every other animal on the farm had been killed (*Guardian* 25 April 2002).

As the spread of disease lessened, the survival of Phoenix became a marker for a new policy of not having to cull healthy animals from surrounding farms. In fact there was always an alternative to the wholesale slaughter, but that is another story. Phoenix was greeted and treated like a child survivor from an earthquake, miraculously arising from the ashes of destruction. The timing of this was crucial in that the calf was found on Good Friday, and the Christian Easter festival is concerned with death and renewal. There must have been a relief for those caught up in the wholescale slaughter to be able to rescue a live animal.

Would this calf have been saved if it had not been pure white, symbolizing the purity of infancy, hope, and peace?

XYZ: the end

Bibliography

Ainsworth, M. D. S., Bell, S. M. and Stayton, D. J. (1971) 'Individual differences in strange situation behaviour of one-year-olds', in H. R. Schaffer (ed.) *The Origins of Human Social Relations*, pp. 17–57, London: Academic Press.

Aldridge, F. (1998) 'Chocolate or shit: aesthetics and cultural poverty in art therapy with children', *Inscape*, 3: 2–9.

Allen, L. D., and Budson, R. D., (1982) 'The clinical significance of pets in a psychiatric community residence', *American Journal of Social Psychiatry*, 2 (4): 41–3.

Alvarez, A. (1992) *Live Company*, London and New York: Tavistock Routledge.

—— (1996) 'Addressing the element of deficit in children with autism: psychotherapy which is both psychoanalytically and developmentally informed', *Clinical Child Psychology and Psychiatry*, 1 (4): 525–37.

Alvarez, A. and Reid, S. (1999) *Autism and Personality*, London and New York: Routledge.

Amini, F., Lewis, T. and Lannon, R. (1996) 'Affect, attachment, memory: contributions toward psychobiologic integration', *Psychiatry*, 59: 213–39.

Anderson, F. (1995) 'Catharsis and empowerment through group clay-work with incest survivors', *The Arts in Psychotherapy*, 22 (5): 413–27.

Anderson, R. K., Hart, B. and Hart, L. (eds) (1984) *The Pet Connection*, University of Minnesota Press: Censhare.

Anderson, R. S. (ed.) (1975) *Pet Animals and Society*, London: Balliere-Tindall.

Anthony, S. (1973) *The Discovery of Death in Childhood and After*, Harmondsworth: Penguin Education.

Arkow, P. (1984) (ed.) *Dynamic Relationships in Practice*, California: The Latham Foundation.

Astor, J. (1995) *Michael Fordham – Innovations in Analytical Psychology*, London and New York: Routledge.

Aulich, L. (1994) 'Fear and loathing: art therapy, sex offenders and gender', in M. Liebmann (ed.) *Art Therapy with Offenders*, London and Bristol, PA: Jessica Kingsley, pp. 165–96.

Axline, V. (1986) *Dibs in Search of Self*, New York: Ballantine Books.

Balbernie, R. (2001) 'Circuits and circumstances: the neurobiological consequences of early relationship experiences and how they shape later behaviour', *Journal of Child Psychotherapy*, 27 (3): 237–55.

Balint, M. (1968) *The Basic Fault*, London: Tavistock.

Barrows, K. (2000) 'Shadow Lives: a discussion of *Reading in the Dark*, a novel by Seamus Deane', in J. Symington (ed.) *Imprisoned Pain and its Transformation*, London and New York: Karnac, pp. 66–83.

Barrows, P. (2003) 'Change in infant–parent psychotherapy', *Journal of Child Psychotherapy*, 29 (3): 283–300.

Baun, M. M., Bergstrom, N., Langston, N. F. and Thomas, L. (1984) 'Physiological effects of petting dogs: influences of attachment', in R. K. Anderson, B. Hart and L. Hart (eds) *The Pet Connection*, University of Minnesota Press: Censhare, pp. 162–171.

Baynes, H. G. (1940) *The Mythology of the Soul*, London: Routledge & Kegan Paul.

Beck, A. M., Seraydarian, L. and Hunter G. F. (1986) 'Use of animals in the rehabilitation of psychiatric inpatients', *Psychological Reports*, 38: 63–6.

Bettelheim, B. (1967) *The Empty Fortress: infantile autism and the birth of the self*, New York: Free Press.

—— (1978) *The Uses of Enchantment*, Harmondsworth: Penguin (Peregrine).

Bick, E. (1964) 'Notes on infant observation in psychoanalytic training', *International Journal of Psychoanalysis*, 45: 558–66.

—— (1968) 'The experience of skin in early object relations', *International Journal of Psychoanalysis*, 49: 484–6.

—— (1986) 'Further considerations of the function of the skin in early object relations', *British Journal of Psychotherapy*, 2 (4): 292–9.

Bion, W. R. (1957) 'Differentiation of the psychotic from the non-psychotic personality', *International Journal of Psychoanalysis*, 38: 266–75.

—— (1959) 'Attacks on linking', *International Journal of Psychoanalysis*, 40: 308–15.

—— (1962a) *Learning from Experience*, London: Heinemann.

—— (1962b) 'A theory of thinking', *International Journal of Psychoanalysis*, 43: 306–10.

—— (1967) *Second Thoughts*, New York: Jason Aronson.

Black, D. and Newman, M. (1996) 'Children and Domestic Violence', *Clinical Child Psychology and Psychiatry* 1 (1): 79–88.

Blackburn, S. (1994) *The Oxford Dictionary of Philosophy*, Oxford: Oxford University Press.

Blenzel, R. (1966) 'Introduction', in L. Levy-Bruhl, (1966) *How Natives Think*, New York: Washington Square Press.

Blount, T. (1656) *Glossographia*, reprinted Hildesheim: Georg Olms, 1972.

Bollas, C. (1987) *The Shadow of the Object: psychoanalysis of the unthought known*, London: Free Association Books.

Boronska, T. (2000) 'Art therapy with two sibling groups using an attachment framework', *Inscape*, 5 (1): 2–10.

Borossa, J. (1997) 'Case histories and the institutionalisation of psychoanalysis', in I. Ward (ed.) *The Presentation of Case-Material in Clinical Discourse*, London: Freud Museum Publications, pp. 45–63.

Bowlby, J. (1988) *A Secure Base: clinical applications of attachment theory*, London: Tavistock Routledge.

Brazelton, T. B., Koslowski, B. and Main, M. (1974) 'The origins of reciprocicity: the early mother–infant interaction', in M. Lewis and L. A. Rosenblum, (eds) *The Effect of the Infant on its Caregiver*, New York: John Wiley, pp. 49–74.

Brenkman, J. (1999) 'Introduction', in M. Mannoni (1923) *Separation and Creativity:*

refinding the lost language of childhood; trans Susan Fairfield (1999) New York: Other Press.

Brickell, C. M. (1986) 'Pet-facilitated therapies', *Clinical Gerontologist* 15: 309–332.

Britton, R. (1989) 'The missing link: parental sexuality in the Oedipus complex', in J. Steiner (ed.) *The Oedipus Complex Today: clinical implications*, London: Karnac, pp. 11–28.

—— (1997) 'Making the private public', in I. Ward (ed.) *The Presentation of Case-Material in Clinical Discourse*, London: Freud Museum Publications.

Brown, L. T., Shaw, T. G. and Kirkland, K. D. (1972) 'Affection for people as a function of affection for dogs', *Psychological Reports*, 31: 957–8.

Bruner, J. (1986) *Actual Minds, Possible Worlds*, Cambridge, MA and London: Harvard University Press.

Burke, E (1757) 'A Philosophical Enquiry into the Origin of our Ideas of the Sublime and the Beautiful', in T. O. McLoughlin and J. T. Boulton (eds) *The Writings and Speeches of Edmund Burke Vol.1 The Early Writings*, Oxford: Clarendon Press (1997).

Butterworth, G. (1992) 'The ontology and phylogeny of joint visual attention', in A. Whiten (ed.) *Natural Theories of Mind, Evolution, Development, and Stimulation of Everyday Mindreading*, Oxford: Basil Blackwell.

Cantle, T. (1983) 'Hate in the helping relationship: the therapeutic use of an occupational hazard', *Inscape*, October: 1–10.

Carrithers, M. (1991) 'Narrativity: mindreading and making societies', in A. Whiten (ed.) *Natural Theories of the Mind: evolution, development and simulation of everyday mind reading*, Oxford: Blackwell, pp. 305–17.

Case, C. (1986) 'Hide-and-seek: a struggle for meaning – art and play therapy with bereaved children', *Inscape*, Winter: 20–24.

—— (1987) 'A search for meaning: loss and transition in art therapy', in T. Dalley, C. Case, J. Schaverien, F. Weir, D. Halliday, P. Nowell Hall, D. Waller (eds) *Images of Art Therapy: new developments in theory and practice*, London and New York: Tavistock Publications, pp. 36–73.

—— (1990a) 'Reflections and shadows: an exploration of the world of the rejected girl', in C. Case and T. Dalley (eds) *Working with Children in Art Therapy*, London and New York: Tavistock Routledge, pp. 131–60.

—— (1990b) 'Heart forms: the image as mediator', *Inscape*, Winter: 20–6.

—— (1994) 'Art therapy in analysis: advance/retreat in the belly of the spider', *Inscape*, 1: 3–10.

—— (1995) 'Silence in progress: on being, dumb, empty, or silent in therapy', *Inscape*, 1: 21–6.

—— (1996) 'On the aesthetic moment in the transference', *Inscape*, 1 (2): 39–45.

—— (1998) 'Brief encounters: thinking about images in assessment', *Inscape*, 3 (1): 26–33.

—— (1999) 'Foreign images: images of race and culture in therapy with children', in J. Campbell, M. Liebmann, F. Brooks, J. Jones and C. Ward. (eds) *Art Therapy, Race and Culture*, London and Philadelphia: Jessica Kingsley, pp. 68–84.

—— (2000a) 'Our Lady of the Queen: journeys around the maternal object', in A. Gilroy and G. McNeilly (eds) *The Changing Shape of Art Therapy*, London and Philadelphia: Jessica Kingsley, pp. 15–54.

—— (2000b) 'Santa's grotto: an exploration of the Christmas break in therapy', *Inscape* 5 (1): 11–18.

—— (2002) 'Animation and the location of beauty', *Journal of Child Psychotherapy*, 28 (3): 327–43.

—— (2003) 'Authenticity and survival: working with children in Chaos', *Inscape*, 8 (1): 17–28.

—— (2005) 'Observations of children cutting up, cutting out and sticking down', *International Journal of Art Therapy*, Inscape 1: 2.

Case, C. and Dalley, T. (eds.) (1990) *Working with Children in Art Therapy*, London and New York: Tavistock Routledge.

Case, C. and Dalley, T. (1992) *The Handbook of Art Therapy*, London and New York: Tavistock Routledge.

Catlin, G. (1903) *The North American Indians*, Edinburgh in Levy-Bruhl, L. (1966) *How Natives Think*, New York: Washington Square Press.

Chadwick, T. (1994) *The Fate of the Elephant*, San Francisco: Sierra Club.

Chetwynd, T. (1982) *A Dictionary of Symbols*, London: Paladin/Granada.

Cirlot, J. E. (1962) *A Dictionary of Symbols*, London and Henley: Routledge & Kegan Paul.

Cochrane, A. and Callen, K. (1992) *Dolphins and their Power to Heal*, London: Bloomsbury.

Corson, S. and Corson, E. (eds) (1980) *Ethology and Nonverbal Communication in Mental Health*, Oxford: Pergamon Press.

Corson, S. A., Corson, E., Gwynne, P. H. and Arnold, L. E. (1977) 'Pet dogs as nonverbal communication links in hospital psychiatry', *Comprehensive Psychiatry*, 18: 61–72.

Crittenden, P. (1985) 'Maltreated infants: vulnerability and resilience', *Journal of Child Psychology and Psychiatry*, 26: 85–96.

Cusack, O. (1988) *Pets and Mental Health*, New York: Haworth Press.

Dalley, T. (1990) 'Images and integration: art therapy in a multi-cultural school', in C. Case and T. Dalley (eds) *Working with Children in Art Therapy*, London and New York: Tavistock Routledge, pp. 161–98.

—— (2000) 'Back to the future: thinking about theoretical developments in art therapy', in A. Gilroy and G. McNeilly (eds) *The Changing Shape of Art Therapy*, London and Philadelphia: Jessica Kingsley, pp. 84–98.

Dalley, T., Rifkind, G. and Terry, K. (1993) *Three Voices of Art Therapy: image, client, therapist*, London and New York: Routledge.

Davis, J. M. and Valla, F. R. (1978) 'Evidence for the domestication of the dog 12,000 years ago in the Natufian of Israel', *Nature*, 276: 608–10.

Daws, D. (1989) *Through the Night: helping parents and sleepless infants*, London: Free Association Books.

De Astis, G. (1997) 'Thoughts about the development of a potential space in the psychoanalytical treatment of infantile psychosis', *Journal of Child Psychotherapy*, 23 (3): 351–71.

De La Mare, W. (1912) 'The Listeners', in D. Cecil and A. Tate (eds) (1958) *Modern Verse in English 1900–50*, London: Eyre and Spottiswoode.

De Pauw, K. P. (1984) 'Therapeutic horseback riding in Europe and America', in R. K. Anderson, B. Hart, and L. Hart (eds) *The Pet Connection*, University of Minnesota Press: Censhare.

De Vries, J. I. P. (1988) 'The emergence of fetal behaviour 3: Individual differences and consistencies', *Early Human Development*, 16: 85–103.

De Vries, J. I. P., Visser, G. H. A. and Prechtl, H. F. R. (1982) 'The emergence of fetal behaviour, 1: qualitative aspects', *Early Human Development*, 7: 301–22.

Diamond, J. (1992) *The Rise and Fall of the Third Chimpanzee*, London: Vintage.

Dismuke, R. P. (1984) 'Rehabilitative horseback riding for children with language disorders', in R. K. Anderson, B. Hart, and L. Hart, (eds) (1984) *The Pet Connection*, University of Minnesota Press: Censhare, pp. 131–41.

Dobbs, H. (1991) *Dolphin Therapy Centres – A Vision for the Future*, Humberside: International Dolphin Watch.

Douglas, M. (1966) *Purity and Danger*, London: Routledge & Kegan Paul.

Dubinsky, A. (1997) 'Theoreticl Overview', in M. Rustin, M. Rhode, A. Dubinsky and H. Dubinsky (eds) *Psychotic States in Children*, London: Duckworth, pp. 5–26.

Dubinsky, A., and Dubinsky, H. (1997) 'Discussion', in M. Rustin, M. Rhode, A. Dubinsky and H. Dubinsky (eds) *Psychotic States in Children*, London: Duckworth, pp. 89–100.

Dubowski, J. (1984) 'Alternative models for describing the development of children's graphic work: some implications for art therapy', in T. Dalley (ed.) *Art as Therapy: an introduction to the use of art as a therapeutic technique*, London: Routledge, pp. 45–61.

—— (1990) 'Art versus language (separate development during childhood)', in C. Case and T. Dalley (eds) *Working with Children in Art Therapy*, London and New York: Tavistock Routledge, pp. 7–22.

Edwards, D. (1997) 'Endings', *Inscape*, 2 (2): 49–56.

—— (1999) 'The role of the case study in art therapy research', *Inscape*, 4 (1): 2–9.

Evans, K. (1998) 'Sharing experience and sharing meaning: art therapy for children with autism', *Inscape*, 3 (1): 17–25.

Evans, K. and Dubowski, D. (2001) *Art Therapy with Children on the Autistic Spectrum: beyond words*, London and Bristol, PA: Jessica Kingsley.

Evans, K. and Rutten-Saris, M. (1998) 'Shaping vitality affects, enriching communication: art therapy for children with autism', in D. Sandle (ed.) *Development and Diversity: New Applications in Art Therapy*, London and New York: Free Association Books, pp. 57–77.

Fogle, B. (ed.) (1981) *Interrelations between people and pets*, Illinois: Charles C. Thomas.

Fonagy, P. and Target, M. (1997) 'Attachment and reflective function: their role in self-organisation', *Development and Psychopathology*, 9: 679–700.

—— (1998) 'An interpersonal view of the infant', in A. Hurry, (ed.) *Psychoanalysis and Developmental Theory*, London: Karnac.

Fonagy, P., Steele, M., Moran, G., Steele, H. and Higgett, A. (1992) 'Measuring the ghost in the nursery: an empirical study of the relation between parents' mental representations of childhood experiences and their infants' security of attachment, *Journal of American Psychoanalytical Society*, 41 (4): 957–89.

Fordham, M. (1976) *The Self and Autism*, Library of Analytical Psychology, London: Academic Press.

Foster, F. (1997) 'Fear of three-dimensionality: clay and plasticene as experimental bodies', in K. Killick, and J. Schaverien (eds) (1997) *Art, Psychotherapy and Psychosis*, London and New York: Routledge, pp. 52–71.

Foucault, M. (1970) *The Order of Things: An archaeology of the human sciences*, London: Tavistock.

Fouts, R. (1997) *Next of Kin*, New York: William Morrow.

Fox, L. (1998) 'Lost in space: the relevance of art therapy with clients who have autism or autistic features', in M. Rees (ed.). *Drawing on Difference: art therapy with people who have learning difficulties*, London and New York: Routledge, pp. 73–90.

Fraiberg, S., Adelson, E. and Shapiro, V. (1975) 'Ghosts in the nursery: a psycho-analytical approach to the problem of impaired infant-mother relationships', *Journal of American Academy of Child Psychiatry*, 14: 387–422.

Frazer, J. (1890) *The Golden Bough* (this edition two volumes in one; 1981), New Jersey: Gramercy.

Freud, S. (1900) *The Interpretation of Dreams*, in J. Strachey (ed.) The Standard Edition Vol. 1V, London: The Hogarth Press and the Institute of Psychoanalysis.

—— (1913) *Totem and Tabo*, in J. Strachey (ed.) The Standard Edition Vol. X111, London: The Hogarth Press and the Institute of Psychoanalysis.

—— (1917) 'Mourning and melancholia', in J. Strachey (ed.) The Standard Edition Vol. XIV, London: The Hogarth Press and the Institute of Psychoanalysis.

—— (1919) *The Uncanny*, in J. Strachey (ed.) The Standard Edition Vol. XV11, London: The Hogarth Press and the Institute of Psychoanalysis.

—— (1975) 'Letter to Marie Bonaparte' (HRH Princess George of Greece), 12/6/36, 8/37, in *The Letters of Sigmund Freud*, New York: Basic Books.

—— (1980) Case Histories 1 'Dora (1905) and Little Hans (1909)' in Vol. 8, The Pelican Freud Library, Harmondsworth: Penguin.

—— (1981) Case Histories 11 'The Rat Man (1905a), Schreber (1911), The Wolf-Man (1918)' in Vol. 9, The Pelican Freud Library, Harmondsworth: Penguin.

Frith, U. (1989) *Autism: Explaining the Enigma*, Oxford: Blackwell.

Fuller, P. (1980) *Art and Psychoanalysis*, London: Writers and Readers.

Gaddini, R. (1969) 'On imitation', *International Journal of Psycho-analysis*, 50 (4): 475–84.

Gampel, Y. (1993) 'Access to the non-verbal through modelling in the psychoanalytic situation', *British Journal of Psychotherapy*, 9 (3): 280–90.

Gardner, H. (1985) *Frames of Mind: the theory of multiple intelligences*, London: Paladin.

Gerity, L. A. (1999) *Creativity and the Dissociative Patient*, London and Bristol, PA: Jessica Kingsley.

Glaser, D. (2000) 'Child abuse and neglect and the brain: a review', *Journal of Child Psychology and Psychiatry*, 41(1): 97–116.

Goldsmith, A. (1986) 'Substance and structure in the art therapeutic process: working with mental handicap', *Inscape*, Summer: 18–22.

—— (1992) correspondence, quoted in T. Dalley (ed.) (1992) *The Handbook of Art Therapy*, London and New York: Tavistock Routledge, pp. 40–46.

Gordon, R. (1965) 'The concept of projective identification', *Journal of Analytical Psychology*, 10 (2): 127–49.

Graham, B. (1999) *Creature Comforts: animals that heal*, London and Sydney: Simon and Schuster.

Grahame, K. (1927) *The Wind in the Willows*, London: Methuen.

Gray, J. (2002) *Straw Dogs: thoughts on humans and other animals*, London: Granta Books.

Greenwood, H. (1994) 'Cracked pots: art therapy and psychosis', *Inscape*, (1): 11–14.
—— (2000) 'Captivity and terror in the therapeutic relationship', *Inscape*, (5): 53–61.
Greenwood, H. and Layton, G. (1991) 'Taking the piss', *Inscape*, Winter: 7–14.
Haag, G. (1997) 'Psychosis and autism: schizophrenic, perverse and manic-depressive states during psychotherapy', in M. Rustin, M. Rhode, A. Dubinsky, H. Dubinsky (eds) (1997) *Psychotic States in Children*, London: Duckworth.
Hallam, J. (1984) 'Regression and ego integration in art therapy with mentally handicapped people', in *Conference Proceedings: Art Therapy as Psychotherapy in Relation to the Mentally Handicapped*, St. Albans: Hertfordshire College of Art and Design, pp. 8–15.
Hama, H., Yogo, M. and Matsuyama, Y. (1996) 'Effects of stroking horses on both humans' and horses' heart-rate responses', *Japanese Psychological Research*, 38 (2) 66–73.
Hamilton, B. (1981) *The Medieval Inquisition*, London: Edward Arnold.
Hanes, M. (1997) 'Producing messy mixtures in art therapy: a case study of a sexually abused child', *American Journal of Art Therapy* 35: 70–4.
Hannah, B. (1992) *The Cat, Dog and Horse Lectures*, D. L. Frantz (ed.) Illinois: Chiron Publications.
Harris, M. (1975a) 'Some notes on maternal containment in "good enough" mothering', *Journal of Child Psychotherapy*, 4: 35–51.
—— (1975b) *Thinking about Infants and Young Children*, Perthshire: Clunie Press.
Harris, M. and Meltzer, D. (1977) *A Psychoanalytic Model of the Child-in-the-family-in-the-Community*, Geneva: WHO.
Hartmann, E. (1973) *The Functions of Sleep*, New Haven, CT: Yale University Press.
—— (1984) *The Nightmare*, New York: Basic Books.
Hartnup, T. (1999) 'The therapeutic setting: the people and the place', in M. Lanyado and A. Horne (eds) *The Handbook of Child and Adolescent Psychotherapy*, London and New York: Routledge, pp. 93–105.
Heaney, S. (1996) 'To a Dutch Potter in Ireland', in *The Spirit Level*, Boston and London: Faber and Faber.
Hediger, H. (1965) 'Man as social partner of animals and vice versa', *Symposium of the Zoolological Society of London*, 14: 291–300.
Heimann, P. (1942) 'A contribution to the problem of sublimation and its relation to processes of internalisation', in M. Tonnesmann (ed.) *About Children and Children-no-Longer: collected papers* 1942–80, London and New York: Tavistock Routledge 1989, pp. 26–45.
Henley, D. (1991) 'Facilitating the development of object relations through the use of clay in art therapy', *American Journal of Art Therapy*, 3: 67–73.
—— (1994) 'Art of annihilation: early onset schizophrenia and related disorders of childhood', *American Journal of Art Therapy*, 32: 99–107.
—— (2001) 'Annihilation anxiety and fantasy in the art of children with Aspergers syndrome and others on the autistic spectrum', *American Journal of Art Therapy*, 39: 4.
—— (2002) *Clayworks in Art Therapy*, London and Philadelphia: Jessica Kingsley Publishers.
Henry, G. (1974) 'Doubly deprived', *Journal of Child Psychotherapy*, 3 (4): 15–28.
Hershkowitz, A. (1998) 'Art therapy in acute psychiatry: brief work', in D. Sandle (ed.) *Development and Diversity: new applications in art therapy*, London and New York: Free Association Books, pp. 160–67.

Hillman, J. (1981) *The Thought of the Heart*, Eranos Lectures 2, Dallas, TX: Spring Books.

—— (1983) *Healing Fiction*, New York: Station Hill.

—— (1997) *Dream Animals*, New York: Chronicle Books.

Hindle, D. (2000) 'The Merman: recovering from early abuse and loss', *Journal of Child Psychotherapy*, 26 (3): 361–91.

Hindle, D. and Smith, M. V. (eds) (1999) *Personality Development: a psychoanalytic perspective*, London and New York: Routledge.

Hinshelwood, R. D. (1991) *A Dictionary of Kleinian Thought*, London: Free Association Books.

Hirsh-Pasek, K. and Treiman, R. (1982) 'Doggerel: motherese in a new context', *Journal of Child Language*, 9: 229–37.

Hobbs, R. (1995–7) *The Farseer Trilogy*, London: HarperCollins.

Hobson, P. (1993), *Autism and the Development of Mind*, Hove: Lawrence Erlbaum.

Holliday Willey, L. (1999) *Pretending to be Normal*, London: Jessica Kingsley.

Hopkins, J. (1998) 'From baby games to let's pretend: The achievement of playing', in B. Kahr (ed.) *The Legacy of Winnicott*, London: Karnac.

Houzel, D. (1995) 'Precipitation anxiety', *Journal of Child Psychotherapy*, 21 (1): 65–78.

—— (2001) 'The "nest of babies" fantasy', *Journal of Child Psychotherapy*, 27 (2): 125–38.

Hughes, R. (1984) 'Destruction and repair', in *Conference Proceedings: Second Conference on Art Therapy and the Mentally Handicapped*, St. Albans: Hertfordshire College of Art and Design.

Hutchings, M. and Caver, M. (1970) *Man's Dominion: our violation of the animal world*, London: Rupert Hart-Davis.

Jolly, A. (1972) *The Evolution of Primate Behaviour*, London: Macmillan.

Jones, P. (1984) 'Therapeutic story-making and autism', in *Conference Proceedings: Second Conference on Art Therapy and the Mentally Handicapped*, St. Albans: Hertfordshire College of Art and Design.

Jung, C. (1956) *Symbols of Transformation*, CW 5, Princeton, NJ: Bollingen.

—— (1959) *The Archetypes and the Collective Unconscious*, CW 9, Princeton, NJ: Bollingen.

—— (1960) *The Transcendent Function*, CW 8. Princeton, NJ: Bollingen.

—— (1963) *Memories, Dreams and Reflections*, London: Collins and Routledge Kegan.

Kacirk, J. (1997) *Forgotten English*, New York: Quill William Morrow.

Kaldegg, A. (1948) 'Responses of German and English secondary school boys to a projection test', *British Journal of Psychology*, 39, 1.

Kanner, L. (1944) 'Early infantile autism', *Journal of Paediatrics*, 25: 211–17.

Karbin, B. and West, A. (1994) 'Working as an art therapist in a regional secure unit', in M. Liebmann (ed.) *Art Therapy With Offenders*, London and Bristol, PA: Jessica Kingsley Publishers, pp. 135–64.

Katcher, A. H. and Beck, A. M. (eds) (1983) *New Perspectives on our Lives with Companion Animals*, Pennsylvania: Pennsylvanian Press.

Katcher, A. H., Segal, H. and Beck, A. M. (1984) 'Contemplation of an aquarium for the reduction of anxiety', in R. K. Anderson *et al.* (eds) *The Pet Connection*, University of Minnesota Press: Censhare, pp. 171–79.

Kidd, A. H. and Feldmann, B. B. (1981) 'Pet ownership and self-perceptions of older people', *Psychological Reports* 48: 867–75.

Killick, K. (1987) 'Art therapy and schizophrenia: a new approach', (unpublished M.A. thesis), Hertfordshire College of Art and Design, St. Albans.

—— (1991) 'The practice of art therapy with patients in acute psychotic states,' *Inscape*, Winter: 2–6.

—— (1993) 'Working with psychotic processes in art therapy', *Psychoanalytical Psychotherapy*, 7 (1): 25–38.

—— (1995) 'Working with psychotic processes in art therapy', in J. Ellwood (ed.) *Psychosis: understanding and treatment*, London, Bristol, PA: Jessica Kingsley.

—— (1997) 'Unintegration and containment in acute psychosis', in K. Killick and J. Schaverien (eds) *Art, Psychotherapy and Psychosis*, London and New York: Routledge.

—— (2000) 'The art room as container in analytical art psychotherapy with patients in psychotic states', in A. Gilroy and G. McNeilly (eds) *The Changing Shape of Art Therapy*, London and Philadelphia: Jessica Kingsley Publishers, pp. 99–114.

Killick, K. and Greenwood, H. (1995) 'Research in art therapy with people who have psychotic illnesses', in A. Gilroy and C. Lee (eds) *Art and Music: therapy and research*, London: Routledge.

Killick, K. and Schaverien, J. (eds) (1997) *Art, Psychotherapy and Psychosis*, London and New York: Routledge.

Klauber, T. (1998) 'The significance of trauma in work with the parents of severely disturbed children, and its implications for work with parents in general', *Journal of Child Psychotherapy*, 24 (1): 85–107.

—— (1999) 'The significance of trauma and other factors in work with the parents of children with autism', in A. Alvarez and S. Reid (eds) *Autism and Personality*, London and New York: Routledge, pp. 33–48.

Kleimann, D. G. (1967) 'Some aspects of social behaviour in the canidae', *American Zoologist*, 7: 279–88.

Klein, J. (1987) *Our Need for Others and its Roots in Infancy*, London and New York: Routledge.

Klein, M. (1921) 'The development of a child', in *Love, Guilt and Reparation and Other Works 1921–1945*, London: Hogarth (1981), pp. 1–53.

—— (1928) 'Early Stages of the Oedipus Complex', in *Love, Guilt and Reparation and Other Works 1921–45*, London: Hogarth (1981), pp. 186–98.

—— (1929) 'Infantile anxiety situations reflected in a work of art and in the creative impulse', in *Love, Guilt and Reparation and Other Works 1921–45*, London: Hogarth (1981), pp. 210–18.

—— (1940) 'Mourning and its relation to the manic-depressive states', *International Journal of Psychoanalysis*, 21 (1): 317–40.

—— (1961) *Narrative of a Child Analysis*, London: Hogarth.

—— (1975) 'Early stages of the oedipus conflict and super-ego formation', in M. Klein, *The Psychoanalysis of Children*, London: Hogarth Press, pp. 123–48. First published 1932.

Kramer, E. (1979) *Childhood and Art Therapy*, New York: Schocken.

—— (1999) 'Preface' in L. A. Gerity *Creativity and the Dissociative Patient*, London and Philadelphia: Jessica Kingsley, pp. 9–11.

Kwaitkowska, H. (1978) *Family Therapy and Evaluation Through Art*, Springfield, ILL: Charles C. Thomas.

Lane, R. D., Chua, P. and Dolan, R. J. (1999) 'Common effects of emotional valence, arousal and attention on neural activation during visual processing of pictures', *Neuropsychologia*, 37: 989–997.

Langer, S. (1963) *Philosophy in a New Key*, Cambridge, MA: Harvard University Press.

Langer, S. (1967) in *The Oxford Dictionary of Twentieth Century Quotations*, London: Oxford University Press, p. 180.

Lanyado, M. (1999) 'Holding and letting go: some thoughts about the process of ending therapy', *Journal of Child Psychotherapy*, 25 (3): 357–78.

Leach, E. (1964) 'Anthropological aspects of language: animal categories and verbal abuse', in E. H. Lenneberg (ed.) *New Directions in the Study of Language*, Cambridge, MA: MIT Press, pp. 23–64.

Leslie, A. M. (1987) 'Pretence and representation: the origins of theory of mind', *Psychological Review*, 94: 412–26.

Levinson, B. (1969) *Pet-oriented Child Psychotherapy*, Springfield, ILL: Charles C. Thomas.

—— (1972) *Pets and Human Development*, Springfield, ILL: Charles C. Thomas.

—— (1978) 'Pets and personality development', *Psychological Reports*, 42: 1031–8.

—— (1980) 'The child and his pet: a world of nonverbal communication', in S. Corson, and E. Corson (eds) *Ethology and Non-verbal Communication in Mental Health*, Oxford: Pergamon Press.

Levy-Bruhl, L. (1966) *How Natives Think*, New York: Washington Square Press.

—— (1975) *The Notebooks on Primitive Mentality*, first published 1949, trans. from the French by Riviere, P. (1975), Oxford and New York: Basil Blackwell and Mott Ltd and Harper Row Publishers.

Lewis, C. S. (1950–1956) *The Narnia Series*, Harmondsworth: Penguin (Puffin).

Lovejoy, A. (1960) *The Great Chain of Being*, New York: Harper Torch Books.

Lyddiatt, E. M. (1971) *Spontaneous Painting and Modelling*, London: Constable.

Macdonald, G. (1967) *The Princess and the Goblin*, New York: Airmont Publishers.

Maclagan, D. (1995) 'The biter bit', in A. Gilroy and C. Lee (eds) *Art and Music: therapy and research*, London: Routledge.

—— (2001) *Psychological Aesthetics: painting, feeling and making sense*, London and Bristol, PA: Jessica Kingsley Publishers.

Mahler, M., Bergman, A. and Pine, F. (1975) *The Psychological Birth of the Human Infant*, New York: Basic Books.

Main, M. and Hesse, E. (1990) 'Parents' unresolved traumatic experiences are related to infant disorganised attachment status: is frightened and/or frightening parental behaviour the linking mechanism?', in M. Greenberg, D. Cicchetti and M. Cummings (eds) *Attachment in the Preschool Years*, Chicago: University of Chicago, pp. 161–82.

Main, M. and Solomon. J, (1986) 'Discovery of a new, insecure/disorganised/ disoriented attachment pattern', in *Affective Development in Infancy* (eds) T. B. Brazelton and M. Yogman, Norwood, NJ: Ablex, pp. 95–124.

—— (1990) 'Procedure for identifying infants as disorganised/ disoriented during the Ainsworth Strange Situation', in M. Greenberg, D. Cicchetti and M. Cummings (eds) *Attachment in the Preschool Years*, Chicago: University of Chicago, pp. 121–60.

Main, M. and Weston, D. (1981) 'Quality of attachment to mother and to father: related to conflict behaviour and the readiness for establishing new relationships', *Child Development*, 52: 932–40.

Mannoni, M. (1999) *Separation and Creativity: refinding the lost language of childhood* (1923), trans. Susan Fairfield (1999), New York: Other Press.

McCulloch, M. J. (1983) 'Animal-facilitated therapy: overview and future directions, in A. H. Katcher and A. M. Beck (eds) *New Perspectives on Our Lives with Companion Animals*, Philadelphia: University of Pennysylvania Press, pp. 410–27.

McDougall, J. (1980) 'A child is being eaten', *Contemporary Psychoanalysis*, 16 (4): 417–59.

—— (1986) *Theatres of the Mind*, London: Free Association Books.

—— (1989) *Theatres of the Body*, London: Free Association Books.

McDougall, J. and Lebovici, S. (1969) *Dialogue with Sammy: A psychoanalytical contribution to the understanding of child psychosis*, London: Hogarth.

McNiff, S. (1990) 'Hillman's aesthetic psychology: from psychoanalysis to psycho-aesthetics', *Canadian Art Therapy Association Journal*, 5 (1): 27–38.

Meltzer, D. (1967) *The Psychoanalytical Process*, Strath Tay: Clunie Press.

—— (1973) *Sexual States of Mind*, Strath Tay: Clunie Press.

—— (1975) 'Adhesive identification', *Contemporary Psychoanalysis*, 2 (3): 289–310.

—— (1992) *The Claustrum, An Investigation of Claustrophobic Phenomena*, Strath Tay: Clunie Press.

Meltzer, D. and Williams, M. (1988) *The Apprehension of Beauty*, Strath Tay: Clunie Press.

Meltzer, D., Bremner, J., Hoxter, S., Weddell, H. and Wittenberg, I. (1975) *Explorations in Autism*, Strath Tay: Clunie Press.

Meltzer, D. (1986) *Studies in Extended Metapsychology: clinical applications of Bion's ideas*, Strath Tay: Clunie Press.

Menninger, K. A. (1951) 'Totemic aspects of contemporary attitudes towards animals', in G. B.Wilbur and W. Muensterburger (eds) *Psychoanalysis and Culture*, New York: John Wiley and Sons, pp. 42–74.

Messent, P. R. and Serpell, J. A. (1981) 'A historical and biological view of the pet owner bond', in B. Fogle (ed.) *Interrelations between People and their Pets*, Springfield, ILL: Charles Thomas, pp. 5–22.

Midgley, M. (1984) *Animals and Why They Matter*, Athens, GA: University of Georgia Press.

Miller, L., Rustin, M., Rustin, M. and Shuttleworth, J. (eds) (1989) *Closely Observed Infants*, London: Duckworth.

Milne, A. A. (1926) 'Winnie the Pooh', in *The Complete Collection of Stories and Poems*, London: Methuen (1973).

Milner, M. (1955) 'The role of illusion in symbol formation', in M. Klein, P. Heiman, and R. E. Money-Kyrle (eds) *New Directions in Psychoanalysis*, London: Maresfield Library (1977).

—— (1969) *The Hands of the Living God – an account of a psycho-analytic treatment*, London: Hogarth.

—— (1971) *On Not Being Able to Paint*, first published 1950 under the pseudonym, Joanna Field, London: Heinemann Educational.

Morra, M. (2002) 'Some considerations about personality structure in child psychosis', *Journal of Child Psychotherapy*, 28 (3): 283–305.

Murphy, J. (1998) 'Art therapy with sexually abused children and young people', *Inscape* 3 (1): 10–16.

Murray, L. (1997) 'Post-partum depression and child development', *Psychological Medicine*, 27: 253–60.

Nathanson, D. E., De Castro, D., Friend, H. and McMahon, M. (1997) 'Effectiveness of short-term dolphin-assisted therapy for children with severe disabilities', *Anthrozoos*, 10 (2): 3.

Naumberg, M. (1973) 'A study of the art work of a behaviour problem boy as it relates to ego development and sexual enlightenment', in M. Naunberg, *An Introduction to Art Therapy*, New York and London: Teachers College Press, pp. 157–95.

Nelson, C. A. and Bosquet, M. (2000) 'Neurobiology of fetal and infant development: implications for infant mental health', in C. H. Zeanah (ed.) *Handbook of Infant Mental Health*, 2nd edn, New York: Guilford Press.

Nez, D. (1991) 'Persephone's return: archetypal art therapy and the treatment of a survivor of abuse', *The Arts in Psychotherapy*, 18 (2): 123–30.

Oremland, J. (1997) *The Origins and Psychodynamics of Creativity*, Madison, CT: International Universities Press.

O'Shaughnessy, E. (1964) 'The absent object', *Journal of Child Psychotherapy*, 1: 34–43.

Pally, R. (2000) *The Mind-Brain Relationship*, London and New York: Karnac.

Palombo, S. (1978) *Dreaming and Memory*, New York: Basic Books.

Pankow, G. (1961) 'Dynamic structurization in schizophrenia', in A. Burton (ed.) *Psychotherapy of the Psychosis*, New York: Basic Books.

—— (1981) 'Psychotherapy: a psychoanalytic approach. An analytic approach employing the concept of the body image', in M. Dongier and E. Wittkower (eds) *Divergent Views in Psychiatry*, New York: Harper and Row.

Papousek, H. and Papousek, M. (1997) 'Fragile aspects of early social integration', in L. Murray and P. Cooper (eds) *Postpartum Depression and Child Development*, New York and London: Guilford Press.

Pearson, M. (1984) 'Exploration of regression and containment as illustrated by the art therapy work of a young mentally handicapped woman', in *Conference Proceedings: Art Therapy as Psychotherapy in Relation to the Mentally Handicapped*, St. Albans: Hertfordshire College of Art and Design, pp. 155–60.

Perez-Sanchez, M. (1990) *Baby Observation*, Strath Tay: Clunie Press.

Perry, B. D. (1997) 'Incubated in terror: neurodevelopmental factors in the "cycle of violence" ', in J. D. Osofsky (ed.) *Children in a Violent Society*, New York: Guilford, pp. 125–49.

Perry, B. D., Pollard, A., Blakeley, T., Baker, W. and Vigilante, D. (1995) 'Childhood trauma, the neurobiology of adaptation, and "use-dependent" development of the brain: how "states" become "traits",' *Infant Mental Health Journal*, 16 (4): 271–91.

Piontelli, A. (1992) *From Foetus to Child: An Observational and Psychoanalytic Study*, London: Routledge.

Potter, H. W. (1933) 'Schizophrenia in children', *American Journal of Psychiatry*, 89: 1253–70.

Pratchett, T. and Pratchett, L. (2001) *The Amazing Maurice and his Educated Rodents*, London: Corgi.

Prechtl, H. F. R. (1989) 'Fetal behaviour', in A. Hill and J. Volpe (eds) *Fetal Neurology*, New York: Raven Press.

Pullman, P. (1995–2000) *His Dark Materials Trilogy*, London: Scholastic.

Pundick, M. (1999) 'Carmen: despot or subject: the discovery of beauty in a wilful passionate child', in A. Alvarez and S. Reid (eds) *Autism and Personality*, London and New York: Routledge, pp. 171–85.

Quasha, G. (1983) 'Publishers preface,' in J. Hillman *Healing Fiction*, New York: Station Hill, p. ix.

Rabiger, S. (1984) 'Some experiences of art therapy in a special school', in *Conference Proceedings: Art Therapy as Psychotherapy in Relation to the Mentally Handicapped*, St. Albans: Hertfordshire College of Art and Design, pp. 106–13.

Raphael-Leff, J. (1993) *Pregnancy: the inside story*, London: Sheldon Press.

Reid, S. (1990) 'The importance of beauty in the psychoanalytic experience', *Journal of Child Psychotherapy*, 16 (1): 29–52.

—— (1997) *Developments in Infant Observation: the Tavistock Model*, London and New York: Routledge.

Rey, H. (1975) 'Liberté et processus de pensée psychotique', *La Vie Médicale au Canada Français*, 4: 1046–60, referenced in J. Steiner, *Psychic Retreats*, London: Routledge and the Institute of Psychoanalysis.

Rhode, M. (1997) 'Discussion', in M. Rustin, M. Rhode, A. Dubinsky, H. Dubinsky (eds) *Psychotic States in Children*, London: Duckworth, pp. 172–88.

Robbins, A. (1987) *The Artist as Therapist*, New York: Human Sciences Press.

Rosenfeld, H. (1947) 'Analysis of a schizophrenic state with depersonalisation', reprinted in *Psychotic States*, London: Hogarth (1965).

—— (1952) 'Notes on the psycho-analysis of the super-ego conflict in an acute schizophrenic patient', reprinted in *Psychotic States*, London: Hogarth (1965).

—— (1971) 'A clinical approach to the psychoanalytic theory of the life and death instincts: an investigation into the aggressive aspects of narcissism', *International Journal of Psychoanalysis*, 52: 169–78.

Rowling, J. K. (1999) *Harry Potter and the Prisoner of Azkaban*, London: Bloomsbury.

Rubin, J. (1978) *Child Art Therapy*, New York and London: Van Nostrand Reinhold.

Rustin, M. (2001) 'The therapist with her back against the wall', *Journal of Child Psychotherapy*, 27 (3): 273–84.

Rustin, M., Rhode, M., Dubinsky, A. and Dubinsky, H. (eds) (1997) *Psychotic States in Children*, London: Duckworth.

Ryder. R. (1992) 'An Autobiography', *Between the Species*, 8: 168–73.

Ryz, P. and Wilson, J. (1999) 'Endings as gain: the capacity to end and its role in creating space for growth', *Journal of Child Psychotherapy*, 25 (3): 379–403.

Sagar, C. (1990) 'Working with cases of child sexual abuse', in C. Case and T. Dalley (eds) *Working with Children in Art Therapy*, London: Tavistock Routledge.

Sartre, J.-P. (1999) 'Qu'est-ce que la littérature?' in P. Kemp (ed.) *The Oxford Dictionary of Quotations*. Oxford: Oxford University Press. First published in *Les Temps Moderne*, 1947.

Savage-Rambaugh, S. and Lewin, R. (1994) *Kanzi: The Ape at the Brink of the Human Mind*, London: Doubleday, pp. 89–114.

Savishinsky, J. S. (1983) 'Pet ideas: the domestication of animals, human behaviour, and human emotions', in A. H. Katcher and A. M. Beck (eds) *New Perspectives on our Lives with Companion Animals*, Philadelphia: University of Pennsylvania Press, pp. 112–31.

Schaverien, J. (1987) 'The scapegoat and the talisman: transference in art therapy', in T. Dalley, C. Case, J. Schaverien, F. Weir, D. Halliday, P. Nowell Hall, D. Walles *Images of Art Therapy*, London and New York: Tavistock Publications, pp. 74–108.

—— (1989) 'The picture within the frame', in A. Gilroy and T. Dalley (eds) *Pictures at an Exhibition*, London and New York: Tavistock/Routledge, pp. 147–55.

—— (1992) *The Revealing Image: Analytical Art Psychotherapy in Theory and Practice*, London and New York: Routledge.

—— (1993) 'The retrospective review of pictures: data for research in art therapy', in H. Payne (ed.) *Handbook of Inquiry in the Arts Therapies: one river many currents*, London and Philadelphia: Jessica Kingsley Publishers, pp. 91–103.

—— (1994) 'The transactional object: art psychotherapy in the treatment of anorexia', *British Journal of Psychotherapy*, 11 (1): 46–61.

—— (1995a) *Desire and the Female Therapist: Engendered Gazes in Psychotherapy and Art Therapy*, London and New York: Routledge.

—— (1995b) 'Researching the esoteric', in A. Gilroy, and C. Lee (eds) *Art and Music: therapy and research*, London: Routledge.

—— (1998) 'The scapegoat: Jewish experience and art psychotherapy groups', in J. Campbell, M. Liebmann, F. Brooks, J. Jones and C. Ward (eds) *Art Therapy, Race and Culture*, London and Philadelphia: Jessica Kingsley, pp. 56–67.

—— (2002) *The Dying Patient in Psychotherapy*, Hampshire and New York: Palgrave Macmillan.

Schore, A. N. (1994) *Affect Regulation and the Origin of the Self: the neurobiology of emotional development*, New Jersey: Erlbaum.

—— (2001a) 'The effects of early relational trauma on right brain development, affect regulation, and infant mental health', *Infant Mental Health Journal*, 22 (1–2): 201–69.

—— (2001b) 'Effects of a secure attachment relationship on right brain development, affect regulation and infant mental health', *Infant Mental Health Journal*, 22 (1–2): 7–66.

—— (2001c) 'Minds in the making: attachment, the self-organising brain, and developmentally-oriented psychotherapy', *British Journal of Psychotherapy*, 17 (3): 299–328.

Segal, H. (1991) *Dream, Phantasy and Art*, London and New York: Tavistock Routledge.

Seigal D. J. (1999) *The Developing Mind: towards a neurobiology of interpersonal experience*, New York: Guilford Press.

Serpell, J. (1986) *In the Company of Animals*, Oxford: Basil Blackwell.

Serrano, J. (1989) 'The arts in therapy with survivors of incest', in H. Wadeson (ed.) *Advances in Art Therapy*, New York: Harper and Row, pp. 114–26.

Sewell, E. (1960) *The Orphic Voice*, New York: Harper.

Sharpe, E. Freeman (1937) *Dream Analysis*, London: Hogarth Press.

Sharefkin, B. D. and Ruchlis, K. (1974) 'Anthropomorphism in the lower grades', *Science and Children*, March.

Shuttleworth, J. (1989) 'Psychoanalytic theory and infant development', in L. Miller, M. Rustin, M. Rustin and J. Shuttleworth (eds) *Closely Observed Infant*, London: Duckworth, pp. 22–51.

Sinason, V. (1986) 'Secondary mental handicap and its relationship to trauma', *Psychoanalytic Psychotherapy*, 2: 131–54.

—— (1992) *Mental Handicap and the Human Condition*, London: Free Association Books.

Sinclair, D. and Murray, L. (1998) 'The effects of postnatal depression on children's adjustment to school', *British Journal of Psychiatry*, 172: 58–63.

Smith, B. A. (1983) 'Project Inreach: A program to explore the ability of Atlantic bottlenose dolphins to elicit communication responses from autistic children', in A. H. Katcher and A. M. Beck (eds) *New Perspectives on our Lives with Companion Animals*, Philadelphia: University of Pennsylvania Press.

Spence, D. (1997) 'Case reports and the reality they represent: the many faces of *nachträglichkeit*' in I. Ward (ed.) *The Presentation of Case-Material in Clinical Discourse*, London: Freud Museum Publications, pp. 77–94.

Spensley, S. (1984) 'Reflections on the contribution of art therapy to the understanding of psychic development', in *Conference Proceedings: Art Therapy as Psychotherapy in Relation to the Mentally Handicapped*: St. Albans: Hertfordshire College of Art and Design, pp. 1–7.

—— (1995) *Francis Tustin*, London and New York: Routledge.

Spurling, L. (1997) 'Using the case study in the assessment of trainees', in I. Ward (ed.) *The Presentation of Case-Material in Clinical Discourse*, London: Freud Museum Publications, pp. 64–76.

Stack, M. (1998) 'Humpty Dumpty's shell: working with autistic defence mechanisms in art therapy', in M. Rees (ed.) *Drawing on Difference*, London: Routledge, pp. 91–110.

Stern, D. N. (1985) *The Interpersonal World of the Infant: a View from Psychoanalysis and Developmental Psychology*, New York: Basic Books.

Stokes, A. (1955) 'Form in art', in M. Klein, P. Heimann and R. E. Money-Kyrle (eds) *New Directions in Psychoanalysis: the significance of infant conflict in the pattern of adult behaviour*, London: Maresfield Library, pp. 406–20.

—— (1972) *The Image in Form: Selected Writings of Adrian Stokes*, ed. R. Wollheirn, Harmondsworth: Penguin.

—— (1973) 'Form in art: a psychoanalytic interpretation', in E. Rhode (ed.) *A Game that Must be Lost: collected papers*, Manchester: Carcanet.

Symington, N. (1986) *The Analytic Experience: Lectures from the Tavistock*, London: Free Association Books.

Tehrani, N. (2002) 'Healing the wounds of the mind', *The Psychologist*, 15 (12): 598–99.

Terr, L. (1981) 'Forbidden games: post-traumatic child's play', *Journal of the American Academy of Child Psychiatry*, 20: 741–60.

Tester, K. (1991) *Animals and Society: the humanity of animal rights*, London: Routledge.

Thomas, K. (1983) *Man and the Natural World: Changing Attitudes in England 1500–1800*, London: Allen Lane, pp.100–20.

Tipple, R. (2003) 'The interpretation of children's art work in a paediatric disability setting', *Inscape*, 8 (2): 48–59.

Tischler, S. (1971) 'Clinical work with the parents of psychotic children', *Psychiatry, Neuralgia, Neurochirurgia*, 74: 225–49.

—— (1979) 'Being with a psychotic child: a psychoanalytical approach to the problems of parents of psychotic children,' *International Journal of Psychoanalysis*, 60: 29–38.

Trevarthen, C. and Neisser, U. (1993) *The Perceived Self: ecological and interpersonal sources of self knowledge*, Cambridge: Cambridge University Press.

Trevarthen, C., Aitken, K., Papoudi, D. and Robarts, J. (1996) *Children with Autism: diagnosis and intervention to meet their needs*, London and Bristol, PA: Jessica Kingsley.

Tronick, E. and Weinberg, M. K. (1997) 'Depressed mothers and infants: failure to form dyadic states of consciousness', in L. Murray and P. Cooper (eds) *Postpartum Depression and Child Development*, New York and London: Guilford Press.

Tuan, Yi-Fu, (1984) *Dominance and Affection: the making of pets*, New Haven, CT: Yale University Press.

Tustin, F. (1972) *Autism and Childhood Psychosis*, London: Hogarth.

—— (1990) *The Protective Shell in Children and Adults*, London: Karnac Books; New York: Brunner-Mazel.

—— (1992) *Autistic States in Children* (revised edn), London and New York: Tavistock Routledge.

Veevers, J. E. (1985) The social meaning of pets: alternate roles for companion animals', in M. B. Sussman (ed.) *Pets and the Family*, New York: Haworth Press, pp. 11–30.

Waddell, M. (1998) *Inside Lives: psychoanalysis and the growth of the personality*, London: Duckworth.

Waldau, P. (2002) *The Specter of Speciesism: Buddhist and Christian views of animals*, Oxford: Oxford University Press.

Waldman, J. (1999) 'Breaking the mould', *Inscape*, 4 (1): 10–19.

Ward, I. (ed.) (1997) 'Introduction' in *The Presentation of Case-Material in Clinical Discourse*, London: Freud Museum Publications, pp. 5–10.

White, T. H. (1939) *The Once and Future King*, this edition 1974, Book Club Associates.

Whyam, M. (1997) 'The human animal bond – companion animals in prisons', *The Society of Companion Animal Studies*.

Williams, D. (1992) *Nobody Nowhere*, London: Doubleday.

Williams, G. (1997) *Internal Landscapes and Foreign Bodies: eating disorders and other pathologies*, Tavistock Clinic Series, London: Duckworth.

Wing, L. and Attwood, A. (1987) 'Syndromes of autism and atypical development', in D. Cohen and A. Donnellan (eds) *Handbook of Autism and Pervasive Developmental Disorders*, New York: Wiley.

Winnicott, D. W. (1945) 'Primitive emotional development', in *Collected Papers*, London: Tavistock (1958).

—— (1947) 'Hate within the countertransference', in *Through Paediatrics to Psychoanalysis*, London: Hogarth Press 1975; reprinted London: Karnac Books, (1992).

—— (1949) 'Mind and its relation to psyche-soma', in *Collected Papers*, London: Tavistock (1958).

—— (1951) 'Transitional objects and transitional phenonema', in *Through Paediatrics to Psychoanalysis*, London: Hogarth Press, 1975; reprinted London: Karnac Books, (1992).

—— (1956) 'Primary maternal preoccupation', in *Through Paediatrics to Psychoanalysis*, London: Hogarth Press, 1975; reprinted London: Karnac Books, (1992).

—— (1958) 'The capacity to be alone', *International Journal of Psychoanalysis*, 39: 416–20.

—— (1960) 'The theory of the parent-infant relationship', in *The Maturational Processes and the Facilitating Environment*, London: Hogarth Press (1965).

—— (1962) 'The theory of the parent-infant relationship – further remarks', in *The Maturational Processes and the Facilitating Environment*, London: Hogarth Press (1965).

—— (1964) *The Child, the Family and the Outside World*, Harmondsworth: Penguin.

—— (1971) *Playing and Reality*, Harmondsworth: Penguin.

—— (1977) *The Piggle – an account of the psychoanalytic treatment of a little girl*, London: Hogarth.

Wittenberg, I. (1999) 'Ending therapy', *Journal of Child Psychotherapy*, 25 (3): 339–56.

Wood, C. (1997) 'Facing fear with people who have a history of psychosis', *Inscape*, 2 (2): 41–8.

Wright, K. (1991) *Vision and Separation: between mother and baby*, New Jersey: Aronson.

Yates, J. (1987) Project Pup: the perceived benefits to nursing home residents', *Anthrozoos*, 1 (3): 188–92.

Zahn-Waxler, C., Hollenbeck, B. and Radke-Yarrow, M. (1984) 'The origins of empathy and altruism', in M. W. Fox and L. D. Mickley (eds) *Advances in Animal Welfare Science*, Washington: Humane.

Zeanah, C. H., Boris, N. W. and Larrien, J. A. (1997) 'Infant development and developmental risk: a review of the past ten years', *American Academy of Child and Adolescent Psychiatry*, 36 (2): 165–78.

Index